A Clear Mirror

A CLEAR MIRROR

The Visionary Autobiography of a Tibetan Master

Traktung Dudjom Lingpa
Supreme Treasure Revealer and Buddhist King

Translated by Chönyi Drolma

Rangjung Yeshe Publications 2011

Rangjung Yeshe Publications
55 Mitchell Blvd., Suite 20
San Rafael, CA 94903 USA

www.rangjung.com
www.lotustreasure.com

Distributed to the book trade by:
Perseus Books/Ingram

1 2 3 4 5 6 7 8 9

First Paperback Edition 2011
Printed in the United States of America

Publication Data:
Traktung Dudjom Lingpa
Full Title: A Clear Mirror, The Visionary Autobiography of a Tibetan Master
Foreword by Lama Tharchin Rinpoche.
Translated from the Tibetan by Chonyi Drolma (Anne Holland).
ISBN 978–962–7341–673 (pbk.)
Religious Life—Buddhism. 2. Buddhism—Doctrines.
3. Vajrayana—Tibet.

Cover design by Maryann Lipaj

Table of Contents

The Secret Autobiographies   203

The Secret Autobiography That Briefly Relates Replies to the Queries of a Wisdom Dakini 277

A Supernova of Blessings 285

Foreword

MY TEACHER, one of the highest, most realized lamas in Tibet, His Holiness Dudjom Rinpoche, gave this advice: "If you want to engage in Buddhist practice to attain fully enlightened buddhahood, it's very important to read the life stories of past sublime beings. You will come to understand how they attained realization, what practices they did, and what kind of realization they gained. You can then follow their example. If you aim to accomplish your practice, these sublime beings' words and stories will act as your witness."

Following Dudjom Rinpoche's advice, I read many life stories, and they proved to be the most effective, profound teachings. Such stories offer models on two levels: how these masters practiced and the level of realization they gained. I would always measure where I was against these two examples, my aim being to emulate those masters' integrity in practice and their profound realization.

This doesn't apply only to me—all past masters have followed the path of sublime beings before them. We say in Tibetan, "In life, we imitate others; whoever is the best imitator succeeds." Similarly, because all Buddhists imitate the Buddha, whoever imitates him best will become a buddha.

These days, however, people have become disconnected from the source of their practice—the lama. Patrul Rinpoche once said, "In ancient times, people would sit around drinking tea and chatting. Mostly they discussed things like, 'My lama says this, my lama does that.' These days when people sit together and have tea, all they talk about is, 'My horse is better, my gun is better.' They never talk about their practice or lama anymore."

Generally, according to the Vajrayana point of view, the sole source of happiness is the sublime teachings—the Dharma—yet what is the source of all teachings? It is the lama. The lama's qualities are equal to those of all buddhas, yet in terms of kindness in relation to us, the lama is kinder than any buddha. To explain, the lama's qualities are equal to those of all buddhas because he or she has completely realized the dharmakaya level of enlightenment, beyond sentient beings' field of experience. The lama's kindness exceeds that of all buddhas because he or she makes their experience available to us in a tangible form, the nirmanakaya. We can see them and hear their teachings. Therefore, talking about the lama, thinking about the lama, and following the lama's example is most important for us.

Almost all lamas have received their education and training from other human teachers, yet Dudjom Lingpa's story is completely shocking and unique. Particularly now, among this generation, he remains a most powerful master. No human guide educated Dudjom Lingpa; his connection came straight from different buddhas' teachings and empowerments. His lineage is truly direct, unlike any other. He didn't even learn to read and write from a human lama, but from Yeshe Tsogyal. In his visions, he was like Yeshe Tsogyal's child and Yeshe Tsogyal was like his mother. In his autobiography, Dudjom Lingpa describes how, even as a baby, he traveled to various pure lands and buddha fields.

Now, especially in this degenerate time, we don't have such a model. Although we have plenty of intellectual, knowledge-based models for our lives, realization models are very rare. Before Dudjom Lingpa's time, his life was prophesied in the ancient treasure texts of twenty treasure revealers. What follows is a brief account of those predictions.

One day in Tibet, Guru Rinpoche and Yeshe Tsogyal were talking as they walked up a mountain. At one point, they sat and meditated. Yeshe Tsogyal heard Guru Rinpoche say, "Ah ka ka!" which means "Oh no!"

"Rinpoche," she asked, "Why did you say 'Ah ka ka!'?"

Guru Rinpoche answered, "In this degenerate time, sentient beings' afflictive emotions are very wild and turbulent. Such gross emotions are difficult to subdue by any buddhas and any teachings. A really terrible time will come in the future."

Hearing this, Yeshe Tsogyal offered prostrations to Guru Rinpoche, respectfully placed his feet on her head, and cried as she requested, "Since these kinds of wild sentient beings are impossible to tame, please send an emanation powerful enough to subdue them!"

Guru Rinpoche said, "Yes my daughter, you're right to ask this. Among my twenty-five main disciples—all mahasiddhas, realized beings—the most powerful one, with realization equal to my own, is Drokben Kye-u Chung Lotsawa. Therefore, he will be this emanation's body aspect. Yeshe Tsogyal, you and I have a connection over many lifetimes, and in this lifetime, you're my consort. I have given you every teaching and prophecy, and I've empowered you to teach my entire doctrine now and for future generations. I've asked you, my heart student, to seal these teachings as treasure texts. You are powerful, so you will be his speech aspect. As Padmasambhava, I will be his mind aspect. Among Guru Rinpoche's eight manifestations, Dorjé Drolö riding on a tiger will emanate in Eastern Tibet as Traktung Dudjom Dorje."

This incredible prophecy is unlike that of any other lama. Realizing this, when we have trust, faith, and devotion, we will receive blessings. Our original buddha nature is like fire and these blessings are like adding oil—it makes our buddha nature blaze forth.

For me, reading Dudjom Lingpa's life stories inspired me to want to practice the Dudjom lineage. Dudjom Lingpa is inseparable from His Holiness Dudjom Rinpoche, with whom I found myself connected. I've experienced so much satisfaction in having focused my personal practice on the Dudjom tradition. I've spent many years with this lineage, and discovered that the entirety of the Buddha's teachings in eighty-four thousand categories, as well as the sixty-four hundred thousand Great Perfection tantras, are complete and perfected within the Dudjom lineage. Nothing is missing from the Dudjom Tersar tradition of Dudjom Lingpa and his reincarnation Dudjom Rinpoche. I gained my connection with these teachings by reading Dudjom Lingpa's life story. It is that inspiring.

Now I'm truly happy that Chönyi Drolma has completed this translation. Until now, we could read it in Tibetan but not in English. Chönyi is also a follower of the Dudjom Tersar lineage. She's my vajra sister and recently finished a three-year, three-month retreat at the retreat center known as Drupnyi Dojö Ga-tsal, Joyful Wish-fulfilling Grove of the Two Aims, at Pema Osel Ling, Land of Lotus Light, this Dudjom-lineage Buddhist center on the West Coast of North America. She is continuing to do a total of six years of retreat focused on Dudjom Tersar practice. Chönyi maintains Dharma activities such as these, and I truly rejoice in her effort and motivation. I'm also requesting all readers, anyone at all connected with Dudjom Lingpa's life stories, to make their connection meaningful: Please read this book and take Dudjom Lingpa's life as a wonderful model to follow.

This is presented by the worst student of His Holiness Dudjom Rinpoche, father and son, the one by the name of Ngakben Tsédrub Tharchin, who wandered away from Eastern Tibet and who comes from the Repkong yogi family lineage of Palchen Namké Jikmé. I offer this with aspiration prayers and the utmost respect.

Lama Tharchin Rinpoche
September 2010
Drup-nyi Dojö Ga-tsal
Corallitos, California

Publisher's Preface

IN THE LATE FALL OF 2009 and early winter of 2010, an incredible event took place. A modern-day emanation of Padmasambhava in the flesh, Dungsé Thinley Norbu Rinpoche, blessed the people of Nepal by turning the wheel of the Dharma for three months in Pharping, a holy site of Padmasambhava located there. His generosity in bestowing teachings, reading transmissions, and empowerments was extraordinary. Merely being in his presence was a shower of blessings and resounding confirmation that living buddhas still exist among us.

Nearly every night during those three months, Rinpoche practiced with a diverse group of people—high incarnate lamas, khenpos, monks, nuns, yogis, and yoginis of various backgrounds, Tibetan, Nepali, Bhutanese, Indian, Chinese, and Western. Each person participated in whichever way that they could, following along with the texts of the pujas, reciting mantras, or meditating. Everyone was extremely dedicated and well behaved. The power of the deep realization of Thinley Norbu Rinpoche's wisdom mind captivated all our ordinary minds and kept us, as much as possible, mindful of the opportunity we were granted. It was completely inspirational.

Thinley Norbu Rinpoche is seventy-nine years old and not in the best of health, as he frequently reminds us. Yet his commitment to the lineage of which he is the holder and foremost propagator, the Dudjom Tersar, is astonishing. Pushing himself to the limit of his physical abilities, he did not refuse any Dharma requests. On the last night, when Rinpoche was receiving ceremonial scarves with love and respect from about five hundred people, I got a chance to talk to Pat, Rinpoche's remarkable longtime attendant. She said that Rinpoche took this hardship with no thought for himself because he felt that there were so many sincere practitioners, some of whom showed true signs of accomplishment. I was not able to go every night for those three months, but I do not see the slightest difference between Thinley Norbu Rinpoche and Padmasambhava.

Personally, my strongest karmic link is to another hidden-treasure lineage known as the Chokling Tersar, propagated by the three nineteenth-century masters Jamyang Khyentsé Wangpo, Jamgön Kongtrul, and Chokgyur

Dechen Lingpa. It has always been a bit perplexing to me to have the good fortune to have received the Dudjom Tersar—which I consider profound, beautiful, and astounding—from its major lineage holders and yet not practice it. Still, I study the instruction manuals by these lineage masters and I wanted to find a way to repay their kindness in revealing these teachings and bestowing them upon those of us lost in this dark age.

I had not found a way to express my appreciation until I met Chönyi Drolma. She quietly and fortuitously came into my life, as if an answer to my prayers, during the Tibetan New Year of the Tiger, 2010. Chönyi is a practitioner of the Dudjom Tersar who has completed a traditional three-year retreat under the guidance of Lama Tharchin Rinpoche. She was one of those devout people who went every night to be in the presence of Thinley Norbu Rinpoche and as this book was being published, she entered another extended retreat on the Dudjom Tersar practices.

When we met the second time, it was next to the Boudha Stupa. She wanted some advice on producing a text she had translated, "The Life Stories of Dudjom Lingpa." Over tea at my place, she showed me her manuscript. I was immediately awestruck; the work was beautiful and appeared, upon that first cursory glance, to have been exceptionally well done. Here was my opening to show my sincere gratitude to the lineage of Dudjom Tersar, and I immediately offered to publish her manuscript.

You might think that this is what publishers do—acquire manuscripts and publish books—so why am I making a big deal about this? Other publishers do, but Rangjung Yeshe Publications had only ever published translations by my partner Erik Pema Kunsang and myself. However, as I read this life story, I felt as if the blessings of Thinley Norbu Rinpoche had descended upon me, and that motivated me to offer enthusiastically to produce Chönyi's work. I am overjoyed to do so.

Chönyi and I made aspirations at the stupa on the tenth day of the lunar month by lighting a butter lamp together. We finalized our agreement on the fifteenth day of the Miracle Month.

Since that time, I have checked the Tibetan original with her translation, to the best of my ability, and my initial enthusiasm has deepened and increased. Chönyi has done a remarkable job of translating the difficult, obscure, and poetic language of the text into English. The story and teachings will speak for themselves—what a wonderful journey you, the reader, will embark upon, and many thanks to Chönyi for having given us the ticket to travel along.

So with my deep love for the Dudjom Tersar Dharma and my devotion to the supreme and exalted Thinly Norbu Rinpoche, I offer this small token of thanks, my involvement in bringing out this book. I will conclude with the aspiration prayer that I made as Chönyi and I held up the butter lamp at the Boudha Stupa:

This illuminating lamp of original pure awareness
I offer to the mandala deities of Vidyadhara Padmakara.
May all beings, my mothers, wherever awareness pervades,
Attain the dharmakaya level of aware emptiness.

MARCIA DECHEN WANGMO

About This Translation

THIS TRANSLATION HAS ORIGINS both humble and incredibly exalted. Its humble origins are in a small cabin in a Dudjom-lineage three-year retreat center under the direction of Kyabjé Dungsé Thinley Norbu Rinpoche, in the Santa Cruz Mountains of California, where I began reading these autobiographies in Tibetan during intervals between meditation sessions. Reading yielded to wanting to fully understand and apply every single thing I read, which led to questions and finally to a translation. I figured if Dudjom Lingpa's autobiographies had changed my mind and practice so radically, then my retreat companions, and by extension, Westerners in general, might benefit as well.

This book's exalted origins, beyond that cabin and my earnest but imperfect aspirations, are the lamas of the Dudjom lineage who very generously and patiently fed me the nectar-teachings of the Dudjom Tersar tradition, which includes both Dudjom Lingpa's legacy as well as that of his immediate reincarnation, His Holiness Dudjom Rinpoche. These incomparable lamas include Dungsé Thinley Norbu Rinpoche and Lama Tharchin Rinpoche, whose teachings formed the core of our retreat experience, as well as Dzongsar Khyentse Rinpoche, Lopön Nikula Rinpoche of Bhutan, Loppön Jigme Rinpoche, Lama Tséring Gyaltsen, Lama Pema Dorje, Orgyen Chöwang Rinpoché, Dzatrul Rinpoche, Namkha Drimed Rinpoche, and Lama Sonam Tséring, the last of whom tirelessly manages both the three-year retreat center and the public center at Pema Osel Ling. It is only through the patient care of these lamas, whose teachings I gratefully received and whose kindness I have no way of repaying, that I was able to understand and profit from the incredible stories and instructions found in Dudjom Lingpa's autobiographies. Despite my extremely limited qualities as a practitioner, as I slowly cultivated my experience based on the lamas' vajra words, I found any questions that arose were answered both by my teachers as well as in the pages of this book. On some days, while I was reading, answers would magically appear mere moments after doubts or confusion had emerged in my mind. With deep appreciation for the Dudjom lineage, and for the lamas and disciples dedicated to this extraordinary and complete tradition, I resolved to see this translation through to its conclusion.

Dudjom Lingpa's writings, from recitations to meditation instructions, stand out as much for their profundity and beauty as for being, simply put, readable. In these translations, I endeavored to preserve those qualities, with a heavy emphasis on readability. Further, although the command to pen these texts came from the heights of Yeshe Tsogyal's wisdom speech, Dudjom Lingpa wrote them with a timbre that feels like home. When I read his accounts during retreat, it felt as if I was sitting at the feet of my lamas—as if the incredible stories and profound meditation instructions were being conveyed in the comfort of our own shrine room. Dudjom Lingpa's tone is familiar and accessible, and the language he uses is often quite colloquial (perhaps as a nod to his Khampa roots, a people renowned for not being stuffy in the least). So in my harrowing mission to imitate Dudjom Lingpa's style—elegant yet conversational in the same pen stroke—I've tried to preserve that sense of an intimate storytelling, even though the storyteller is one of the greatest masters of our era. That was my vision in general.

As for specifics throughout the book, the titles of all texts are translated into English. Most individual names, human, deity, and otherwise, are written in phonetic Tibetan with English translation on their first occurrence. In the case of central deities, English translation is paired with Tibetan names throughout the narrative. (Some names translate more gracefully than others, but in my limited experience, it's helpful or at least interesting to know what they mean.) Most terrestrial place names are left in Tibetan; the names of pure lands are translated. All endnotes after the first one are my own.

Regarding the three autobiographies,[6] for the outer account, the first and longest of the three, I have kept the form consistent with the Tibetan, rendering prose and verse as they appear in the original. In keeping with the English language custom of having long works divided into chapters, I used a phrase from the actual text to create each chapter division. The second text, the first of the two secret autobiographies is a treasure revelation written almost exclusively in verse in the original. I chose to render some sections in prose for the sake of flow and readability, keeping what appeared to be songs in verse. I also inserted several chapter breaks into what was otherwise a continuous text. The second secret autobiography, also a treasure revelation, is written entirely in verse, and has been translated as such.

One of the impressions I had while reading these texts in Tibetan was a sense of deep, continuous immersion in Dudjom Lingpa's reality. I felt like this consummate master was inviting me to go as far I dared to. With that in mind, I decided to let Dudjom Lingpa's narrative speak for itself. Rather than attach a lot of informative notes to the translation, I placed supplementary information in the introduction, appendices, and bibliography. Although every person, place, and incident Dudjom Lingpa recounts is likely a font of helpful and intriguing information, for the sake of preserving that sense of immersion, I decided to let readers stay in the narrative and see how deep it takes them. For fact-lovers, I suggest starting by investigating the books in the bibliography, keeping a copy of Gyurme Dorje's *Tibet Handbook* handy, and delving into the online wish-fulfilling jewel that is the Tibetan Buddhist Resource Center (www.tbrc.org).

Any errors in meaning, word choice, or understanding are entirely my own, and I ask forgiveness of the deities and guardians of the doctrine for all mistakes made out of unawareness, lack of experience, or otherwise. May this book be a source of inspiration and illumination, and may all beings benefit.

Acknowledgments

THIS BOOK IS THE RESULT of incredibly fortunate circumstances and a network of supportive individuals that stretches around the world. I must first express my deepest and completely inadequate gratitude to my amazingly kind and patient wisdom lamas, with whom I pray to remain inseparable throughout all my lifetimes—Kyabjé Dungsé Thinley Norbu Rinpoche and Lama Tsédrub Tharchin Rinpoche. Though it's utterly impossible to repay your kindness, I make sincere aspirations to follow your enlightened example as closely as possible.

The teachings of these lamas, and those mentioned elsewhere, form the core of this translation. Further, Lama Tséring Gyaltsen who completed three-year retreat under His Holiness Dudjom Rinpoche's direction, and attended Sanskrit University in India at his bequest, acted as the primary consultant for questions about the translation. He applied the depth of his personal practice and knowledge to answering hundreds of questions throughout the process, leading me to new levels of insight regarding the teachings in this book. Lama Ngawang Zangpo, my Tibetan language teacher for close to a decade, found time in his busy schedule to help me with the translation at every stage, including serving as a second reader when the translation was nearing completion. I must also thank my retreat companions, who inspired me to start translating the autobiographies into English.

During the period of time following retreat when I re-emerged into the world and was determined to finish the translation, without funding, and find a publisher, without a clue, my incredible family and friends supported me in every way. In particular, I'm grateful to my parents, Gloria and Rob Holland, and my sister Susan, for their bemused support throughout my Buddhist life and budding translation career. The same goes for my grandparents (one grandmother is sure I was in retreat with "that nice actor Richard Gere"), and my California family, Paul Holland and Linda Yates, as well as Don and Jane Yates. Many thanks to my friends in Brooklyn and Manhattan, who found me work so I could continue with the translation, and frequently took me in for indeterminate periods. Great swaths of this translation came together over many meals in the apartments of my dear friends, Aaron J. Wong, Rabbi

Jordie Gerson, and Alison Laichter, director of the Jewish Meditation Center of Brooklyn.

This book only exists as a book due to a serendipitous encounter one evening in Nepal, paired with the intrepid vision of Marcia Dechen Wangmo, who decided to take on the project and provide her considerable skills as an editor and organizer. Her generosity of spirit, long-term experience as a translator and editor, and, most importantly, deep personal practice have all informed this translation and seen it through to completion. In addition, thanks go to the front-matter editor, Michael Tweed; the copy editor, Meghan Howard; the book designer, Joan Olson; the cover artist, Maryann Lipaj; and the proof readers, Dr. Lynn Schroeder and Michael Yockey.

Finally, sincere gratitude and appreciation goes to Richard Gere and the Gere Foundation with its magnanimous director Mollie Rodriguez for their support in this production. May this work serve as a meaningful connection to the incredibly alive, deeply pure lineage of the Dudjom Tersar tradition, and may all beings benefit.

Translator's Introduction

YOU ARE ABOUT TO EMBARK on an autobiographical account of a saint, a genius, a virtuoso. He has given us full access to his incredible inner life, which runs from the mystifying to the magical. I have translated his three autobiographical accounts in their entirety, now in your hands, but whether in their original language or in English, I am left breathless, awestruck, by this chronicle. To say the least, Dudjom Lingpa (1835–1904) was not your run-of-the-mill saint. Then again, what saint is?

If across cultures and religions we share any conventional presuppositions concerning the lives of the saints who seem to grace all lands and peoples, it may be the expectation that they experience a bolt from the blue—a confrontation with a larger, higher truth—followed by a life of service to that inspiration. Be it Saul on the road to Damascus or Mother Teresa on the train to Darjeeling, the arc of a saint's life can appear familiar or known. In Western religions, sainthood (whether the individual so named is recognized by ecclesiastical authorities or not) is something thrust upon its recipient by a divine being or by a worldly crisis that conspires to elevate the saint among us.

Things are a little more complicated in the East. In India for example, cultural expectations allow that avatars, saints, and other great beings are regularly born, generation after generation, to seemingly random families throughout the country. These individuals become authentic spiritual guides. Indian saints can become so by dint of religious training that leads to a significant spiritual breakthrough, through a life shift or flash of inspiration, or simply by being born that way. In the Tibetan world, that of Dudjom Lingpa, the situation gains an entirely new level of complexity: The culture's spiritual renewal was and is still based upon the recognition of reincarnate saints and their training to reassume their previous life's (or lives') work.

Whatever mold we might have for saints' lives—Western, Indian, or Tibetan—Dudjom Lingpa shatters it in this series of autobiographies. The scope of his inner life of visions and dreams is simply too overpowering. He informs us obliquely at the outset that he knows the conventions of normal autobiographical accounts, by treating us to a few daunting pages of detailed family history, acknowledging his ancestors before leaning across the table, smiling, and searching our face, then saying, "Well, if you really want to know who I am . . ."

And then we are lost, drawn into his tale spanning almost seventy years with rarely a nod to the outer world and its reference points. He composed twenty-one volumes of writing (this trio of autobiographical works comprises one of them), fathered eight reincarnate sons by several mothers, lived in perpetual motion, built at least one major Buddhist center, and filled Tibet with his disciples. Yet throughout his narrative, we rarely surface to register a change in his circumstances before hurtling once again into the maw of his inner life.

The incredible lives of saints go beyond ordinary human bounds—this is why they achieve timeless eminence. Yet be they Hindu, Christian, Buddhist, or otherwise, these individuals have a background of belief systems that make it possible to understand how their lives unfolded, and to follow in their wake. While Dudjom Lingpa's experience often leaves known reality behind and may at times startle even seasoned Buddhists, we must endeavor to understand some outlines of his belief system in order to accompany him along the way.

I find myself in the somewhat uncomfortable position of being your unqualified guide for this journey. I can only offer the limited experience of having immersed myself in the study and practice of Dudjom Lingpa's writings and meditations, guided by some of the leading holders of his lineage. In the following introduction to his shared accounts, I will try to prepare you, as much as one can, for engagement with Dudjom Lingpa's amazing reality. What threads, spiritual and mundane, can we follow among the fantastical events of his life? Who are the members of the endless cast of characters he meets—masters, wisdom deities, dakinis, gods, and demons? How did his corpus of work take shape? What impact did this unique life have beyond its time? Exhaustive answers to these questions lie beyond the limits of this book. I hope in this introduction, in the appendices, and in the bibliography to provide some indications as to where readers who find this saint as compelling as I do can learn more about him and his world.

PRESSED TO WRITE a single sentence to situate Dudjom Lingpa in the world of Buddhist discourse, I would say this: He was a treasure revealer and Great Perfection master in the Nyingma, or Ancient Tradition, order of Buddhism in Tibet.

Although every word in that sentence belongs to the English language, only "Buddhism" and "Tibet" may carry any meaning for most people. We might reasonably expect that reading the autobiographies translated here will better inform us, but such hopes are in vain. Dudjom Lingpa's life story accelerates quickly into the miraculous, with little or no indication of what the above description means. Faced with this lack of basic information on classic Tibetan Buddhist reference points, I will survey the panorama of his accounts from two vantage points, starting with the philosophical and moving to the tangible.

I begin this introduction by presenting some of the background information necessary for us to understand the major landmarks in Dudjom Lingpa's life—his spiritual compass. This necessarily begins with a brief introduction to Guru Rinpoche and Yeshe Tsogyal, the primary founders of Dudjom Lingpa's belief system. This pair lived in Tibet a thousand years before Dudjom Lingpa was born, yet they consistently appeared to him throughout his life, providing his main source of guidance and inspiration.

Second, I will briefly address the theoretical underpinnings of Dudjom Lingpa's experiences. For the sake of our journey, I will focus on the areas of Buddhism he embraces, masters himself, and then teaches to others throughout his life—Tantra and the Great Perfection. These topics may initially seem formidable to some, however I can offer firsthand assurance that everything Dudjom Lingpa relates is part of a well-tread path happily relied upon by all sorts of people worldwide. That said, we will jump into the deep end of Buddhism, and some Buddhist jargon or code words are regrettably unavoidable. These will include a glimpse of the belief system at the heart of Dudjom Lingpa's spiritual legacy, the view of all phenomena as self-manifest in infinite purity, evenness, and emptiness.

This perspective, signature Dudjom Lingpa, will help us better understand the next topic—a brief exploration of the origins, cast members, and purpose of the prolific and incredible visionary experiences that form the main fabric of his life stories. The introduction ends by delving into various key aspects of the amazing life that unfurls from these reference points and beliefs.

IT IS VERY RARE to receive such an intimate glimpse into a saint's life, so it's worth our while to try to understand where Dudjom Lingpa is coming from. For Buddhists, this is a book filled with essential, clear instructions. Yet this

is not merely a Buddhist book; it's a book about awakening, about manifesting our deepest altruistic potential beyond any presupposed limits—that seed
within each of us that compels us to explore, to meditate, to read on, and to
trust ourselves to discover and tread paths that might at first appear uncertain, but in time prove to be right and noble. Many great individuals have
gone before us on these paths. Shared accounts such as this one bring their
timeless, brilliant presence into our lives, opening us suddenly to new and
unforeseen possibilities.

Wisdom Guides

WE HAVE THE DEEP PRIVILEGE of exploring Dudjom Lingpa's reality in the
company of two spiritual revolutionaries who established Buddhism in ninth-
century Tibet—Guru Rinpoche and Yeshe Tsogyal. We encounter them at
the start of this great nineteenth-century master's narrative, not as historical
figures but as living presences. In compassionate concern for the state of the
world, they press Dudjom Lingpa to take rebirth, then repeatedly strengthen
and reassure their envoy in visions throughout his life. Guru Rinpoche
appears to Dudjom Lingpa on at least twenty occasions, Yeshe Tsogyal even
more frequently.

Guru Rinpoche's previous incarnation, Shakyamuni Buddha, is familiar
to most people. Born Prince Siddhartha Gautama in northern India in the
sixth century BC, his life story has long served as an epic adventure and source
of inspiration. Shakyamuni Buddha stated that he would return in a future
emanation to give teachings related to Tantric, or Secret Mantra, Buddhism.
In *The Concise Tantra of the Complete Unsurpassable Meaning,* he foretells,
"Twenty years after passing into enlightenment, I, the victor most supreme
among all worlds, will emerge in the land of Oddiyana. Called Lotus-Born,
I will expound the teachings of Secret Mantra." Shakyamuni Buddha did
return as the individual known as Padmasambhava, the Lotus-Born, and
became renowned as Guru Rinpoche, the universal lama to whom tantric
practitioners pray for spiritual accomplishment with deep faith and gratitude—the one who established the tradition, taught an exalted circle of disciples, and ensures the continuation of Tibetan Buddhism to the present day.

Yeshe Tsogyal was one of Guru Rinpoche's original disciples, as well
as a principal lineage holder and his spiritual consort. During her life, she

assumed a variety of exceptional roles to ensure Buddhism would endure and flourish. Like Guru Rinpoche, Yeshe Tsogyal vanished from the human world. Yet she remains constantly accessible to practitioners at any level. To synthesize her limitless qualities, Yeshe Tsogyal has a threefold role within Tantric Buddhism, three aspects which figure prominently in Dudjom Lingpa's life stories. First, as a historical figure, she was a model of Buddhist practice, particularly in her unwavering devotion to her spiritual master, that art which is so central to Tantric Buddhism's unique and swift effectiveness. She accomplished, preserved, and conveyed every teaching she received. This includes the immense task of recording and concealing teachings and objects known as terma, or treasures, such as those Dudjom Lingpa revealed and propagated. Second, as a visionary persona, she continuously reveals herself in dreams, visions, or real life to guide and inspire faithful practitioners. Third, her human incarnations continue to be reborn in the world, guiding others in whatever capacity is needed, impartially working for the welfare of the Buddhist doctrine and all beings.

When we define Dudjom Lingpa as a master in the Ancient Tradition order of Tibetan Buddhism, that order traces its central roots to Guru Rinpoche and Yeshe Tsogyal, who are still considered the prime catalysts for accomplishing one's spiritual aims within that tradition.

A View from the Summit

AN ALTITUDE ADJUSTMENT is necessary as we journey through Dudjom Lingpa's life. In Guru Rinpoche and Yeshe Tsogyal's Ancient Tradition, many worthy approaches to reach enlightenment exist. There are nine in fact, each replete with different teachings, structures, and meditation techniques. One can begin at the beginning and progress from one to nine; it is equally acceptable to start elsewhere, at level three for example, and assimilate what has preceded one's entry point. As readers traveling on the Dudjom Lingpa express, however, we advance directly to the summit: Tantra and Great Perfection.

Tulku Thondup Rinpoche explains, "In *tantric* teachings, the view is indivisibility of cause and result. . . . [T]he world and beings are equally as pure as the Buddhas and Buddha-fields." While it may be difficult to fathom reality experienced in this say, this startling insight is the view relied upon by realized guides like Dudjom Lingpa. Referred to as "pure view," this is the recognition of all-encompassing purity, not glimpsed after arduous self-improvement, but right now, corresponding to every creature's and every thing's inherent nature.

Primordially pure, all phenomena are a seamless tapestry woven from the spontaneously perfect qualities of enlightenment. As Dudjom Lingpa states, "I, a practitioner of Great Perfection, realize all phenomena to be naked awareness."

Dudjom Lingpa's narrative returns to this direct perception of awareness again and again, amid epic visionary voyages. His is an immediate experience of the all-encompassing equanimity and infinite purity of all phenomena. Good or bad, enjoyable or unwanted, everything seen, felt, and known has equal value, and most importantly, nothing is "out there," other. Dudjom Lingpa wrote volumes on this view of reality, on its many implications and subtleties, and on the path that leads to this summit of all Buddhist theory and practice. This is a key aspect of this great master's revealed experience throughout his life stories, and a hallmark of his doctrine.

Metameetings: Layers of Visionary Engagement

IN ORDER TO SHOW others his path to awakening, Dudjom Lingpa shares with us his process of self-revelation. This takes place mainly in copious visionary encounters (both in waking life and in dreams), and these occur within the context of his belief systems—Tantra and Great Perfection—with which he assumes readers are comfortably familiar.

How does Dudjom Lingpa gain access to his alternate world of pure vision? More often than not, mystical female figures are the conductors of his visionary life. Almost all his expeditions to visit deities and pure lands are led by ephemeral entities called dakinis. *Dakini* is a Sanskrit word that in Tibetan (khandro) translates literally as "one who moves in space." Dakinis are considered mysterious and powerful, manifesting as both worldly and wisdom beings. Worldly dakinis can be caring, or capricious, or even misleading. Their transcendent counterparts include Yeshe Tsogyal. Rather than languishing in the enclosure of ordinary dualistic reality, wisdom dakinis operate in the space of the nature of reality—they move unhindered within the expanse of the wisdom of nondual awareness. It is to these mystical beings that precious troves and teachings have been entrusted, sometimes concealed for centuries until a suitable audience appears in the world. In many stories, dakinis pluck the seminal teachings and sacred objects meant for Dudjom Lingpa and his disciples from the timeless space between layers of solid reality.

On this level of the narrative of his autobiography, the "how" question concerning Dudjom Lingpa's visions is easy to answer. In many cases, he accepts female enlightened beings' invitations to leave the mundane world behind. The "why" question—what was the purpose of these meetings?—has a number of answers.

Some of Dudjom Lingpa's visionary encounters are largely practical in nature. They are the context in which he receives the transmissions of tantric teachings. Tulku Thondup Rinpoche explains, "The transmission of teachings and the esoteric power that comes from the primordial Buddha through master to disciple is the basis of the tantric tradition." Tantric Buddhists at all levels accept as part of their spiritual path the task of seeking and receiving transmission from qualified lamas. This is a deeply important part of their training. Conventionally, such transmission transpires between a human master and a human disciple, but Dudjom Lingpa's experience, however, completely defies such convention. Instead, the dakinis who possess the blueprints to his visionary journeys often have him meet exalted figures such as buddhas, deities, and past adepts of India and Tibet called awareness holders, whose accomplishment during their lifetimes affords them timeless eminence. From them he receives the transmissions needed for spiritual practice wholesale, en masse. His visionary rendezvous dispel the limitations of time and space, as if the entire timeline of tantric history has folded upon itself and spread out before him. Directly from the source, Dudjom Lingpa receives his share of the inheritance of the Buddhist wisdom of the ages. He then cultivates its experience in his personal meditation practice and passes its transmission to his disciples.

According to Buddhist taxonomy, the deities he meets in such visions belong to the different categories of Tantra. These meetings fill in a major gap in Dudjom Lingpa's experience as a Buddhist practitioner: He has no human meditation teachers. Awareness holders and deities act in their stead, offering the guidance, criticism, and confirmation normally provided by an individual's lama. For his part, Dudjom Lingpa condenses the usual process of gradual training into an instant of pure awareness—he vaults directly into the middle of each deity's universe.

In his autobiographies, Dudjom Lingpa's sole explicit organizing principle is chronological—this happened, then later that year this occurred, and so on. He presents the facts without much commentary, and we accompany him on a series of amazing but seemingly haphazard visions. To appreciate that there might be a method, a logic, to the kaleidoscope of his reality, we must look to Dudjom Lingpa's seminal work, *Buddhahood Without Meditation.* There, he provides bare transcripts of teachings he received during visionary encounters with over a dozen deities and awareness holders. Yet he does not give us the keys to understanding the framework of his progress. Is there a pattern here? Why does this vision follow the last? The translator of that book kindly includes a text by Dudjom Lingpa's reincarnation, His Holiness Dudjom Jikdral Yeshe Dorje, entitled *Structural Analysis and Outline.* Even if we do not entirely comprehend the topics mentioned, the text still allows us to realize that every vision and teaching represents an identifiable step along a well-charted path. It all makes perfect sense, or if not to us, then at least to Great Perfection masters. (Incidentally, if a similar *Structural Analysis and Outline* existed for *A Clear Mirror,* I would have been delighted to include it as an appendix in this volume.)

Dudjom Lingpa's visions also function as a conduit for his activity as a treasure revealer. Tantric Buddhism's great strength is its spiritual technology; the treasure tradition is basically a very sophisticated information delivery system, as will be explained in more detail later. While many teachings have endured for centuries through pure lineages, passed from one individual to another, such lineages are subject to the vagaries of human existence. When a line of transmission grows thin and breaks, teachings tragically disappear. The immediacy of treasure transmission solves this problem. Over the centuries in Tibet, hundreds of men and women, reincarnations of Guru Rinpoche's first Tibetan disciples, have served as revealers of such treasures and thus restored some defunct practices and reinvigorated others. Dudjom Lingpa is one such individual. Many of his pure visions revolve around his destiny and role as treasure revealer. In visions, he receives key information and prophecies regarding the locations of his treasures, who his consorts and doctrine custodians should be, and how he should live his life so as to actualize his potential as an authentic treasure revealer. Further, the treasures themselves are sometimes delivered to him in encounters with enlightened beings.

While there is obvious purpose in these divine visionary engagements, what of the demonic? From infancy Dudjom Lingpa is plagued by apparitions and demonic incursions, and throughout his life "demons" in many forms challenge him or members of his entourage. Such events, experienced as crises, force Dudjom Lingpa to evaluate himself and to flex his meditative muscles. As if to say, "resistance to the present moment is futile," he uses these encounters to demonstrate the difference between reacting to experience as being "out there" versus owning it as being self-manifest. He chooses not to recognize challengers from a place of knee-jerk defensiveness, instead seeing them, with the poise of awareness, to be his own phenomena. We see this most dramatically in his encounters with demonic forces, yet the same spirit underlies even his grandest visions of buddhas and pure lands.

In the midst of his visions, everything appears just as solid and real to Dudjom Lingpa as our selves and surroundings do to us, and for the sake of his narrative he portrays what transpires in visions as external. Yet *A Clear Mirror* contains a number of "gotcha" moments. There are points at which the deities who appear to him in all their enlightened splendor question Dudjom Lingpa's experience of them as being "other," as being anything else than self-manifest expressions of his inherent enlightened nature. They mock him for allowing himself to be momentarily duped into believing that the length and breadth, heights and depths, of cyclic existence and the boundless majesty of displays of enlightenment's qualities are anything else than self-manifest adornments of the indwelling luminous nature of his own being.

Revealing an Outer Autobiography

WE NOW MOVE from the philosophical to the tangible, the circumstances of Dudjom Lingpa's life. If only this were the easy part.

In Tibet's literary culture, the genre of spiritual biography and autobiography is quite common. These accounts are generally identified as outer, inner, or secret, either explicitly by the author or implicitly due to their content. An outer account of a life focuses on worldly events, often describing important people and places, teachings received and given, institutions established, and so forth. Inner memoirs provide a more personal perspective, often including private reflections and some recounting of meditative experiences, dreams, visions, and prophecies. With secret narratives, readers are privy to the author's deep spiritual processes and self-reflections. Therefore, secret accounts can be far more esoteric; some sections may even be written in code or terminology that only practitioners with like experiences can fathom. At the very least, as Westerners living in a media-saturated culture where tell-all autobiographies are common, we open books deemed "secret" with the expectation of an intimate view on the person's life. In the Tibetan context, however, such access does not necessarily include details of the individual's public or private life, and the people, places, and intrigues that filled it. Conversely, outer or inner levels of autobiography could divulge such information without touching on the secret level of the person's being—the domain of their creativity, what made them grow and learn, live and breathe, at their innermost level.

Dudjom Lingpa's first and longest autobiography is deemed to be an outer account, although its content resembles an inner or even secret account. While engrossing, he reveals very little about his public life. It's as if, instead of learning about Beethoven's career, family, and social life, we were able to read his private journal instead and gain a glimpse of that genius from inside his head and heart. This is exactly what Dudjom Lingpa does in his trilogy of autobiographies. Although he was brilliantly successful in his multifaceted career as a teacher to incalculable outstanding disciples, a prolific writer with at least twenty-one extant volumes of composition that are still studied around the world, a treasure revealer in the teaching system unique to Tantric Buddhism, and a father of eight remarkable children, his stories offer us something else. In this book, we are shown the very thing that high lamas regard as most sacred and intimate—spiritual evolution via the lens of their innermost visionary life, cinematic in scope, filled with buddhas and beings both divine and demonic. Dudjom Lingpa grants readers access to his enlightenment process as only he could have experienced it.

As for the rest—details on the messy task of navigating an uncooperative reality and bringing together the conditions necessary to fulfill his impressive destiny—Dudjom Lingpa leaves us on our own. While thoroughly absorbing, *A Clear Mirror* reveals very little about the chart of his spiritual growth, rise to prominence, and formation of an enduring lineage of vast scope. For this, we often have to read between the lines. Dudjom Lingpa often leverages his visionary encounters as celestial therapy sessions. By using them to express doubts, seek clarification, and assess his own qualities and orientation in the world, he reveals in his own unique fashion his maturation process. In this most intimate and inspiring account, it is for us to search among the abundant gold and jewels he strews about to find the pieces of common rock and earth with which to construct the outer story of his life. This includes themes and patterns we can all relate to, such as the challenges and successes in his saga that are patently human.

Isolation and Independence

THE SOLITARY, unrecognized genius: What could be a more predictable cliché? Yet, throughout most of Dudjom Lingpa's life, isolation was in fact the norm. He consistently lacked a peer group, whether familial, social, or spiritual. In his youth, he mentions no fellow classmates. Even as he grew older and gained prominence, he had no consistent companions at his own level. From an institutional perspective, Dudjom Lingpa was equally isolated. He never sought monastic ordination, nor did he live in a temple with a large community. He was never involved in the tulku system, in which individuals, often as infants or children, are recognized and sometimes enthroned as the official reincarnation of a great master's previous lifetime. One implication of this lack of recognition was that Dudjom Lingpa didn't receive training with other reincarnate youths, nor was he ever returned to the institution of a former incarnation, as is so often the case.

In Tibet, it was not uncommon for high-ranking Tibetan teachers to have other lamas or practice companions with whom they collaborated. Dudjom Lingpa's own contemporaries and geographical neighbors formed such an alliance. The trio of Jamyang Khyentsé Wangpo (1820–92), Jamgön Kongtrul (1813–1900), and Chokgyur Dechen Lingpa (1829–70) served as lama and disciple to one another. Their treasure revelations represented a concerted effort whose success relied upon a symbiotic dynamic. As portrayed in Dudjom Lingpa's life stories, such relationships were absent from his own career as a teacher and treasure revealer.

While isolation can foster unfettered independence, Dudjom Lingpa frequently lamented to his visionary guides that he had no support network. While he demonstrated from a young age the ability to command respect from above (in visions) and eventually gathered a vast following of disciples, his complaints rang true. Especially early in life, he had very little lateral support and plenty of detractors. Dudjom Lingpa's claims to be a treasure revealer contributed to further distance and suspicion from those who might have otherwise been inclined to ally with him. It should be noted that in a culture where charismatic individuals who call themselves treasure revealers (whether authentic or fraudulent) can quickly achieve celebrity status, skepticism is a healthy attitude. Even revered masters sympathetic to the treasure tradition, such as Jamgön Mipam Rinpoche (1846–1912), wrote texts exposing the transgression of false treasures and their so-called revealers.

Dudjom Lingpa's standing as an authentic treasure revealer was consistently challenged, in both this-world and visionary confrontations. Among the great teachers of his time, Jamgön Kongtrul, Jamyang Khyentsé Wangpo, and Jamgön Mipam Rinpoche were early skeptics. Initially they did not regard Dudjom Lingpa, who lacked a title, institutional endorsement, and formal education, as an authentic treasure revealer. Nor were his writings taken seriously, due in part to the occasional use of unconventional structures or statements that did not match classical Tibetan composition. (As so often happens, such deviation was not recognized as an indication of genius.) It was only after the rise of Dudjom Lingpa's star—as his doctrine flourished and his disciples showed true signs of spiritual maturation—that this trio of superlative masters came to regard Dudjom Lingpa as a true treasure revealer. This shift is confirmed by the fact that Jamgön Kongtrul eventually requested to be allowed to include Dudjom Lingpa's work in his encyclopedic *Compendium of Precious Treasure Teachings*. (Dudjom Lingpa respectfully declined.)[1] In addition, Jamyang Kyentsé Wangpo sent one of his closest disciples, Gyurmé Ngédön Wangpo (19th—20th centuries), to Dudjom Lingpa. He ending up staying with Dudjom Lingpa until his passing and served as teacher to his reincarnation. Further, Jamgön Mipham Rinpoche is reported to have written to Dudjom Lingpa, stating that having read his treasure texts, he found them, and their fresh, nontraditional Buddhist vocabulary, both profound and authentic sound.[2] In the end, Dudjom Lingpa's spiritual evolution, teachings, and exceptional disciples inspired validation.

Perhaps his isolation and lack of approval allowed him to heed the stern advice of visionary teachers. Unlike many of his peers, especially those with prestigious titles and heavy institutional responsibilities, Dudjom Lingpa was free to do as he (and the deities) pleased—to practice meditation in retreat, focus on his writings, and amass a circle of exceptional students at his own pace.

The Persistence of Poverty

DUDJOM LINGPA'S EVENTUAL TRIUMPHS were preceded by decades of solitary struggle. Although his inner panorama—fantastic adventures and rapid spiritual progress—was rich with marvels, he found that miracles didn't pay the bills. A Tibetan saying has it that if your finances are sound, it is at the expense of your spiritual practice, whereas if your meditation is going well, your money situation is awful. As someone who did not follow any conventional, reasonable route to worldly success, this was true throughout most of Dudjom Lingpa's life. Much of his prosperity was based on trusting in advice prescribed through supernatural avenues. He would confide to visionary teachers his concerns regarding wealth and resources, and receive scant reassurance. Even in the case of positive indications or predictions of prosperity, he was more often than not forced to wait until later in life to enjoy the fruition of such prophecies.

For instance, at age twenty-one, Dudjom Lingpa received a magic egg in payment for bringing rain to a suffering naga community.[3] This gift was meant to increase his wealth, but even such a lucky charm failed to help his situation. Sometimes deities responded to his plight. At age thirty-six, while he meditated upon Great Wealth Lord Apara, the deity actually appeared. Having endured nine years with only bare-minimum resources, the deity announced he would grant Dudjom Lingpa whatever he desired. The following year he could afford to build a house.

Yet balancing a domestic life with deep spiritual commitment was precarious, as it remains for so many devoted spiritual practitioners today. Throughout his life, seeking payments for religious services was a recurring topic, replete with pejorative and cautionary messages (usually involving demons). At one point Dudjom Lingpa bemoaned having to seek provisions when he only wanted to practice meditation. In response, a visionary guide called Supreme Hungkara told him he had to choose between losing himself to "undeserved payments (*kor*)," or persevering in spiritual practice. The Tibetan word *kor* has several meanings, including "religious wealth or materials offered out of faith." However, one definition of a kor-la (literally, a material lama) is "a lama who performs rituals in houses solely for the sake of wealth, without studying, thinking, meditating, practicing, and so forth."[4] Dudjom Lingpa found himself in need of food and clothing, yet acting as lama-on-call was clearly not the answer. Shabkar Tsokdruk Rangdrol (1781–1851), another itinerant adept who defied convention, sings a teasing song on this very subject:

> *Are the mountain hermits under attack by bandits?*
> *Why do I ask? Because they don't remain up in the mountains,*
> *But keep coming down to the villages, looking for food.*

While no ideal solution presented itself, just as his isolation fostered independence, a dearth of ready resources was not entirely detrimental to Dudjom Lingpa's spiritual life. Deities and dakinis warned him on several occasions to avoid seeking payments for religious services. They even gave him strict guidelines as to when to seek alms and when to stay in retreat. These impoverished, yet unfettered, conditions contributed to Dudjom Lingpa's full embrace of a tantric adept's lifestyle, allowing him to wander freely and maintain strict retreat as needed. Even after his rise to prominence, he remained obligated to trust the advice of his visionary, if insufficiently bountiful, guides.

The Emergence of Gili Tertön

DUDJOM LINGPA'S STATUS as a treasure revealer was so central to his persona that throughout his autobiographies he is referred to as Terchen Rinpoche, "Supreme Treasure Revealer," and Gili Tertön, "Treasure Revealer of the Gili family" (his major patrons). This aspect of his life is key to understanding Dudjom Lingpa's impact and resulting legacy.

Treasure revelation in Tibet is yet another area of Dudjom Lingpa's life that defies linear explanation, although it does involve as much method as magic. During Guru Rinpoche's lifetime, sacred objects and seminal teachings were miraculously concealed so that destined masters can reveal them at an ideal moment in the future when they will be of most benefit. Treasures pass directly from Guru Rinpoche, Yeshe Tsogyal, or a comparable master to a destined recipient like Dudjom Lingpa. While there are numerous systems for classifying treasure, the two primary kinds are earth treasures and mind treasures, named for the location of their initial concealment.

Earth treasures can include an array of articles—statues, ritual daggers, and so forth—as well as manuscripts, such as meditation guides and rituals.

Most texts concealed as earth treasures were encoded in symbolic script on parchment. These scrolls were hidden, often in adamantine vessels within rocks, underwater, in temples, or in myriad other sites. While earth treasures are substantial in nature and physically concealed in an external environment, they aren't ordinary things subject to weather and decay. These objects, and their assigned guardians, endure to meet their owner due to the power of enlightened vision and the collective good karma of those meant to discover and benefit from such treasures.

Once the appropriate master locates the treasure, the symbolic script, sometimes just a few characters or lines, acts as a catalyst. It unlocks the complete meaning that was once planted in the treasure revealer's mind, often during a past life as a disciple of Guru Rinpoche. The revealer or a colleague then transcribes the symbolic script into human language, a unique process whose delicacy Dudjom Lingpa notes in numerous episodes.

Mind treasures are accessed in the minds of treasure revealers either through cognitive perception of symbolic scripts that catalyze discovery of the whole teaching or through direct apprehension of the teaching itself. Tulku Thondup explains:

> Concentrating his enlightened mind, Guru Padmasambhava concealed the teachings, by the power of aspirations, in the essential nature of the minds of his disciples, or in the expanse of their awareness state. If the teachings had been concealed in an external object or in the ordinary state of mind, they might be affected by changing circumstances. Concealed in the natural state of the mind, which is pure and changeless, they will remain stable until the time of discovery.

Thus, unlike earth treasures, mind treasures are not reliant on external or material support. Although many lifetimes may pass from the time the treasure teaching is planted until a great master unearths it in his or her own mind, when it manifests, it is pristine and timely.

A third category is known as vision treasures. As we have seen, life stories of accomplished adepts are often replete with visions. Yet only when such visions act as a catalyst to unlock mind treasures are the ensuing teachings considered vision treasures.[5] Not all teachings that result from these encounters are considered to be treasure. Even universally revered instructions given in visions to a treasure revealer are not considered vision treasures if they do not satisfy that criterion. This distinction is clear in Dudjom Lingpa's own account of receiving his vision treasures. He reports an instantaneous emergence of the teachings, complete and intact.

Dudjom Lingpa's qualities as a treasure revealer were rarely acknowledged early on. However, nonhuman and visionary recognition was swift and definitive. When Dudjom Lingpa was just three, a sorcerer approached him. This sorcerer recognized the child as Guru Rinpoche's emanation, to whom a treasure had been bequeathed. Three years later, the deity Dorjé Pakmo told the young boy to expect his mind treasure at age twenty-two, and his earth treasure two years later. This constitutes the earliest prediction of his future career. Prophecies such as these validate treasure revealers, often far in advance (sometimes lifetimes) of their actual activity. As events unfolded, Dudjom Lingpa's earth treasure revelation took place when he was twenty-five.

Also in his twenty-fifth year, Dudjom Lingpa for the first time plainly states that he taught students, conducted rituals for patrons, and through those intercessions, was able to heal sick people. The confluence of assuming the role of spiritual guide and the subsequent revelation of his earth treasure was no mere coincidence. This was the result of profound inner evolution thanks to the rigors of meditation practice and intensive retreat. Dudjom Lingpa is in fact renowned for having revealed four cycles (or bodies) of treasure: one earth treasure and a trio of vision treasure cycles, which belong to the category of mind treasure. Incredibly and improbably, these teachings spread far and wide in Tibet during his lifetime and throughout the world today.

Evolution of a Writer and Teacher

THE BUDDHA is said to have accepted requests for teachings only after having been asked to do so on three separate occasions. Disciples often begin guiding others only when their lamas or visions of deities or past masters tell them the time has come to do so. For example, Jikmé Lingpa reports a vision during which Longchenpa tells him, "Noble son, just now the understanding of the meaning-continuum has been transferred to you through appointment and aspiration! So implant a life-staff of practice and teach widely to the fortunate ones! Your songs come forth extremely well." Jikmé Lingpa is then blessed with the realization necessary to transcribe his treasure texts, encouraged to continue with his meditation practice, and receives confirmation that it is time to teach others.

Likewise, Dudjom Lingpa stands on his own, without formal recognition or any tangible acknowledgment, yet he receives ample and insistent visionary validation and encouragement. Thus he teaches without having received invitations from such-and-such a monastery to give specific teachings, as would traditionally be the case. In many instances, students find him after he's directed to certain locales through visionary counsel.

For three years after Dudjom Lingpa discovered his earth treasures, he has no recorded human encounters. He finally reports being approached by a man named Anam Wangchen. The significance of this encounter is twofold. First, Anam Wangchen had been cited in a vision sixteen years prior as someone who would play a pivotal role in the development of Dudjom Lingpa's lineage. Second, this interaction illustrates how his renown has spread. Anam approaches him on the recommendation of a master Dudjom Lingpa held in high esteem. The circumstances of this meeting herald his full acceptance of the powerful role of treasure revealer and lama.

Although Dudjom Lingpa remained immersed in his personal practice, retreat spaces and teaching venues eventually merged. As students began to seek him out and find him, a deity advised him to avoid transcribing lengthy texts from the raw material of his treasures. This directive to keep his work pithy, in both length and essence, was about more than just books. His writing style preserves the magic of the treasure tradition, which allows teachings to emerge fresh, direct, and unadulterated to a contemporary audience hungry for their particular methods and blessings.

Wrathful Virtuoso

ANY READER WHO VISITS Dudjom Lingpa's world will likely find many aspects of his life unfamiliar; we might even conclude that some parts of his persona defy logic, be it conventional or Buddhist. One of these areas outside our rational mind's bandwidth is his renown as a wrathful virtuoso, or in more common language, as a sorcerer. In common Tantric Buddhist terms, he was a master of wrathful activity, an accomplishment gained through harnessing the power of meditation, and this constitutes another aspect of his service to the world and the Buddhist doctrine.

Dudjom Lingpa regularly reports confrontations with humans and demons who prove so insoluble that he needs to enter states of nondual wrathful compassion. In Tantric Buddhism, demonic beings—those especially laden with negativity, hatred, and a strong will to harm others and block paths that inspire goodness—are considered particularly excellent candidates for compassion. The ability to stay the hands of would-be hostile beings before they create even more negative karma constitutes Dudjom Lingpa's rare wrathful virtuosity.

In overpowering these malicious entities, whether they take the form of an army, a witch, or a horse thief, Dudjom Lingpa forcefully liberates beings from their evil patterns. In some cases, this entails separating mind from body and sending the demonic consciousness to a pure land—an environment conducive to the practice of virtue. From a Buddhist perspective, if such entities were left to continue in their habitual cycle of destruction, their next destination would be many aeons in a hell realm. Wisdom guides such as Dudjom Lingpa aid demonic beings by giving them a karmic discount of sorts. Such wrathful activity is never harmful or hurtful, and is always compassionate and liberating.

As we read of Dudjom Lingpa's repeated struggles with human and non-human entities we might well ask if, besides being a wrathful virtuoso, he was also simply an angry person. It may not be surprising to note that he does not portray himself as such. According to his own report, he rises to challenges but does not deliberately instigate confrontations. So he says. His reputation, as likely embroidered (to what degree?) over the hundred years since his death, paints him as a free spirit and nonconformist who owed nothing to the social networks and hierarchies—familial, collegial, religious, political, financial, and so on—that tend to keep us all in check. In oral histories, he is remembered as an unpredictable individual who did and spoke as he pleased, traits he shared to some degree with the people of his region Golok, who are less constrained by formal social manners and verbal honorific forms than their Central Tibetan sisters and brothers. Nevertheless, the verdict of his own and others' accounts, whether friendly or skeptical, seems to indicate that he could definitely be awe-inspiring, intimidating, or even terrifying, but he is not cast as an angry, aggressive, or belligerent character.

Lifestyle "Choices"

BEING A TREASURE REVEALER usually comes prepackaged with a lifestyle. Most were followers of tantric discipline and had families, homes, and possessions. In Dudjom Lingpa's case, his first revelation of earth treasures, at the age of twenty-five, coincided with a visionary message that his retrieval of long-concealed teachings was half as successful as it might have been. Had his destined female partner (her identity then unknown to him) accompanied him, he would have been allowed to recover the entire trove.

At another point in his life, Dudjom Lingpa is told in a vision that if he doesn't meet a qualified consort, his realization will not overflow and that this could result in writings inconsistent with the tantras. This had historical precedents, including that of Jomo Menmo, an emanation of Yeshe Tsogyal who was a thirteenth-century treasure revealer. As the consort of the treasure revealer Guru Chöwang, Jomo Menmo,

> unraveled the knots of his energy channels, whereby he realized all the symbols and meanings of the Great Esoteric Instructional Tantra of the Eight Transmitted Precepts, the Consummation of Secrets . . . which he had not been able to establish previously; he translated it into Tibetan. Consequently their union, which was one of mutual advantage, came to be unsurpassedly beneficial.

Alluded to in numerous prophecies, Dudjom Lingpa's many consorts were not ordinary women. Dudjom Lingpa's eight sons—all reincarnations of past masters—were also heralded in visionary missives. As we read of his experiences and his responses to visionary guidance in this aspect of his life, we do not gain the impression that he chose his sexual partners (and whether or not to have children with them) as men and women of his own place and time did. Even the identities of the women and children with whom he shared his life are known to us only from sources outside his autobiographies.

At the risk of making a too-sweeping generalization, the choices of mates, whether to have children, and where to live number among the most personal for persons of most modern cultures, especially in the West. Encountering an individual who entirely abstains from participating in these life-defining choices is surprising, even troubling. Yet we find our hero, a renowned treasure-revealing virtuoso, an adult man without any societal pressures, has completely abdicated his choices in these departments. He lives in and according to his visions, for better or worse.

Beyond family matters, this is further highlighted by the fact that Dudjom Lingpa was bound to be a lifelong itinerant. Present day Tibet remains a society filled with pastoral nomads wed to fierce seasons. In addition, religious encampments, both nomadic and stationary, still exist and thrive, particularly in Dudjom Lingpa's homeland of Eastern Tibet. Tracing their origins to the thirteenth century, these often highly organized communities uniquely accommodate both monastic and lay disciples, allowing lamas and their diverse groups of followers to live near one another for the sake of teachings and study. In Dudjom Lingpa's case, his nomadic encampment moved from one monastery, retreat center, or like community to the next as he gave teachings.

Nevertheless, even in a society so accustomed to transience, this great master's lack of choice regarding how and where he lived is striking. At age thirty-seven, Dudjom Lingpa built a house near the Mar River in Eastern Tibet. Immediately upon its completion, he identified a portent signaling that he wouldn't stay there. Four years later, he had a surreal dream in which a woman mocked his monastery, Kalzang Gonpa, making similar remarks about his transience.

Even at age sixty, he continued to receive unsolicited advice on the matter of his lodgings. He's informed by an audacious dream persona to abandon his hopes of staying in a house and live in a nomadic encampment instead. Later, just a few years before his death, Dudjom Lingpa is still unable to settle down. Even at the height of his renown, a noncorporeal authority forces him out of comfortable accommodations at a Buddhist center and back onto the road. Dudjom Lingpa and his entourage embark on transient tent life as recommended. This visionary injunction causes him to return to Dzagyal Monastery, where he is received with great honor, as was the case seventeen years earlier.

Why all the flux? Like many treasure revealers before him, Dudjom Lingpa accepts the directives of Guru Rinpoche and Yeshe Tsogyal above any others, including his personal preferences. With this lifestyle comes an overwhelming form of renunciation. He gives up, either motivated by intuition or (often unwelcome) prophetic counsel, his homes, his monasteries, even his children. Ultimately, he renounces his own trajectory and plans.

Dudjom Lingpa never did find a place in this world where he fit in, where he belonged. No happy ending resolved his lifelong struggle with life on human level. He gained a certain notoriety as a treasure revealer, writer, sorcerer, and visionary, but he never retired, never signed a truce or set aside his visionary compass. He might seem to be the paragon of a stubborn, untethered savant, but what other teacher before or since can claim to have guided thirteen disciples to the attainment of rainbow body?

The Outer Autobiography

A Clear Mirror

*Expressions of Pure Display within
the Nature of Reality's Magical Illusion*

An Account of My Secret Meditative Experiences

Namo Guru Padmakara Yé
Homage to the Lotus-Born Lama!

Wisdom body of all victors of the past, present, and future,
Supreme treasure of omniscience, love, and capability:
Lotus-Born, you abide indivisibly with me as the ornament of the wheel
    at the crown of my head.
Having accepted me as your lineage holder, grant me assurance of your
    blessing!

Writing down ordinary individuals' accounts
That detail a variety of karma and deeds within limitless cyclic existence
Would cause me to become depressed and aggravated.
Knowing this, I never even considered putting my own such stories into
    writing.
Nevertheless, I could no longer withstand my disciples' insistent
    requests to do so.
If I recount in detail my myriad visions, these ripples on water,
I could never finish,
So here I will succinctly recount my pure visionary experiences.

The Origin of My Clan

To COMMENCE, if I don't briefly relate the origin of my clan, failure to demonstrate knowledge of my ancestors' family line would cause me to be scorned like a monkey in the jungle. Therefore, I will explain this concisely.

The archives of the illustrious district governor Lhazik Repa state, "The three clans are Ga, Dong, and Dru; a fourth is Dra; Nuwo and Pa Nga make six in all." These words from an important individual constitute a reliable source, so I accept this as valid information.

Ancient stories list the four major clans as Mutsa Ga, Abo Dong, Sengkyung Dra, and Ahchak Dru. Together with two minor clans, Pa and Nga, it is said there are six [Tibetan] clans. This seems to concur with the above statement.

In the Chinese tradition, treatises of elemental astrology correlate the five families with the five elements, five colors, and so forth. According to this system, the brown Dong family is related to the earth element, the white Dra family to the metal element, the blue Dru family to the water element, the red Ga family to the fire element, and the green Go family to the wood element. The major clans are gathered into these five groups, so it has been said. In terms of this system, it's not a great inconsistency to organize them as such. Among the six clans above, the pair Nuwo and Pa Nga are given their own names. When they are not divided as they would be in an extensive version, they are merged into one. For that reason, among the five families above, these two are combined under the name Go. Based on this tradition of elemental astrology, it is appropriate to group the original six into the five major clans.

Of these, I have been told that I come from the Ahchak Dru clan or the blue Dru family. That is the case, as I will now relate: In the past, one branch belonging to the blue Dru family arrived in the Nup region [of Central Tibet]. Among them were Sangyé Yeshe, Wisdom of Enlightenment, who dwelled on the levels of awakening of holy supreme bodhisattvas; the monk Namké Nyingpo, Essence of Space, heart son of the second Buddha; and others who took human rebirth in that region among those who had become known as the Nup family. One part of this Nup family, of the same line as those masters, gradually left that region due to conditions of time and place, and went to Eastern Kham. They settled in the middle of the Makok region close to the Trishok Gyalmo Lake.

There, Nup family descendants reached the summit of valor in worldly terms. Some rivaled the best in swordsmanship and archery skills. One among them lived in Rungchen; he was called Rungta, which become akin to his clan name. Henceforth, the family descended from him was known as Rungta.

In the end, a Mongolian king sought to gather all external areas entirely under his dominion. He dispatched an enormous army; the Nup families were expelled from that area. They gradually traversed many regions and reached a southern range of lower Amdo, known as Dra Chakung. They settled in Upper Dra Chakung, named after a local Chinese iron mine. To that point, those people of the Rungta families are called the earlier Rung line of the Nup family. Concurrently, Nuzok, Tongpön, Doshul, and Rungta are some of the different names that developed for the same clan.

To what area does Dra Chakung belong? It sits within the six mountain ranges of lower Eastern Tibet [Amdo and Kham], in the section of land of the eastern Minyak Range. It numbers among the twenty-five supreme locations of sacred ground in Kham and is called the White Cliff of Venerable Ba or the White Lion Cliff of Washul. In the past, a great student of Ba Mipam Gönpo consecrated this region as a practice site of the heruka. On the cliff's right, the place where water always falls is called Dra Chakung. The people who reside in that region's villages, along with the upper area's distant nomads, are called by the general name Chakung.

Among the early Rung line of the Nup family who lived there was a household with three brothers. Each brother's respective lines of sons, grand-sons, great-grandsons, and great-great-grandsons were said to form a major, a middle, and a minor line. Collectively, these became known as the later Rung line of the Nup family.

Among the descendants of the minor line, Tarpé Gyaltsen, Victory Banner of Freedom, gained accomplishment by relying on the excellent tradition of the Martsang Kagyu; Géwé Gyaltsen, Victory Banner of Virtue, was a master of scriptures and realization. Shakya Gyaltsen, Victory Banner of the Shakyas, had superlative realization of the two phases [of tantric meditation]. They were known as the three victory banners. In later times, a master known as Targé Shakya Gyaltsen, Virtuous Freedom Victory Banner of the Shakyas, and other holy individuals appeared in that family as well.

Moreover, among the minor Rung line of the Nup family, two men called Kyonglo and Dukar gradually journeyed eastward to the upper part of Gyalmo Rong. This was an area known as Do-ser Marsum, where three rivers diverged. The older man named Kyonglo reached the upper area of Dakok. The younger man was named Dukar; he also had an honorific name, Ah-duk, and a nickname, Duklo. He went to the eye of the earth [an especially powerful area], called Seryul Dünying Go, and settled there. Three sons were born to him—the eldest Paldrak, Glorious Renown; the middle Gönkyab, Guardian; and the youngest Dargyé, Increase.

Gönkyab took land in Upper Do. His family line, called Serkor, spread out in Dzutö. The brother named Paldrak went to Lower Do, where, because the family originated from Dra Chakung, his clan was known by that name. Additionally, those who settled in the upper and lower regions became known as the upper-area and lower-area Chakung families. The brother named Dargyé stayed in his homeland, and his family became known as Chokmo Ru.

In that way, the family line that issued from the brother named Gönkyab was called the later family line. My father, named Ah-ten, descended from this line. My mother, named Bo-dzok, belonged to the Mutsa Ga clan. I was born to them in the Female Wood Sheep Year of the fourteenth sixty-year cycle [1835].

Based on this evolution, my family belongs to the minor Rung line of the Nup family, among the trio of So, Zur, and Nup, renowned as kings of mantra practice. In the past, the reincarnation of the awareness holder Mati Ratna, Shartér Chenpo, was born in this family, as were numerous other holy individuals. Since I emerged from this line, I was an exceptional child in a distinctive family of a very pure line of individuals. As for the sections of the Dru Nup family, the major line included a host of skilled warriors. The middle line was very wealthy. The distant line boasted a prevalence of holy individuals who were accomplished meditators.

With that, I've concluded a brief discussion of my parents' family lines and clans.

> In the doctrine of Tüpwang, the Mighty Sage [Shakyamuni Buddha],
> Family and clan are not emphasized,
> Yet to show that karma is not irrelevant,
> Many great individuals took rebirth in this world,
> Appearing in families of renown.
> Likewise, I demonstrated taking rebirth
> Within an especially exalted family of this country.
> I've elucidated this in just a few words.

Namo Guru Manjushri Yé
Homage to Lama Gentle Splendor!

Resplendent with the might of ten million forms of merit,
Your orange youthful body blazes with the brilliance of the dawning
    sun.
Fearless upon a blue lion, boldly magnificent:
Jampal Mawé Sengé, Gentle Splendor Lion of Speech, bestow joy and
    good fortune [upon me for this composition].

Here, an amazing and praiseworthy life story
Like those of supreme, exalted holy individuals
Who possess the three secrets' inconceivable qualities
Cannot be found, and what does appear is very unlikely to help others.

However, to enhance the faith of those with impartial minds,
I burden myself with the hardship
Of expressing what is now certain and undistorted in my mind—
Words that describe this old man just as I am.

An Envoy of Enlightened Activity

So THEN, IN THE PAST, Supreme Buddha Dorjé Chang, Vajra Bearer, the body of ultimate enlightenment (dharmakaya), arose as a guide in the experience of disciples. He assumed a form body of enlightenment (nirmanakaya) for the welfare of the Buddhist doctrine and beings. Known as the powerful adept Nüden Dorjé, Vajra of Capability, he bestowed empowerment upon the thousand buddhas of this aeon and himself received investiture as a Buddhist king of the three realms. He made aspirations to help beings on a vast scale: "Until the teachings of this Fortunate Era's thousand buddhas come to an end, may my sublime and holy emanations constantly appear. May I carry out prodigious acts for the sake of others in ways attuned to their needs and circumstances."

By the force of these pure aspirations, hundreds of his emanations served beings in any number of eras and circumstances. Among them, during the time of our teacher [Shakyamuni Buddha], he was the reincarnate hearer Shariputra; later, Awareness Holder Supreme Hungkara, Drokben Khyé-u Chung Lotsawa, Katok Dampa Deshek, Karnakpa of Drum, and Hépa Chöjung. Once known as Awareness Holder Dudul Dorjé, and later Dudul Dorjé Rolpa Tsal, he converted to Buddhism a profusion of demon hordes called Lokar-nak in this region now known as Drakar Dranak. In [1824], the Male Wood Monkey Year, [my previous incarnation] Dorjé Rolpa Tsal, Demon Vanquisher Vajra Manifest Adept, passed away and advanced to the Lotus Light Celestial Palace of Tail-Fan Island. There Guru Rinpoche empowered, enthroned, and made aspirations for me to suppress the hostile barbarian Chinese, Mongolian, and foreign armies that would come to Tibet's frontiers later in the five hundred year cycle of the degenerate age. Then, gazing upward into the vastness of the open sky, Guru Rinpoche spoke:

Kyé Ma! Alas! So pitiful are beings of this degenerate age!
Corrupt aspirations, heretical substances, mantras, and trance states
Possess their minds and they deceive one another.
They trust nothing and cannot even rely upon themselves.
As their amassed livestock vanish like the wealth of dreams

And frost lays waste to the harvest of sown seeds,
The durushka demons of disease, famine, and weapons torment them.
It's possible that a few are my disciples—
Men and women connected to me through aspirations and karma—
Yet there are no spiritual mentors to show them the path.
Fooled, as if blind and without a guide,
A mob of frauds who hold corrupt views assume the guise of lamas
And lead them into the abyss of endless cyclic existence.
Those guides teach obscured meditation, fixated on ordinary mind and
    bereft of the sacred view.
They cling to and prize the concepts they pursue.
Viewing mind with mind [rather than wisdom], they search for
    happiness and suffering [to which they're attached].
In the end, considering theirs to be the ultimate view
They nonchalantly let loose the mind into nonactivity
And deceptively affirm that Great Perfection and Supreme Seal are "this
    and this alone."
Having accumulated such karma propels them to the state of form
    realm gods.
Clouds veil the sun of the Great Perfection:
Look at how they see a firefly as the sun!

Having spoken, he settled in natural repose.
Dakini Yeshe Tsogyal, Queen of the Victors' Oceanic Wisdom, requested:

Kyé Ma Kyi Hu! Alas, alack, Guru Rinpoche!
The time has arrived when the five forms of degeneration are rampant.
Sheltering these cruel, deluded sentient beings is hard,
Yet to you some are connected through aspirations and karma.
Led down false paths into darkness,
They roam through the abodes of endless cyclic existence.
To tame these beings, I beseech you, arise in the form
Of an emanated sacred awareness holder, an envoy of enlightened
    activity!

Guru Rinpoche responded to her plea:

Wisdom Dakini Tsogyalma, listen to me!
There are individuals with karmic destiny from past training:
A vestige of the sunlight of Secret Mantra teachings
Still shines in Do Kham, the lower region of the land of Tibet.
Although some disciples live there,
They lack stability and independence,
Overpowered by masters who cling to their own views as supreme.
The might of the adept Nüden Dorjé 's aspirations
Wields a force capable of guiding a few disciples.
Apart from the illustrious awareness holder Dudul Dorjé, there is no else:
His enlightened wisdom must arise in human form!
If he relies on Khamsum Wangchuk, Ruler of the Three Realms, teacher
    to the gods [as a protector],
He will master others' phenomena.
Right now, all of you awareness holders and male and female adepts
Within ten million leagues:
Throw flowers, hold paths of silks, and create a symphony
To escort the wrathful Dudul [back to the world].

Moved by his words, I considered my own disappointment and aggravation with cyclic existence, and how very troublesome it is to tame beings of our degenerate age. Pondering this, I respectfully joined my hands in prayer and appealed,

Kyé Ho! Supreme eternal refuge, Orgyen Rinpoche,
Superb universal embodiment of all buddhas of the past, present, and
    future:
Heed me with your love and compassion,
And grant me permission [not to return].

Guru Rinpoche again issued the same command:

Listen to me, Dudul Drakpo Tsal!
Sentient beings of this degenerate age are difficult to guide,
Yet there are three thousand fortunate individuals
Connected to you through their previous lifetimes' aspirations and
    karma:

These are your disciples.
More than five hundred sublime beings among them
Can gain freedom in one lifetime.
Reincarnations of the king and his subjects
Will arise as twenty-five envoys of your activity.
Moreover, ten emanations of treasure revealers
Will truly serve beings.
Emanations of seven Secret Mantra teachers
Will reincarnate as your own children.
They will benefit beings—have no doubt!
Therefore, you, sovereign awareness holder,
Arise as the wisdom body of Dorjé Drolö,
And these fierce dharma protectors will accompany you as companions.
You will appear as a child
To parents with whom you have a previous karmic connection.
The time to enact my enlightened activity has arrived. Now go!

I was incapable of refusing Guru Rinpoche's imposing command. As I examined who these parents were with whom I had a previous karmic connection, I saw that the parents of Katok Dudul Dorjé, my previous incarnation, had both passed away and gained the support of a human rebirth. As mentioned earlier, my father belonged to the Ahchak Dru clan in Eastern Kham and my mother belonged to the Mutsa Ga clan. Through the strength of their aspirations, they had again married each other. Seeing that I had a karmic connection with them, I left Guru Rinpoche's presence accompanied by an immeasurable assembly of spiritual heroes and dakinis casting a rain of flowers, and entered my mother's womb. From then on, in her dreams my mother always saw a multitude of spiritual heroes and dakinis guarding her and performing ablution rituals. I was born during the night of the tenth day[7] in the Bird Month of the Female Wood Sheep Year [1835]. At sunrise, everyone saw rainbows entirely encircling our yak-hair tent. The tips of the rainbows reached inside our home.

On that occasion, an individual named Lama Jikmé, Fearless, was invited. He gave me longevity empowerments and proclaimed, "When I married the two of you I had the sense that it would be very fortunate if you stayed together. Now the tips of rainbows extend into your tent home. These two experiences coincide. Furthermore, today I have the impression that this child of yours is an incomparable reincarnate master. Even if a monastery doesn't claim him, he will awaken to his spiritual heritage: It seems certain he will help others. Therefore, make it a point to keep him very clean and periodically exert yourself in making smoke offerings and ablution rituals."

Henceforth, for the next three years I actually saw dakinis dancing beautifully and singing melodious songs. My mother repeatedly dreamt of this as well. Very often during the night, hordes of male ruler demons, female sorceress demons, and vow-violation spirits threatened my life—I saw battles ensue as they clashed with spiritual heroes and dakinis. I was constantly terrified and would cry in panic to my mother. Though I wanted to express myself, I didn't know how to talk, so I just rolled around in bed and wailed. Unable to sleep, both mother and child suffered.

Your Father's Wealth

I TURNED THREE in the Bird Year [1837].[8] On the eighth day of the second month, I watched as my venerable mother prepared to go dig for wild sweet potatoes. "I'm going to follow her," I thought. As she was leaving, she tied me with the rope attached to the tent door and departed. I cried until I collapsed. At that moment a woman came along—I imagined it was my mother returning. Thinking this, I looked up as a very beautiful white dakini arrived. She said, "I'm your mother. Come here," and took me on her lap. I nursed from her breast and my entire body and mind instantly became intoxicated with bliss. When the woman said, "My child, do you want to go to your mother's grove?" she immediately led me off, and the experience of traveling unfolded: We went north, crossing in a moment over many world systems to the wide and spacious panorama of a pure land illuminated by the light of lapis jewels. It was circled by wish-fulfilling trees; at its center stood a celestial palace with four walls and four doors, decorated with myriad flowers. Elegant and beautiful in formation, the palace was captivating.

Within its delightfully charming interior stood a jeweled throne. Upon a seat made of a lotus, sun, and moon sat a buddha known as Dön Mizawa Gyalpo, Transcendent Conqueror Undoubtable King, adorned with the buddhas' marks and signs of physical perfection. His right hand displayed the gesture of giving refuge, while his left made the gesture of abiding in evenness. He wore the three Buddhist robes and sat in cross-legged vajra posture. To his right was a bodhisattva called Salkyab Wangpo, Chief Encompassing Clarity, and to his left was a bodhisattva called Nampar Drolwé Gyalpo, King of Liberation; both were white and red in color and blazed with light. They ceaselessly emanated clouds of offerings to the central buddha and praised him with respectful words.

Furthermore, congregations of male and female bodhisattvas, as numerous as stars clustered in the sky, bowed with deep reverence to that buddha, praising him with many poetic verses. Likewise, even I expressed myself by saying,

Namo! Homage to the sublime epitome of all sacred circles and buddha families:

Buddha Transcendent Conqueror, to you I bow.
Liberate all beings, others and myself, who wander in cyclic existence,
From the worldly ocean and grant us assurance of freedom!

Thus I respectfully rendered homage. Once I made that supplication, five colored light rays emerged from the buddha's heart and dissolved into my own—I experienced the wisdom of bliss-emptiness. Then that transcendent being spoke:

Child, I acclaim you as my regent.
I empower you in the vajra Secret Mantra approach.
You have already gained supreme and common spiritual attainments.

He placed a crystal box in my hands. Inside appeared the shapes of the syllables *Om Ah Hung,* as if painted clearly in white, red, and blue. "This is your share of your father's wealth. Without harboring any doubts, swallow it." Just as he instructed me, I gulped it down. This caused me to remember a multitude of teachings; it renewed my aptitude for everything I had learned and trained in throughout my previous lifetimes, including every creation- and completion-phase meditation practice. These all became vivid in my mind as if a precise copy had been made. I rested for a while within that luminous state.

Then, as if I was waking from a dream, everything vanished into basic space. Just then my mother returned. Since I had cried myself into a faint, she said, "Either he's dead or struck by disease!" Sobbing, she told my father to call for a lama. He invited Lama Jikmé, who then gave me a longevity empowerment and performed many rituals for summoning the forces of my longevity. He told them, "This child hasn't been struck by disease: It seems that his karmic propensities from previous training have awakened."

At that moment I gazed at him with clairvoyance. I saw that through the momentum of positive aspirations, a man called Tsampuk Gomchen, Great Meditator Cave-Dwelling Hermit, who was the paternal uncle of my former incarnation, Dudul Dorjé, had been reborn as this man, who was now my lama and a local leader. From that point on, the opportunity for demonic obstructers to harm me and any turmoil caused by gods and demons vanished on its own.

This Appearance of a Young Boy

THAT SAME YEAR at night on the tenth day of the first summer month, a woman appeared in my dream saying, "I have come from the celestial pure land of Orgyen Dakpa, Pure Orgyen. My child, do you want to go to the western land of Orgyen?" She led me, and we shot like an arrow more than a league upward into space. Once we crossed over numerous regions and countries, I saw that all the mountains were made of dried skeletons ablaze with light. No trees grew—only groves of different arsenals, from which spark-like weapons flew, as in a tempest. All water flowed as lakes and surging rivers of blood, with bubbles the size of yak-hair tents carrying the corpses of humans, horses, tigers, leopards, bears, brown bears, and other beings. The bubbles were filled with these creatures' dead bodies.

The resonance of the four elements and the clamor of living beings reverberated as "Phat! Pem! Kill! Strike!" making a din like the roar of a thousand dragons. I saw all appearing forms as male and female wrathful deities who hoisted aloft innumerable weapons, and hordes of black men and women launching magical weapon wheels. Blazing whirlwinds of fire raged thick upon one another, as loud as thunder.

In the midst of that terrifying, brilliant, and fearsome land stood a three-sided building erected from piles of new and old charnel-ground bones. Inside this immense and tall structure, upon a throne of numerous fresh and withered human corpses, stood the chief dakini Dorjé Pakmo, Vajra Sow. She was dark blue, terrifying, and magnificent with an extremely wrathful demeanor. At the crown of her head a black pig's head jutted upward, squealing. She held a curved knife aloft in space with her right hand and used this to draw under her control hosts of spiritual heroes and dakinis. She transformed all apparent existence into blood in the skull-cup in her left hand, and drank it. Her right leg was drawn up in dancing posture and her left leg was bent. A tantric staff rested at her shoulder, and she wore a complete array of charnel-ground regalia.

When I met her, she stood haughtily in the center of a constellation of dakinis, and sang to me:

> Child, I acclaim you as Lotus-Born's supreme regent!
> These days, foul demon hordes spread,
> While the protective gods that uphold goodness are on the decline.
> In your region especially, a being with corrupt views has assumed the
>   guise of a lama.
> When his bad karma converged, he died by a knife,
> And was then reborn as a malicious, homicidal ruler demon.
> Due to this, he jealously murders all holy, noble lamas
> And people of high standing.
> Under his thrall, they stray into delusion as ruler demons of vow
>   violation.
> Since that creature will attack your life and threaten your doctrine,
> I will protect you and grant you my blessing!

When she finished speaking, the five syllables *Bam Ha Ri Ni Sa* shone on the palm of her hand, and my body was cloaked in layers of five-colored light. The letter *Bam* emerged from the tip of her right breast and entered my heart. My entire body was saturated with red luminosity and appeared to be made of light.

"Now, my child, return to your home. During the latter part of your life, you will be of significant benefit to beings." She stroked my head, and with that I awoke—she disappeared like a magical contraption collapsing.

THAT SAME YEAR, on the morning of the ninth day in the last winter month, I went to play around a sheep corral. I saw a turquoise man riding an iron horse. Holding a lance with a white silk banner in his right hand, he circumambulated me three times, then removed his tiger-skin hat and said,

> Kyé Ho! Greetings Khyé-u Chung Lotsawa!
> If you don't recognize me,
> Outwardly, I am Ngala Taktsé Lak;
> Inwardly, I am a wild sorcerer who takes lives;
> Secretly, I am the nine classes of Zhang ministers.
> In the past, at a place called Drakmar Yerpa,
> Glorious Supreme Master Orgyen granted me empowerment,
> Entrusted me with the stewardship of three great treasures,
> And conferred upon me inconceivable wealth and possessions.

"When the five-hundred-year period of degeneration arrives,
I will live on Earth as a son of the Ahchak Dru clan.
At that time, give me this one treasure," proclaimed Guru Rinpoche.
I wondered, "Is it you?" so I came to see.
Now I recognize you!

He smiled and vanished.

WHEN I WAS FOUR, on the seventh day of the fourth month, I came across a
pile of old hardened ashes along the path where I played. I dug it full of holes,
then left. The next day when I returned to look at that pile, I saw a white field
mouse inside the hollow of one hole. I wanted to grab it but couldn't. After
a while I poked a spoon in the hole. The mouse sat up in a crouch, and said
to me,

Pi Pi Kam Kam Lé Lé Ho!
The sacred refuge is the Three Jewels.
The buddhas' truth is shown by the wisdoms and bodies of
    enlightenment.
The sacred teachings' truth is shown by relative and ultimate truth.
The spiritual community's truth is based on embodying the qualities of
    scripture and realization.
Take refuge in the three supreme jewels.

Sentient beings, ignorant of their own nature, are deluded.
In their flagrant attachment to that delusion, they experience happiness
    and suffering.
All sensations are suffering:
The extent of their delusion is pitiful!

I am Ahchung the Amazing.
I came from Brahma's heaven above.
I am Babo Jawa, child of the gods.
I'm incredible! This is wonderful! I laugh out loud!
I look at you [Shariputra], the son of Sharadhati—
You are said to be one who has defeated his enemies, so who are your
    enemies?

You are said to be liberated, so who is liberated?
You are said to have tamed demons, so what demons have you tamed?
You are said to have transcended, so what have you transcended?
If you are a sentient being, then who has gone beyond sorrow?
I am definitely a sentient being, and you've caused me harm!
If you lack compassion, then what of your intention to awaken for
    others' sake?
Failing to see your own hidden faults brought to light,
Instead you boast. What a terrible shame!

Pick me up and toss me in the water.
This child of the gods is disguised as a child of animals.
This animal will take the guise of a child of nagas.
This child of nagas will go to the land of [Indra,] Lord of the Gods,
A place of wondrous revelry!

He fell into the palm of my hand, instantly became a black frog, and jumped onto the surface of the water. At that moment, a rainbow appeared from the sky and extended until it reached just above the frog, who immediately departed into light and vanished into space.

LATER, ON THE TWENTY-EIGHTH DAY of that same month, I went to play on the banks of the Ser River when it was quite swollen. At the bottom of the Nakté Mountain, a huge boulder sat at the river's center; at its base was an old man with white hair and a white beard. He stared directly at me and I felt a little intimidated. He said, "Hey there!" three times and finally called out, "Well then . . . ?" He peered at my face, so I asked, "Who are you?" He replied,

Yé Yé! This majestic mountain that rises to the midheavens
Is like dust particles collected by the winds of timeless existence.
Above, this light blue sky we see
Is like sentient beings' primordial oblivious delusion.
The space between these is empty blankness,
Like the fault of seeing your inner state manifesting outwardly, yet
    assuming it's something else.
The appearance of stars reflected on this great river's surface

Is like perceiving partitions in space.
A single thing that seems to morph into many
Is like self-manifest perception imprinted with false characteristics.
Given that no one is here, I appear as an old man
Who is like the old fellow in your own confused perception.
This solid stone behind me you can stare at
Is like the reification of your own deluded dualistic fixation.
I am you, as an old man of existence.
In your confused perception of an old man of existence
There is this appearance of a young boy—how astonishing!

"Do you understand my metaphors or not?" he asked, and I told him I did not. "Ha ha!" he laughed, and vanished into basic space like an optical illusion.

THAT SAME YEAR, on the evening of the fifth day of the eighth month, I saw a line of cranes above me in the sky. I listened to their call and heard this:

Kur! Kur! In the past during this fortunate aeon,
The teacher, a glorious buddha, and his circle of followers convened on
    this earth.
Now you don't even hear a trace of the story
Of the happiness of that gathered assembly.

In the middle of this fortunate aeon,
Constellations of illustrious accomplished masters
Turned the wheel of the teachings for their gatherings of accomplished
    followers.
Now the happiness of the disciples born at that time
Is imperceptible—how dull beings' minds have become!

In the latter part of this fortunate aeon,
In this benighted land of demons called Tibet,
The lords Abbot Shantarakshita and Master Guru Rinpoche dawned like
    the sun and moon.
At that time, translators and scholars encircled them, as numerous as
    the stars.

The happiness of Tibet's doctrine and inhabitants
Hasn't endured to the present day—how dismal!

When the end of this fortunate aeon arrived,
Noble accomplished adepts—great treasure revealers—
Were surrounded by their assembled entourage, disciples, and subjects,
And the sun of happiness dawned in Kham and the land of Tibet.
Now that hasn't lasted—it vanished like a dream.

In summertime, the green grass is festooned with flowers
And myriad trees, leaves, and fruits flourish.
Happiness amid that meadow
Now hasn't endured—it vanished like a dream.

We mothers and children are flying south, to Mön.
At the end of this degenerate five-hundred-year cycle,
Beings have become wild and cruel, with coarse emotions.
Although a teacher to subdue them has appeared,
Still these mother and child cranes leave the land of Kham behind.
Future disciples will be difficult to tame—how miserable!
Now we're thinking of leaving for another pure land.
Having observed the borderland barbarians,
It won't be long before the sun of the Buddhist doctrine
Is veiled by the clouds of demons' corrupt views. Look at that!

Then they flew off into the western sky.

I TURNED FIVE in the Pig Year [1839]. On the tenth day of the sixth month, white clouds gathered thick in the southwestern sky, amid which a five-colored halo encircled a canopy of rainbow light. This held a handsome white man in silk garments. He traveled along a rainbow path and arrived before me. Giving me a white crystal rosary, he said, "My child, if you complete one hundred million recitations of the six-syllable mantra, the latter part of your life will be of immense benefit to beings." Then the perception arose that he dissolved into my heart. For the next few days I saw all phenomena as Potala Mountain Pure Land, and not even an iota of impure phenomena arose.

That same year on the twenty-fifth day of the tenth month, I went to play at a place called Yarchen where two valleys met. A red man with a red horse gave me a long-life arrow with silk ribbons and said,

> Kya! This red arrow is made of tamarisk wood, a magnetizing material.
> Since five-colored silks festoon it, you can accomplish the four activities.
> In a future period of your life, in the Rabbit Year,
> If you lodge this where the upper valley begins,
> Your merit, renown, and glory will increase.
> I am Nöjin Shenpa Marnak, Dark Red Noxious Spirit Butcher.
> For many lifetimes I've never experienced separation from you.
> Now I will accompany you in your activity!

Then he vanished like an optical illusion.

That same year on the fifteenth day of the first autumn month, I went to play at midday on the lower plateau, called Yarchung, and spied a rabbit. When I followed it, it became a monkey who crouched down and told me, "I am the wandering spirit of the deceased woman who was your father's wife before your mother."

I asked, "Where has your life force gone? And your consciousness?"

"My life was terminated by a demoness. My consciousness has taken on the body of a female dog in Kongpo," she answered.

"If you don't have a consciousness, where have you come from?" She told me,

> Hé! From the interdependent connection
> Of the mind that clings to an "I" and appears as a self,
> Phenomena as the spirit arises by clinging to the existence
> Of the person left behind, which is deemed "the spirit."
> If not having [a consciousness] causes the spirit not to exist, then it
>   never existed from the start,
> Yet if you grasp to something existent, then it's merely this "I."

Then she vanished without a trace.

Seeing these copious spectacles of illusory visionary appearances

Enhanced my view—the realization that all phenomena are like a
   magical illusion.
Although my physical form was very young in age,
The strength of my realization's body was fully developed.
Compared to sentient beings, my capability was inconceivable.
Although I had immeasurable insight in the realm of meditative
   experience,
Nothing whatsoever appeared apart from the outwardly appearing
   luminosity
That arises from the vast expanse of the basis of being.

Gods and Demons

I TURNED SIX in the Rat Year [1840]. On the morning of the first day of the sixth month, as soon as I awoke I saw a black nine-headed iron scorpion writhing about in the space before me. I was immediately terrified. Unable to bear it, I covered my head and cried for a while. When someone called out, "Ah Ho!" I drew back the blanket and peeked out. A man stood above the scorpion and appeared to speak to me, saying, "Ho! I am known as the scorpion-riding madman. I've come to deliver a message to you. Pema Drakpo, Wrathful Lotus, says, 'When you go to sleep at night, you must meditate on your own body as an iron scorpion blazing with fire. For three years, don't forget this! It's not right to meditate on yourself as an animal forever, yet in this circumstance you must, in order to gain victory over a ruler demon's malice. This is the scorpion. Look at it. Vividly instill it in your mind's domain, just as it is. This is very important! Look well.'" Then they vanished.

THAT SAME YEAR, one evening in the seventh month when I covered my head to rest, I couldn't sleep. Light rose like the dawn and within it swirled a crimson expanse like the bright, colorful streaks of shooting stars and flashes of lightning. A woman saying she was the goddess Tro Nyérchen, Great Wrathful Frown, appeared—wrathful, fierce, light blue, and fearsome, with angry, staring eyes. She said,

> Kyé Ho! Pray to me, noble exalted [Tara].
> Gods and demons attack you:
> Bring me to mind every morning without fail.
> Render homage and take refuge in me. Don't forget. Concentrate!
> When you supplicate me, pray just like this:
> "Noble exalted Drolma, Liberating Mother, heed me!
> Shelter me from all fears and sufferings, I pray!"
> Supplicate me in that way.

Then she vanished.
When I fell asleep, an experience of bliss-emptiness dawned. Through-

out the night, other than the sensation of that single moment, nothing else
arose.

THAT SAME YEAR, on the night of the twenty-fifth day of the tenth month, I
experienced myself arriving at a long golden plain called Laka. In the midst
of a vajra feast attended by one thousand dakinis, the vajra master was identified to me as Dorjé Pakmo, Vajra Sow. Magnificent upon a throne of bloody
human skulls, she said to me,

> Kyé Ho! Holy individual of excellent fortune,
> Rely on your chosen deity, Dorjé Drolö,
> And practice the creation phase as you apply the key instructions and
>   complete the full number of mantra recitations.
> Rely on Jampal Mawé Sengé, Gentle Splendor Lion of Speech,
> And practice the creation phase as you apply the key instructions,
>   reciting his mantra one hundred thousand times for each syllable.
> Cherish the supreme master Orgyen as your crowning jewel:
> Recite "The Seven-Line Prayer" one hundred thousand times
> And the four-line "Prayer for the Spontaneous Fulfillment of Wishes"
>   many times.
> Recite "The Litany of the Names of Gentle Splendor" ten thousand
>   times.

> Once you've completed all those tasks, at the age of twenty-two your
>   mind treasure will overflow.
> At the age of twenty-four, you will bring forth three cycles of earth
>   treasure.
> After the age of forty, you will be of incredible service to beings.
> Further, different kinds of demons with corrupt aspirations
> Will reproach and criticize you, rise up as enemies, and so forth.
> Reject the karmic ripening of their evil intents and deeds.
> At that time, sever your attachment to caring about happiness and
>   suffering, hope and fear.
> Hold to your own ground! This is a key piece of advice.
> By doing just that, every adverse condition will become your ally.

Immediately after speaking, she vanished as if in a dream.

THAT SAME YEAR, at night on the tenth day of the twelfth month, I dreamt that light appeared in the eastern sky, white like the conch color of the fifteenth day's full moon. Within a dense expanse of white clouds, I saw crowds of busy, bustling people and heard the clamor of many different sounds. This sight drew closer and closer until finally it arrived directly in front of my face. In its midst appeared someone saying he was the sublime, exalted Tukjé Chenpo, Supreme Compassion, youthful, bright white, and beautiful to behold. Seated amid one hundred thousand spiritual heroes and dakinis, he showed his radiant smiling face to me and gave me this sacred advice:

> My child, meditate on me.
> Occasionally recite my six-syllable mantra as a supplication.
> Sometimes clearly visualize your body as me
> And recite the six-syllable mantra as my vital essence.
> Your inseparable companion,
> I foresee that I will repel your outer and inner obstacles.

As soon as he spoke, I awoke from that dreamscape. From then on, a child in white garments would sometimes accompany me in my dreams and foretell my own and others' happiness and suffering, fortune and misfortune, and make other predictions. That child was warmly loving towards me.

I TURNED SEVEN in the Ox Year [1841]. To celebrate the arrival of the New Year, we climbed atop a high hill. From a gap in the sky, a rainbow shone, ending directly in front of me. Along its path traveled someone saying he was Awareness Holder Longchen Rabjam, Infinite Expanse. He was youthful, wore monk's robes, and was adorned with the buddhas' marks and signs of physical perfection. He gave me two pills made of vajra feast substances. As I savored their sweet taste, my body and mind became intoxicated with bliss. At that moment, this song dawned in my mind, so I sang,

> É! If you desire a happy blissful abode,
> Above lies Joyful Heaven, land of the gods,
> The result of constant meditative stability.
> If you can meditate, it's not far off—it's so close!

The realm that provides unchanging bliss
Is Celestial Enjoyment Pure Land,
The result of profound creation-phase practice.
If you can meditate, it's not far off—it's so close!

Ultimate Unsurpassable Pure Land, a place self-manifest,
Is the true capital of the body of ultimate enlightenment.
The doctrine of Great Perfection
Will lead you to mastery of your own awareness.
It's not far off—isn't that astonishing?

Longchen Rabjam is my sole father.
Having actually met him today,
He gave me pills that grant liberation upon taste.
Their flavor of bliss-emptiness has inebriated me:
Now I've found the path to freedom!

Friends, assembly of fortunate men and women,
Connected through our past lives' deeds and their fruition,
Focus your minds on positive virtue
And you will seize the path to freedom!

When I sang this song, everyone at the vajra feast gathering rejoiced and was amazed.

THAT SAME YEAR on the fifteenth day of the first winter month, I went to a mountain flank called Puktsa. Its surface was made of stone and earth mixed together, and when I dug into it with a pickax, I struck a small boulder. I pried at it repeatedly with a strong stick and succeeded in dislodging it, leaving a crevice in the mountain. Inside I saw a dense lattice of five-colored rainbow light that held an exquisite, fascinating five-colored sphere. A monk, handsome in face and form, sat within that sphere's expanse. He wore saffron robes; his two hands displayed the gestures of teaching the doctrine and abiding in evenness. He sat in cross-legged posture. With a smiling face he said, "You've opened the door of my dwelling place. Why have you done that? I've stayed here for three thousand human years and haven't encountered an ordi-

nary person. You can only see me because of your previous [good] karma and
aspirations. Even if you couldn't see me, merely by seeing this, my domicile,
you will surely realize the meaning of profound emptiness. So be joyful!"

> Who am I? I am the unfixed basic space of phenomena.
> All phenomena are the five aggregates.
> The five aggregates are things that arise in interdependence.
> View everything as emptiness.

Then he disappeared.

After that, I called to my father and a family friend named Gyaltsé, Victorious Life, who came over. They grew worried as soon as they saw that
cave, saying, "Oh shit! A fissure in this great mountain is definitely not good."
They closed the mouth of the cave with a lot of rocks and earth, and we left.

I TURNED EIGHT in the Tiger Year [1842]. On the morning of the fifteenth
day of the middle summer month, I went along with my sister and a little
neighbor girl down to the waters of the Ser River, which was extremely turbulent. Between the peaks and crests of the massively soaring waves, I saw
the elevated apex of a large boulder. I thought, "I'll go on top of that," and
then I saw a path of rainbow light like an outspread blanket. As I tread along
there, it felt like walking on the ground. I reached the top of the boulder and
sat down. Then two men on horseback called Abo Tarchin and Sokpo Serré
came to the water's edge. They cursed aloud, reprimanding me.

Serré said, "Should the two of us throw ourselves into the water [trying
to reach him]?"

Tarchin said, "I'm definitely unable to give my own life. A demon led that
boy there. If you look at it that way, death by drowning is unavoidable in this
situation. Let's go deliver this news to his family."

As soon as they'd gone, I crossed over the water: Like a waterfowl, I
returned to where I was before. When I arrived home, the two men from
before exclaimed, "An obstructer demon has possessed this boy—an elaborate
rite must be performed for him! Make divinations! Do astrology readings!"
Then they left.

A Lama Who Inspires

In the Rabbit Year [1843], I turned nine. At night on the seventh day of the first winter month, a dakini wearing a blue cotton blanket told me, "My child, next year you must leave here and go to the northwest, where you will meet the supreme master Orgyen incarnate, named Lama Jamyang, Gentle Melody. In the course of his lifetimes, he was Master Namké Nyingpo, Essence of Space. Train in reading and writing with this master—all your happiness and well-being will gradually come into resolution. This is certain."

Saying that, she handed me an exquisite and fascinating skull-cup into which she poured nectar. When I drank it down in a single gulp, I experienced bliss coursing through my whole body. The dakini mounted a sunbeam and departed, vanishing into a gap in the blue sky.

At the start of the Dragon Year [1844], when I turned ten, on the evening of the fifth day of the first spring month, someone approached me riding a white lion. He wore monk's garb and a hat with a round brim. "I am Dorjé Lekpa, Vajra of Excellence. You have a past karmic connection with a lama people are inviting to come. He will arrive on the fourteenth day of the middle summer month. Be joyful and see to it that you are able to meet him." Then he vanished.

That same year, at night on the seventh day of the middle summer month, I witnessed this vision in a dream. A red man with a body made of tongues of flames rode a red fire garuda with wings of wind. He came right up to me in the sky saying, "Kyé! You are an individual in whom exceptional past aspirations and karmic propensities now converge. Since the time of Khyé-u Chung Lotsawa to the present, you and I have never been separated for even a moment. Therefore, I am your protector throughout all your lifetimes. On the fourteenth day of this month, your maternal uncle named Mingyur, Unchanging, will come to summon you. You must go with him!" Then he disappeared.

My maternal uncle did arrive on the fourteenth day. As my dream had indicated, it was crucial that I go with him. I explained this to my parents. My mother said, "When something is lost and he explains where to find it based on his dreams, they've never been false. Therefore, we really must send him, right?"

My father replied, "While that may be true, this boy is so terribly wild that I wonder if he might get in a fight and be killed. Nevertheless if there is no way for him not to leave, he should learn to read. Such training is an absolute necessity."

My uncle said, "Whether or not he gets trained in reading, I'm wondering if he can take over my household and land." Saying that, he didn't promise anything.

So the next day my uncle led me away to live at his house. He kept domesticated animals, including livestock. Since they obliged me to work as a shepherd, I reacted by piercing all the cast iron cauldrons, clay pots, stirrups, containers, and every utensil with a bamboo arrow, smashing them until only fragments remained. Both my grandmother and aunt declared, "A goblin has possessed this boy! If he's trained in reading, he could become a practitioner, right? If that doesn't happen, as a secular layperson, it's certain that he will defeat others and ruin himself."

My uncle replied, "Well, now he must become a practitioner."

In the Snake Year [1845], I turned eleven. On the first day of the first winter month, I was led into the presence of Lama Jamyang, who was very pleased to see me and smiled radiantly. He patted me on the head, gave me sugar and molasses treats, and said, "Last night I had an outstanding dream and today, once again, I experienced a sense of joy and well-being. Based on that, I think you will become an exceptionally outstanding practitioner. Ordinary individuals don't have flawless clairvoyance, and they value mere meditative experiences and dreams above all else. If those hold any truth at all, then my dream is probably also true." Having said that, he taught me the thirty letters of the alphabet three times and recited an aspiration prayer three times. From that point on, the holy lama took me under his care and trained me in reading.

In the Horse Year [1846], I turned twelve; at night on the ninth day of the seventh month, a young woman wearing a blue brocade upper garment, a red wrapped skirt, and a yellow silk belt told me, "Let's go together to Sindu City in the north." She held my fingers and led me away. When we arrived in a city of nonhuman dakinis, I saw absolutely every kind of male and female daka and dakini gathered there like at a marketplace. In their midst loomed a canopy of rainbow light. Within an arc of fine vajras sat the wisdom form of the supreme master Orgyen as if he were a painting, wearing a full set of his customary regalia. He was teaching the definite secret supreme approach to the dakini assembly.

I respectfully bowed before him. The moment I touched his feet, he smiled, placed his right hand upon my head and prayed, "My child, at this very moment may nonconceptual wisdom, the enlightened mindstream of the victors and their spiritual heirs of the three times, shift to your mind. Once your mind reaches spiritual maturity and liberation, may you have the capacity to lead anyone who encounters you to the ground of liberation."

Then he told me, "Sit here before me and listen to my words of explanation." As instructed, I sat there and listened. The supreme master told me, "This lama of yours, called Jamyang, is an emanation of Bodhisattva Dribpa Namsel, Dispeller of Obscurations. You have a connection with him as your spiritual guide throughout five lifetimes. Heed his instructions and you will surely become an individual proficient in language.

"At the end of your life, someone will help this monastery and it will be as if the sun were dawning on a dark continent—he is a holder of the doctrine of clear light Great Perfection [and a reincarnation of] Natsok Rangdrol, Self-Liberated Sensory Spheres, who is Langdro Konchok Jungné incarnate. Further, a lord of my activity, an authentic emanation of the monk Ma Rinchen Chok, known as Anam, will cultivate the doctrine. In the past, Anam forcefully liberated Nyangmi Nangboché, who was reborn by the force of his corrupt aspirations as a ruler demon in Nyilung. He will create obstacles for Anam—in the end, with his life span compromised, he won't be able to help anyone. Anam's subjects and entourage are composed of many individuals connected to him through aspirations and karma. They will become your disciples and uphold the doctrine's tradition."

He then asked, "Before now, did things like frightful apparitions appear to you?"

I offered this in response: "When I was seven years old, during the evening of the eighteenth day of the first winter month, I went with my oldest sister to search for a calf. On top of a boulder we saw bloody flesh and a large pile of mucus. My older sister exclaimed, "Oh no! What is this?" We were both terrified and panic-stricken, so the two us, brother and sister, fled for home. Once we recounted what had happened to our parents, they said it was the miraculous apparition of gods and demons. This made me extremely fearful.

"As soon as I closed my eyes to sleep, waves of blood crashed down from above like a raging river, with a din that could rend heaven and earth. In all directions absolutely everything appeared as a blank void in blackness. Frightened and unable to sleep, I got up again, sobbing intensely. Since then, as soon as I close my eyes I see things like that. Especially in the time since I turned ten or eleven years old, with no sky above and no earth below, I've seen tremendous waves of blood within an expanse of vivid emptiness. These would change into a glowing red inferno like a rainbow, from which shone infinite masses of light, causing the environment and beings of a vast region to appear, like the reflection of the moon on water—an appearance without any intrinsic nature. That experience led me to understand that the entire range of environments and beings is my own manifestation, without any reality, like a dream."

The supreme master said, "Child, red Girti Dakini has explicitly given you the sacred teachings that reveal cyclic existence and transcendence as self-manifest. Based on her instruction, recognize their intrinsic nature. Gain confidence in that!" Then he vanished.

The night when that incident initially frightened me, both my parents said, "It seems as if our boy is possessed by a demon, so tomorrow we will invite a lama. We must request an authorization empowerment." Then they each held my head on their laps. I stayed with them until dawn, although it didn't allay my fear. As they said, the next day they invited someone called Lama Tsenzang, Excellent Attributes, and requested him to perform Severance practice and an empowerment, with an ablution ritual. They also asked for a prediction, to which the lama responded, "Your little boy is not possessed by a demon or hindering spirit. Last night a dakini told me that the little boy I would see tomorrow is not in fact possessed by demons. His karmic propensities from the past have awakened, and this is a portent that he will gain the mastery of realization. Since that dakini's words are definitely true, I've concluded that my services of protection and reversing ill aren't needed." In that way, he reassured us.

IN THE YEAR I TURNED THIRTEEN [1847], at night on the fifteenth day of the ninth month, all phenomena collapsed into the nature of reality, boundless unformulated basic space. At one point, within that pure basic space of empty sky, a vast inferno appeared like a rainbow enveloping absolutely every direction. A black wrathful deity stood amid that blazing expanse, wearing a black cape, brandishing a curved knife and skull-cup, and carrying a sandalwood club at his waist. Fearsome, majestic, and impossible to look at directly, he told me, "My child, don't be frightened! Don't panic! I've come from the gods' realm above. I am a male wrathful deity with the utmost skillful means that overpower the tribe of male protectors; I am also a female wrathful deity with the sublime insight that takes control of the tribe of female protectors. I am your lama's foremost doctrine guardian. Are you aware that a ruler demon down there will interrupt your lama's family line? If your lama doesn't move from this area, his family line will become very thin. The splendor of their wealth will collapse as in a dream. This is certain. Don't forget this. Keep it in mind. Tell your lama!

"The place where he currently resides is the remains of a site of defeat and destruction. The mountain range behind here comes to a halt and the river is bent like a naga demon's lasso. Therefore, fortune and disaster alternate like the sun shining between the clouds. It's very important for your lama to move somewhere else. Instill this fact in your mind!

"This year, your maternal uncle will meet an increasingly powerful hostile ruler demon that will obstruct his longevity. Nevertheless, if starting tomorrow you request the empowerment and scriptural transmission for Nöjin Shenpa Marnak, Dark Red Noxious Spirit Butcher, and exert yourself in supplications and offerings, that ruler demon won't harm you." Then he vanished.

As he commanded, I reported this to my lama. He said, "That was most likely my chief protector, Maning Nakpo, Black Genderless. If I relate this to other people, they will say a child's dreams are untrue. Everyone will ridicule me, so it's inappropriate to tell them. However, I'm going to give you the empowerment and scriptural transmission for Nöjin Shenpa Marnak." After giving those, he entrusted the teachings to me and composed an aspiration prayer.

Child and Guardian

THE YEAR I TURNED FOURTEEN [1848], at night on the tenth day of the first month, a light blue dakini appeared, her body lavishly adorned with turquoise garlands. She told me, "The malicious ruler demon down there has left, carrying away with him the spirits of both your maternal uncle and a monk named Chuk-ngön. Due to this, they will die in the first autumn month. There is a way to prevent this: it will help if Phurba, Dagger, recitation practice is done with great care."

In the morning when I told my uncle, he said, "You don't know anything at all!" He slapped me on the head and left. In the first autumn month during the spread of a virulent epidemic, my uncle's throat swelled, and he died.

AT NIGHT ON THE THIRD DAY of the first autumn month, an older woman and a monk showed up together in my dream. They said, "It's time for you to go. We have a place below that's a very happy land. Let's go there!" As soon as they said this, I prepared to leave with them, and a red man appeared astride a red garuda. He said, "Child, it's not right for you to go! You will be lost to the clutches of murderers. You need to do this visualization precisely. Think like this, bring this to mind."

> Hung! My ordinary body, speech, and mind become empty.
> Within empty space,
> The essence of the lama and chosen deity indivisible
> Becomes Guru Drakpo, Wrathful Guru [Rinpoche].
> He is dark red with one face, four arms,
> A gaping mouth, curled tongue, and bared incisor teeth.
> Sparks blaze from his eyebrows and beard,
> While his dark brown hair surges upward.
> His first two hands hold aloft in space
> A vajra and a three-pronged tantric staff.
> His lower two hands brandish a ritual dagger and an iron scorpion.
> His lower body, red-hot iron, is the blade of a ritual dagger
> That pierces the heart of a hostile ruler demon and a sorceress.

Within the expanse of an inferno, like the fires at the end of time,
The sound of Hung resounds like the roar of a thousand dragons.
Sparks of tiny wrathful deities and iron scorpions
Eradicate all hostile ruler demons and sorceresses.

Om Ah Hung Ah-tsik Ni-tsik Namo Bhagawaté Vajra Kili Kilaya Sarwa
  Bighanen Bam Hung Phat

"Recite that!" he insisted.

I visualized clearly as he had described and recited the mantra. This caused both the ruler demon and sorceress to faint and swoon to the ground. After a short while, as soon as they revived, they fled far away and vanished.

Then the dark red man said, "Since the previous aeon, you and I, child and guardian, have never been separated for even an instant. Due to this, completely entrust your mind and heart to me and I will annihilate all your obstacles!" With that, I awoke.

That same year at night on the tenth day of the middle autumn month, a fearsome red man came along on a red demon horse. He said, "Tell an individual called Tulku Jigka I said this: Regarding the instructions for deity practice that Nöjin Shenpa, Noxious Spirit Butcher, once gave you, he too must meditate and recite the mantra as described. Since the ruler demon of Lower Nyi is constantly roving like a wandering dog, searching night and day for an opportunity to harm him, be heedful of your meditation—this is crucial! Tell him I said that.

"Should those who live in this monastery do a month-long sealed Phurba, Dagger, practice without interruption, it would be best; but since there are very few practitioners here, there is little point in suggesting this. My child, you are Awareness Holder Dudul Dorjé incarnate, although there is no need to make that known right now." Then he vanished.

Three days later, I related what I'd been told to this person named Tulku Jigka, who replied, "Because I'm certain your dream was a sign, now I'm going to perform the Guru Drakpo practice from the Sky Revelation cycle, which has a Phurba text at the end. From today on, that is definitely what I will practice." Making a vow to stay for one month, he entered retreat.

IN UPPER NYI, a large river flowed to the left of Sera Monastery, and there was a cave in a mountain. A nomad encampment was set up at the cave's mouth. That same year at night on the fifth day of the twelfth month, to the west of that encampment, a young boy called my name three times in a clear voice, but I didn't answer his call. I laid down and slept. In the middle of the night, he called me again, though I didn't respond.

At the end of the night when he called me anew, Nöjin Shenpa Marnak, Dark Red Noxious Spirit Butcher, appeared in the realm of space roaring *Kya!* like a thunderclap. "Take this wooden bow and arrow and go where you were summoned," he said. I took hold of the bow and arrow, and went to that place. A naked little boy sat on the stirrup of a horse's saddle. As he stared up at me with wide-open eyes, I shot him with my arrow. This caused him to cry and shrink back. My grandmother heard this as well.

The next morning we saw that my arrow made of barberry wood had pierced straight through the saddle's stirrup. My grandmother said, "Iron pierced by wood—is this a sign of accomplishment or is it the miraculous display of gods and demons?" They asked a lama, who replied, "This child seems to be an exceptional individual, so it's possible this is a sign of accomplishment."

The next night, an extremely savage woman, too terrifying to look at, told me, "As payment for killing my son last night, I'm definitely going to tear out your raw, warm lungs and heart!" When she aimed her iron fingernails, long as a hand is wide, at my chest, out of a gap in space the magnificent Nöjin struck that woman's body with his blazing sword, splitting her like a bamboo stalk. Then she vanished.

THE YEAR I TURNED FIFTEEN [1849], at night on the tenth day of the third month, an old woman told me, "On the second day of the middle summer month, your father will come here. It will then be time for you to return to your homeland. A vow-violation spirit will appear from within a whirlwind turning counterclockwise. You have to shower it with stones infused with the mantra of Namjom, All-Vanquishing. The spirit will sing to you, but it's wrong for you to do what that song tells you." Then she vanished.

On the fifth day of the first summer month, when I went to tend the animals, a black whirlwind spinning counterclockwise pursued me closely. I ran away. When it continued to follow me, I infused many stones with the long mantra of the Unstoppable Fine Vajra, then threw them at the wind. At that moment, someone appeared that I didn't recognize as either a man or a woman. It sang this song:

Yé! Yé! Yé! Listen here, you brainless little boy!
I am truly your divine guardian.
Don't go elsewhere—
Stay here and lead your uncle's homestead!
You will direct the farmwork
And become the chief of many people.
Reciting rough, wrathful mantras is wrong—
It's possible they will become your own executioner!
Meditation on wrathful male and female deities is amiss—
It's possible they will ultimately manifest as demons!
If you listen to my words spoken with a good attitude,
You will surely decide not to become a Buddhist practitioner.
If you exert yourself in the work of worldly existence,
Both comfort and happiness will surely ensue.
My child, lodge this in your mind.
Don't listen to anyone else!

Then the being vanished.

My FATHER ARRIVED during the middle summer month and we embarked together for our homeland. One night on the way there I had this dream. A black man wearing a black cape astride a black horse with rings of white hair above its hooves told me, "There is a regional ruler demon in your homeland—a malicious murderer no one else can vanquish. Therefore, here is the antidote:

"Meditate that from the Unsurpassable Pure Land above, great glorious Dorjé Zhonnu, Vajra Youth, with his retinue, emerges in the form of a blazing inferno that dissolves into you. Further, your heart casts boundless masses of rainbow light, like banks of clouds, inviting dense rainbow clouds of the sacred circles of Guru Rinpoche, in both peaceful and wrathful forms, complete with his pure land and its resident deities, to arise as dense rainbow clouds. These dissolve into you and your own body becomes a mass of light.

"You then transform into the essence of the lama and chosen deity indivisible, the supreme deity Dorjé Drolö. Your body is dark maroon, with one face and two hands. Your right hand hoists aloft a golden vajra while your left aims an iron ritual dagger at the earth. You wear a cape, a lower garment, and orange Buddhist robes. A necklace made of fifty human heads dripping blood adorns you. Your three angry eyes gaze wide open and your teeth are bared downward. Your hair swirls to the right and fiery sparks blaze from your orange beard and eyebrows. You wear the sun and moon as earrings. Astride a striped red Indian tiger, with both legs wide open in an athlete's stance, you stand haughtily within the expanse of wisdom's blazing inferno, emitting sparks of iron scorpions and garudas. In your heart, [the deity that is] your wisdom aspect sits majestic upon a lotus and sun seat, naked without attire or ornaments, with an extremely wrathful demeanor. A golden five-pronged vajra stands erect in his heart. Within the vajra's center space a mantra garland encircles a dark red syllable *Hung*. Meditate that the light rays of the spinning mantra garland cause all sacred circles of peaceful and wrathful deities of vajra basic space to appear in the form of the deity you are meditating upon. They gradually dissolve into you like snow falling on the ocean."

> Hung! In the space of the consort of emptiness, sublime insight,
> Supreme skillful means, which no one can overcome,
> Arise as the illusory wisdom body.
> In its secret heart stands the fundamental heruka.
> Within the innermost secret vajra, in the enclosure of skillful means and
>   sublime insight,
> Sits *Hung*, encircled by the mantra garland:
> *Om Ah Hung Vajra Guru Dro Wo Lö Lo ka Sarwa Siddhi Hung Hung*

Then he disappeared without a trace.

From that point on, throughout my life I was released from hindering obstacles by relying upon these key meditation and recitation instructions.

THAT SAME YEAR at night on the eighteenth day of the first winter month, I saw the face of Dakini Sangwa Yeshe, Secret Wisdom. She rested her hand on my head and spoke to me: "My child, the way to open the gateway of your channel of sublime insight is to meditate upon and perform the recitation of Jampal Mawé Sengé, Gentle Splendor Lion of Speech, and to recite 'The Litany of the Names of Gentle Splendor.' If you exert yourself in those practices, the gateway of your sublime insight-wisdom channel will open, and the expanse of the space treasury of the nature of reality will definitely overflow. Don't forget this method! Keep it in mind."

I replied, "Kyé! Mother dakini of the sphere of wisdom, I promise to do as you've told me!" Then she vanished without a trace.

I TURNED SIXTEEN in the Dog Year [1850]. At night on the tenth day of the last summer month, a woman appeared who was beautiful in body and face, and lavishly adorned. Saying she was Dakini Yeshe Tsogyal, she told me,

> Kyé Ho! I am a wisdom dakini
> In the guise of a human woman,
> Revealed for your eyes.
> Jikmé, Fearless, this region's guide and teacher,
> Is the dance of Lotus-Born's activity.
> Rely on him during this year and cultivate your experience
> In the preliminary practices' systematic approach.
> Auspicious omens of your spiritual accomplishments will arise.
> You have a previous karmic connection with this lama:
> Do not forget this! My child, keep it in mind.

Then she vanished without a trace.

THAT SAME YEAR on the first day of the middle winter month, I went to that lama and entered into a month-long preliminary practices retreat with fifteen companions. On the evening of the fifteenth day, I had this vision: I found myself in the presence of the lama. In space directly in front of him, a yellow man bedecked with various silks floated four cubits above the ground. He sat grandly in the posture of royal ease upon a white lioness, and brandished a victory banner in his right hand and a mongoose in his left. He blazed with light and light rays. A stream of milk descended from the tip of his big toe into a wide copper vessel. The lama told me, "Drink this milk!" As he had ordered me, I drank a large amount. Bliss and joy entirely suffused my body and mind, and the lama told me, "You have received the common spiritual attainments." Both the lama and deity vanished into basic space.

> Awareness holders imbued with the blessings of accomplishment,
> Wisdom deities, and oceans of doctrine guardians:
> I pray that manifestations of your wisdom body and speech grant me
> assurance.

An infinitude of pure phenomena unfold from the symbolic methods
Of your wisdom mind's myriad blessings. The basis for their arising
Is primordial awareness, the innate face of fundamental buddhahood.
Without searching, I've directly encountered that abiding within me.
In the sphere of equal purity, the name of affliction doesn't exist,
Yet many false outlines, signs of obstacles, appeared
Due to the unceasing interdependence of impure concepts.
My indwelling radiance, the assembly of deities, arose as antidotes
Which defeated those obstacles, and I see everywhere the play of
    magical illusion.

The Sacred Practice of Space

In DREAMS, dakinis of wisdom's sphere and a host of spiritual heroes gave me instructions related to the preliminary practices. I relied on those instructions and my understanding unfurled without impediment.

That next year, the Pig Year [1851], I turned seventeen. On the seventh day of the first summer month, I was doing what I called "meditation." Hoping that something would happen that I could see or feel, I sat with my back to a cliff, my body drawn up straight without shifting or movement. On the last of seven days, I fell asleep and dreamt of a young naked boy, one span in size. He ran and jumped across a flower-filled grassy meadow, stared at me with piercing eyes, and said:

> In the body, like an empty city,
> Speech is made by the mind in a constant stream.
> Mind is the creator of all myriad fabrications.

A small girl appeared and responded,

> Very so! In the body, like an empty paper tube,
> Speech is like wind moving through its opening:
> Mind is what carries out various activities.
> Apart from recognizing which is chief among this trio,
> To wait for something you can see or feel, during what you refer to as
>   "meditation," is shocking!

The sound of her raucous laughter woke me up, and I examined that: The body is made by the mind. Due to the appearance of the body, the manifestation of verbal expression occurs through speech. Where there is no body, what only appears as a body is also the mind. Where there is no speech, what arises as verbal expression is also the mind. In fact, there is nothing apart from mind. Having come to that conclusion, I continued to wonder why the young boy explained it as three things.

Once again, I sat with my back to Marshar Cliff. As soon as I focused my attention on a small stick, from the cliff face behind me a tiny red bird sang with a pleasant voice,

> I, the young boy, am not telling lies:
> These days, some teachers do not understand
> The meaning of what only appears as the three doors of body, speech,
>   and mind where there are no doors,
> So they identify and teach them as a trio.
> Therefore, I taught accordingly.
> You've realized the conclusion—
> That the three doors are inseparable and are merely appearances—how
>   wonderful!
> That's it! Within the three vajras' indwelling state,
> [Body, speech, and mind] are inseparable and complete. How right you
>   are!
> Although now you realize that the three doors are only the mind,
> Exactly what is the form, shape, and color
> Of that which creates and does everything—what we refer to as
>   "mind"?
> I deem you incisive if you know the way things actually are.

Then it flew away.

Once again I sat with my back against the cliff. At one point, these words resonated from the space of empty sky: "'Mind is emptiness. Emptiness has no shape or color, no sound, no smell, no taste, no touch, no phenomena.' Analyze this with your mind!" I examined what was said, and I saw and understood that the absence of any objective domain is the essence of pervasive emptiness. However, since I was unsure how I should meditate, I settled in an unfixed state of mind for the time being.

THAT YEAR, AT NIGHT on the tenth day of the twelfth month, as before, an immense river of blood surged and changed into dark blue light like a raging river. My mind became space: I experienced the river of light flowing down from that expanse, and then all apparent phenomena dissolved into it. At that point a youth with a blue body wearing blue attire appeared, saying he was Orgyen Tsokyé Dorjé, Lake-Born Vajra. He said, "Isn't this—your visionary experience—extraordinary?"

I replied, "At first this vision arose as blood, which was terrifying. Later, it appeared as utter darkness, and my mind was exhausted. Finally, it manifested as rainbows. Now it appears like a waterfall of dark blue light. If I examine how this unfolds, I can compare it to a rainbow appearing in space or a reflection appearing upon water. I think that all phenomena are nothing apart from space, yet at the same time, how is it that space is wide-open emptiness, without faults or qualities? As for what is called 'mind,' for example, if there is no fire, there are no sparks; if there is no water, there is no sound of water, and the reflections of planets and stars won't appear. If mind has no basis, thoughts and appearances can't possibly arise. If this mind dwells in my body, outer appearances can't possibly arise. To whom does a dreamscape— earth, rocks, mountains, cliffs, firmness, solidity—appear? In the morning it vanishes without a trace. When I examine that, the true nature of mind appears within mind's expanse. That's what I think."

"You've almost realized the view! Now tell me of your meditation practice."

"Since I don't know how to meditate, you should teach me how," I insisted.

"Oh child of my spiritual family, each master employs a different style of teaching meditation. Some claim that you must block thoughts. Some say that you must gaze directly at thoughts and be aware. Some claim that you have to cultivate thoughts, then rework the negative ones. Some contend you must merge mind and space. It's astonishing the myriad forms of happiness and suffering that occur due to the fault of not [naturally] settling, as is the mind's nature. Some even assert that mind is emptiness, and yet you also have to maintain a very subtle perception of mental consciousness.

"Whatever you name these, however you label them—they are definitely not the correct path! Now, if you wish to enter the true path, [understand that] the pure lands above, impure cyclic existence below, and all environments and beings are nothing other than the nature of reality's space. Once you've recognized their single, innate flavor within space, space is fully evident. Settle undistracted within that continuous nature. What does it mean to be 'undistracted'? It is to have neither a focal point nor clinging, no meditation or fixation, no nurturing or preserving. It is beyond description or expression. Just as it was before, leave [the mind] to itself, unfettered."

I asked, "How should I handle all these thoughts?"

The youth answered, "It's incorrect to block or to hold on to thoughts in any way. Know that without attachment to any sort of understanding, sensation, or experience, let thoughts go."

"Do I look at space with my eyes?"

He said, "Look from within a state of uncontrived natural repose—that's it!"

I asked, "Is looking into space with my eyes incorrect? If mind doesn't see mind, even if space becomes apparent, how can that be helpful?"

"Gazing at mind with mind entails the duality of a looker and something looked upon. Therefore, looking at thoughts with your intellectual mind is like an old person watching a small child's game—it's pointless. All cyclic existence and enlightenment are nothing other than space itself, within which they are of a single flavor. Once you recognize that indwelling state, it is sufficient to not turn your eyes from space. That is meaningful because original awareness perceives the visual consciousness, which has no essence apart from that awareness. A corpse doesn't have eyes to which forms appear; in dreams, appearances of forms manifest without eyes; in the intermediate state, as well, appearances of forms manifest without eyes. Use these examples to understand primordially present insight.

"All sentient beings have not actualized the basis of being, so they are deluded. Putting that aside, you can see that because thoughts or concepts aren't different from the basis of being, there really is no delusion. Look at how all sentient beings are deluded because of their obsessive attachment to thoughts. Therefore, thoughts are something that can be transformed. Once you apprehend the incisive certainty from deep within that all phenomena of cyclic existence and enlightenment never transcend the nature of space, that is called 'pure space.' Throughout the past, present, or future, it's not right to ever stray from [the state in which] that indwelling nature is obvious to you. If you accomplish the vital training of familiarizing yourself with this, in the end, unformulated basic space beyond limits, the nature of reality, will become apparent to you. For example, just as at dawn there can be no darkness, you will surely reach meditation practice free from exertion and effort." Then he vanished.

From that time forth, I made my spiritual path simply not taking my eyes away from space. I cultivated that experience wholeheartedly and arrived directly at basic space free from edge or limits, the nature of reality. My realization overflowed into that openness.

Absolutely everything appears from either cyclic existence or
    enlightenment

Free from the multiplicity of elaboration;
The essence of space is the arena of the original basis of being,
Which cannot be demonstrated by metaphor, other than as space itself.
Even the Buddha's Sublime Insight sutras state
That when you carry out the sacred practice of the perfection of
    sublime insight,
You are actually engaged in the sacred practice of space.
Be aware: This is the ultimate meaning of what has been taught.

As things are outside, so they are inside.
Whether outer or inner, everything is the natural radiance of what's
    within:
Whatever the inner radiance is, it manifests as if outer.

Separate things are exaggerated, given symbols and names;
What is ineffable, inconceivable, and indescribable is expressed and
    thereby made definable.
That inexpressible meaning is presented fully through illustration.
This is the sage approach—the skillful means of the victors of the three
    times—
An entryway that leads to ultimate basic space.

Dualistic mind perceives objects. When your experiential mode has
    shifted to timeless awareness
And supreme sublime insight seals phenomena as the dynamic
    expression of awareness,
Outer and inner become indivisible via the kati crystal secret path
Of the eyes and space, and you recognize emptiness's true nature.

The lion's roar of the discourse of the utmost sovereign spiritual
    approach
Terrifies the lowly minds of herds of wild animals.
The very nature of the extremely profound teachings
Is constantly challenged by ordinary minds.

Inner truth, the primordially present body of ultimate enlightenment,
Is seen with your own wisdom eyes.

If some method exists to teach this to others,
Why did the Buddha say it was profound peace, unformulated, and
   difficult to fathom?

The True Meaning of Sublime Insight

In the year I turned eighteen [1852], on the tenth day of the middle summer month, I took a bucket and went to fetch water at noontime, between meditation sessions. When a torma[9] dropped into my bucket, I looked up into the sky and saw a single raven in flight. I knew it had thrown that torma. Understanding this to be an omen of spiritual attainment, I touched it to my forehead, throat, and heart, then ate it.

That night, a girl saying she was Dakini Salkyab Wangmo, Chief of Encompassing Clarity, told me, "Earlier, that torma came from the Nepalese forest of Swayambu. It was the Nepali Sukha Shri's practice torma, given to a raven-headed protector by Dakini Dorjé Pakmo, Varja Sow: You have definitely received the common spiritual attainments. You should be elated!" Saying that, she vanished.

That same year on the tenth day of the first autumn month, I went to tend the livestock. On top of a boulder along the path sat nine pills the size of mustard seeds, round and completely blue. The moment I saw them, I said, "Kaya Vak Tsitta Sarva Siddhi Pala Ho," touched them to my forehead, throat, heart, navel, and secret place, and then ate them.

That night, a dakini saying she was Namké Yingchukma, Sovereign of Space, said to me,

> Yé Yé! Mother's young child, listen to me!
> Of any number of different Buddhist paths,
> Those expansive treasuries that contain all meanings
> Are the doctrine of Great Perfection.
> Your mother gave you
> What appeared as those nine pills.
> Young boy endowed with sublime insight,
> You recognized them as spiritual attainment
> And you've definitely gained
> Unsurpassable supreme attainment.
> Now if you can apply yourself

To profound meditation,
Three cycles of mind treasure will overflow
And pervade your wisdom mind's expanse:
You will accomplish to a sweeping extent what is beneficial for beings.

She disappeared.

THAT SAME YEAR on the fifteenth day of the third winter month, I went to recite texts for a patron named Gönten, Doctrine Guardian. An older woman told me, "I'm giving you this food to eat. Enjoy it without anything left over," and passed me a handful of small wild sweet potatoes. As I was about to consume them, a red man riding a red horse struck my wrist with a bannered lance. I dropped the food and became enraged. "What are you doing?" I roared.

He answered, "That demoness was planting the seeds of sickness—how could you possibly eat that?"

"Who are you?"

"I am king of the sorcerers, Soklen Marpo, Red Murderer. My job is to dispel your obstacles," he told me.

I asked, "If I make offerings to you, what should I recite?"

"If you don't call me by proclaiming my vows, I won't come. Therefore, call me with this vow proclamation. Say my life force syllable, *Hri,* then:"

Noxious spirit Sorcerer King with your entourage,
With faith I summon you and invoke your strict tantric commitments:
    Come to this place!
By making petitions and offerings to you, may your formidable wishes
    be fulfilled.
Perform enlightened activity according to whatever I wish!

"If you say that, I will come from my own residence." Then he departed on the red sheen of the setting sun.

IN THE YEAR I TURNED NINETEEN, I went into a cave called Draklung. An old woman inside it said to me, "Where are you going? What are you?"

"I want to stay here for one practice session. Who are you?" I asked.

The woman told me, "I am the owner of this place, a sorcerer, a woman

addicted to taking others' life forces. If you stay here I will surely kill you."
Then she poked me in the back with her finger and said, "Over there is an
omen of your death."

I looked outside and saw a weasel dragging a dead snake. That made me
think, "If I die, my killer will surely be this woman. I have to kill her." As I
reached for her hand, she vanished.

I stayed in the cave. While I recited three repetitions of the reversal [of
obstacles] formula using *The Perfection of Sublime Insight Sutra,* this sound
reverberated like an echo from deep within the cave: "Do not stay here! I will
show you dire omens—I swear I'm not jesting."

THAT SAME YEAR in the middle winter month, I entered into a month-long
retreat based on the meditation and recitation practice of Jampal Mawé Sengé,
Gentle Splendor Lion of Speech. At the end, the consecrated pills multiplied
and flew about. That night I actually saw Jampal's face, and he said to me,
"My child, what do you want? I'll give it to you."

"I want skill in writing," I requested.

"It's possible for even some secular laypeople to know how to write well.
What's the use of that?"

"Oh. Well then, I wish for sublime insight." He responded:

> Kyé! Listen well, child of my spiritual family.
> Mere proficiency in reading and recitation is not sublime insight;
> Such training is common knowledge.
> What we know as sublime insight is not that at all.
> When you make evident the indwelling nature of things as they are—
> The nature of reality—and realize the meaning of emptiness,
> This is the true meaning of sublime insight:
> I dwell within the unmoving sphere;
> I am unformulated within magnificent pervasiveness;
> I permeate as great encompassing clarity.
> In the panorama of the nature of reality's sky
> I am the sun of splendid sublime insight.
> When every teaching of path and result
> Overflows from the inexhaustible expanse,
> I have entered your heart.
> When you see all phenomena of cyclic existence and enlightenment

As dreams or magical illusions,
My wisdom mindstream has shifted to your mind.
When you realize that appearances of mind
Are by nature pervasive evenness within the play of space,
My enlightened vision has shifted to your mind.
When space is apparent
Through the wide open wisdom eyes of sublime insight,
You and I then become indivisible.
You have attained sublime insight.
You have even attained the eyes of wisdom.
Now, together, you and I,
Abide within non-duality: Ah.

Then he gave me his means of accomplishment with a mantra, and dissolved into my heart. For a while, I let go within the indwelling nature of reality.

IN THE YEAR I TURNED TWENTY [1854], at night on the eighth day of the middle spring month, a large and spacious land with a grove of myriad blossoming flowers appeared in my dream. Many dakinis there venerated a stupa of accomplishment made of precious conch shell. I approached and saw someone sitting inside the opening of the vase section of the stupa, said to be the Buddha, Transcendent Conqueror Lord Mikyöpa, Immutable, wearing a lama's three Buddhist robes. His two hands displayed the gestures of calling the earth to witness and abiding in evenness. Though he sat there in silence, something like a naturally occurring echo resounded from his form:

Ah É! All composite phenomena in their entirety are a magical illusion
With many illusory false designs.
[Beings are] like a magician deceived by his own magic.
[All phenomena are] are a mirage—the creation of causes and
    conditions.
[Beings are] are like deer gazing vainly into water that is a mirage,
Like dreamers deluded by attachment
To the appearances of their varied dreamscapes.
While you can see a visible reflection,
Apart from the field upon which it arises, it doesn't exist elsewhere.

Even a large city of spirits doesn't otherwise exist
Apart from your impressions.
An echo resounds that doesn't exist
Apart from the single sound of Kʏɪ!
The moon appears on water's surface,
Yet apart from that water, there is no moon.
A rainbow appears in the sky,
Yet doesn't arise anywhere else than that sky.
Those blurred impressions on your eyes
Don't exist apart from an eye malady.
Firelight appears from flame,
Yet doesn't exist apart from that fire.

While something appears external to oneself
Apart from that self, nothing exists.
All appearances of the basis unfold from the basis of being;
Apart from that, nothing exists.
Absolutely all phenomena emerge from mind;
Nothing substantial exists independent of mind.
You fetter yourself by clinging to space as something existent;
You fetter yourself by perceiving what is deemed "the basis of being"
    as something other than what it is.
Maintaining obsessive attachment to the magical projections of
    mind—
Conceptual thought—you bind yourself by considering them the
    enemy.
When thoughts change within themselves to wisdom,
To purposefully cultivate, sustain, alter, or block them is to bind yourself.

Ah is the pure sphere of basic space.
Ah is free from birth and cessation.
By the mere expression of this essence
Of the basic space of phenomena's wisdom, it is all-encompassing.
The basis of all expression is this self-arising Ah.
The two of us, you and I, are indivisible.
We have no good or bad, no hope or fear, no acceptance or rejection.
We have no label of existence or nonexistence.

The basic space of the body of ultimate enlightenment is not something
   you can attain or lose.
When you realize this meaning, you are an adept.

Then he appeared to dissolve into me.

Victor Mikyöpa, my self-manifest teacher,
Did not use the fabricated effort of speech,
But the resonance of unimpeded sound-emptiness from his wisdom
   body of clarity-emptiness,
To show, with various examples, how relative truth is the result of
   interdependent arising.

Using unborn words he revealed the meaning of the fundamental
   nature:
When appearance and emptiness [are recognized] as nondual, this is
   inner basic space without any binding or freeing,
Just as one is liberated or deluded in relation to [understanding] the
   basis and appearances of the basis.
I realized this as he described, and was freed from the precipices of
   eternalism and nihilism.
His enlightened body, speech, and mind and my body, speech, and
   mind became inseparable.

The Union of Bliss-Emptiness

AT NIGHT ON THE FIFTH DAY of the twelfth month, a red woman in a dream told me, "Tomorrow you're really going to see something happen. Pots and kitchen articles will be smashed." Then she vanished.

The next day, my patron Gönten's sister arrived before dawn. An ash-colored child appeared at the same time, laughing loudly and dancing on the hearth. When I saw that, I told my patron, "You should be careful with the things in your kitchen. There's a goblin playing and laughing on the hearth."

He replied, "I will definitely be careful."

Then three pots of different sizes, nested in one another, were loaded on an already burdened yak. When someone went to fetch a rope, the yak rolled on its side, breaking the three pots against a rock.

IN THE YEAR I TURNED TWENTY-ONE [1855], at night on the thirteenth day of the first month, a blue dakini appeared, wearing multiple strands of jewels and a white silk skirt. She arrived in front of me and immediately it seemed as if the sun had risen—everything became bright and a wide, spacious land appeared. The ground was covered with golden flowers, and their light rose into space. Many groups of young and old women there sang this song:

> Yé Yé! In this land of nonhuman dakinis,
> We have no men. We're depressed!
> We don't need sinful worldly companions.
> We need a great-bliss king of supreme skillful means
> Who grants uncontaminated bliss:
> We wonder, "Can we find such a one?"
> We've abandoned all hope.
> If we enter the union of bliss-emptiness
> With the sovereign of great bliss, supreme skillful means,
> We imagine bearing a cherished child.
> Everyone has children who are sinking stones
> In cyclic existence—we don't need those!
> A superb child of the sublime insight of awareness:

No one has that! How do we get such a child?
If we bear one, we will surely create
A great celebration of the treasury of space.

I was enthralled as they sang that long melodious song. The voice of another dakini responded with this drawn-out ballad:

Yé Yé! Joyous is the city of joyous dakinis.
Delightful is this land of delightful celestial beings.
Nowhere—it is nowhere else.
You have it! You have it complete within you.
Understand! You must understand from deep within.
Know! You must gain ultimate knowledge.
Realize! You must realize from within.
Be aware! You must make your awareness manifest.
Liberate! You must be liberated on your own ground.

This song of nonhuman dakinis
Contains indications of future times.
Don't forget! Absolutely don't forget this.
Pervading! It is all-pervading.
Encompassing! It is all-encompassing.
Purity! From the space of primordial purity,
Liberated, I am the primordially liberated dakini—
Present is the spontaneously present magical display
That is your own, your own true reflection.
Benefit! For your own benefit
I will explain, explain with these words.
Now listen to me!

These days, the wish-fulfilling tree [is you]
With fragile branches and leaves
And fruits and flowers that have not ripened.
Since people mistake it for an ordinary tree,
They have no need for it.
Yet that won't stop the tree from growing.

When the energetic white lion
Leaps to the eastern direction
Together with its small lion companion,
They roar their own sound when you meet them.
Once that pleasant melody rings forth,
It makes the throngs of clawed animals pause.
Without traveling, the lions arrive naturally
At the summit of the highest white glaciers.
Spreading their four clawed paws across the ice,
Gazing upward with their eyes,
These two mighty, excellent companions meet.

Twenty white vultures will appear.
Moving slowly in the sky,
Without activity, they take shelter among the cliffs,
And nurture their children with food.

Indian tigers staying in the jungles
Are spiritual heroes of majestic bearing
Whose eyes survey a spacious land.
Enjoying nourishing food of one hundred flavors,
There are thirty of these powerful beings.

Melodious blue cuckoos
Search for food across grassy plains.
They soar to the treetops
And sing sweet songs, four birds in all.

Clutching jewels in their hands,
Seven blue turquoise dragons
Emerge from the depths of the ocean.
Arriving in the sky's arena with perfect mastery,
They fill the three realms of existence with their thunder.

Sixteen resplendent peacocks,
Their five hues blazing with light,

Eat poison as food;
These are the companions of the bodiless dakini.

From the midst of the swamp of existence,
There are one hundred wealthy barons
Who dispel poverty and the decline of wealth.
They attained the precious jewel
That is the reward of great service.

Now is not the time to brandish
The nine-pronged golden vajra:
The southern demons' emissaries
Have amassed a demon army.
There are many miserable lands where karma has ripened.
Their work is war—they dispatch troops into battle.
When they rise up like a storm,
That's a sure portent the time has arrived.

Do not show to anyone
The words you wrote yesterday!
In the midst of foxes and monkeys,
Humans don't sound the war-cry *ki*.
Once that sound strikes their hearts
They run away to far-off lands.

Instill what I've said in your mind,
And you will gradually arrive at a high position.

This place of bodiless dakinis,
A supremely unimpeded zone, lacking a domain,
Is without location, obstruction, or elaboration:
You will wake up from this as if from a dream.

Everything collapsed like the contraption in a magical display.

That same year on the tenth day of the last summer month, I went to
Sergyi Traklung. When I sat there in a grove of splendidly blooming flow-

ers on the plains by the river, an experience of inconceivable joy and bliss dawned in me.

A bee circling a flower appeared to sing this song:

> Bam Bam! In this grove of flowers and green grass,
> I, a small golden bee, am happy—
> Happy, although my delight will surely not last.
> She, the queen of autumn, will come.
> This grove of lotuses abloom will wilt.

> Although this green-festooned grass has grown,
> As for lasting very long—it won't endure.
> The insects from before have all gone away.
> Although a small, black, flesh-eating fly is left behind,
> As for lasting very long—it won't endure.
> Humans from the past have died.
> Although an orphan is left behind,
> As for lasting very long—it won't endure.

> Even if you are installed [as king] at King Trisong Deutsen's capital,
> You will only be burdened with the country's suffering.
> Even if you've become a great lama with power,
> You will still be a leader within cyclic existence.
> Even if you've become a wealthy person with riches,
> You will still experience unbearable hardship.
> Even if you've become a very eloquent chief,
> You will still have only distraction and no leisure.
> Even if you've become a penniless beggar,
> You will still experience unbearable hunger and thirst.

> If you have a female companion,
> She will still be your adversarial opponent.
> If you have cherished children,
> They will still be bandits who steal your wealth.
> If you've become a Buddhist in a state with nothing to be done,
> In this and later lives, you will still be happy.

I, a yellow golden bee, have described what I see:
The city of cyclic existence
Is impermanent, just the same as a dream.
My joyful and foolish song
Is my advice for you, my friend.
I prepare to go to the celestial lands.
You should also follow me!

Then it flew far away.

Eastward toward Golok

THAT SAME YEAR, at night on the eighteenth day of the seventh month, I was told that I was in Great Bliss Celestial Enjoyment Pure Land. In a pleasure grove in that joyful land was a white man, so handsome you could look at him forever and never be satisfied. He rode a castrated buck, leading a female deer wearing silk ornaments. With him was a beautiful girl adorned with jewels. They approached me together and asked, "Do you want to come with us to the spectacle at the summit of the black Chinese mountain Déshen?"

I said that I would, and we went to a single mountain with five peaks. The middle peak rose extremely high. When we reached its summit the white man told me, "You should look upward." As he instructed, I looked up and saw in the sky what looked like a rainfall of red fiery sparks.

"Look to the east." I looked as instructed, and saw a city made of intestinal ropes inside a tent of human skin; its ground was entirely red with blood.

"Look to the south." I looked as instructed and saw a white mountain the color of conch. A milky ocean encircled its base, with water fowl and many other birds frolicking on its banks. A grove of blooming white flowers grew at its peak, which appeared to be cloaked in a mist of five-colored light like the colors of a rainbow.

"Look to the west." I looked as instructed and saw various cities filled with Chinese and Tibetan people.

"Look to the north." I looked as instructed and saw packs of wild animals and poisonous snakes, as well as crowds of humans whose hair and eyebrows were red, yellow, blue, green, and white in color. They were giving the animals meat to eat and pouring blood to drink.

He handed me a white conch and told me to turn to the four directions and blow the conch. When I did as he instructed, to the east a whirlwind rose up, so no sound came out. To the south, snow filled the conch and no sound emerged. To the west it made a great sound that resounded everywhere. To the north it made a noise, but it was blocked by a tall mountain, so the sound faded to only an echo.

I asked the young man, "What is the meaning of all this and who are you two?" Both the girl and the boy sang in unison:

Kyé! Listen to me, youth endowed with awareness!
If you don't recognize me,
I am the god-child Dungi Zur Pü, Topknot of Conch.
My sister is the nonhuman Zulé.

Above, these fiery sparks
Are the dakinis stirring up dust,
Churning the atoms of existence.
They've turned their faces towards Supreme Mountain,
Putting their backs to an evil era.

To the east, this city of ugly humans
Is a wicked barbarian metropolis.
The plain burning with fire
Is the incineration of the fields of liberation.

To the south, the white conch mountain
Is Potala Mountain.
The flocks of various birds at its base
Are spiritual heroes and heroines.
The grove of blossomed lotus flowers
Is the birthplace of pure moral discipline.
The mountaintop cloaked in clouds
Symbolizes how beings with obscurations are unable to see it.

To the west, the humans in those cities
Are the disciples compatible with you.
There are some people wearing blue clothes in the midst of darkness:
That's an obscured city in a Chinese region.

To the north, where there are different kinds of humans,
Stands a city of various venomous demon tribes.
The flesh to eat and blood to drink
Given to savage carnivorous wild animals
[Represents] hostile gods and demons taking control of humans
By altering their minds.

In the east, the conch's call muted by wind
Indicates demons obstructing the sound of the doctrine.

In the south, the conch's sound muffled by snow
Indicates that very few beings are free of the two obscurations—
A sign that it's rare to attain liberation.

In the west, the conch's call roared forth,
A sign that your renown will spread.
Every sunbeam that appears in those areas
Represents one of your disciples.

In the north, the conch's slight sound
Is a sign that, for a while, you will suppress the barbarians.

Do you understand this song or not?
I replied, "I understand well!"

We, the brother and sister, are going to the sphere of space.
As for you, return once again to the regions of existence.
When you reach Great Bliss Lotus Array Pure Land,
We, brother and sister, will surely come to meet you.

With that sound, I awoke.

IN THE YEAR I TURNED TWENTY-TWO [1851], during the seventh month, the matriarch of my patron Gönten's family fell ill. As a healing service they practiced Menla, Medicine Buddha, and I joined the ranks of those performing recitation. On that occasion, at night on the fifteenth day, a beautiful dakini appeared, so gorgeous one could gaze at her forever and never be satisfied. She poured thirteen mustard seeds onto a mirror made from beryl and gave it to me. She told me,

Kyé! My child, listen to me!
Fifteen years in the future,
When a specific time arrives,
You will gradually have students from that point on.

> Once you have gathered many thousands,
> They will travel to the ground of eternal happiness.
> Those who become your especially outstanding disciples
> Will live in unfixed mountain locales.
> They will keep their braids long
> And wear the attire of male and female adepts.
> Thirteen practitioners of magical illusion
> Will accomplish the illusory rainbow body.
> Spiritual hero, these will be your companions.
> These white mustard seeds, blessed by dakini awareness mantras,
> Symbolize that auspicious connection.
> Keep these with you inseparably as a sacred support.

"Child of my spiritual family, keep these white mustard seeds in your pocket and in the future, your disciples will advance in one lifetime to the exalted state of Dorjé Chang, Vajra Bearer. There will definitely be thirteen individuals, their hair twisted in braids at the crown of the head. Keep this mirror at your heart and your realization will equal the bounds of space." She dissolved into my heart and I experienced bliss-emptiness.

That morning I asked Lama Luchuk, Wealthy Naga, about this event. An old monk named Loden, Intellect, was also sitting there who said, "If you have disciples like that, then why doesn't the old dog down here have disciples?"

The lama said, "It's not right to say things like that! This dream portent is very positive. Don't judge it."

Laughing, "Oh ho ho!" the old monk made me feel ashamed.

AT NIGHT ON THE NINTH DAY in the tenth month, a red woman with a very beautiful body and face appeared in front of me and said,

> É É! When a pair of travelers
> Coming from the east reaches this place,
> It's as your worthy lama proclaimed:
> When you arrive in the east [Golok],
> Familiar companions from the past
> Will flank you inseparably as your subjects.
> The glorious qualities of conducive conditions

Will then ever improve and increase,
Like the moon on the first lunar day.

Resources, wealth, food, and possessions
Will seem scarce at the beginning.
In the end, you appear not quite so poor.

When the vital points related to meditation and creation-phase practice
Overflow from the expanse of your mind's nature
Like the sun breaking free from clouds,
Impartial aid for beings will result—this is certain!

You will have several sublime sons,
Like the sun, moon, and major stars,
Who will shine with the doctrine's immense glow.

Don't be weak in asserting your intention and uplifting your mind.
Once the fruit of your store of merit from previous lifetimes ripens,
Your wealth and influence will grow.
When a humble person gains significant power,
It's important to exercise self-control.
When a wealthy person's riches and possessions increase,
It's important to maintain contentment.
When you gather fortunate disciples,
It's important to teach them the profound meditation instructions.

In our land of nonhuman dakinis
We use symbols and sing songs—
It's impossible for us to use human speech.
Since you are very foolish,
I have revealed these symbols with human words.
Do not forget—instill this in your mind!
This information is of great value.

"Next year an excellent companion will appear one morning in the sixth month. At that time, go east with him to the land of Golok. You have a fine disciple there."

I asked, "Elder sister, if I go there, how much tea will I get from this disciple?"

"He's not that sort of disciple. Many disciples like your own heart will appear and you will accomplish what is beneficial for beings on a vast scale." She vanished without a trace.

IN THE YEAR I TURNED TWENTY-THREE [1852], one morning during the last summer month, a man named Gili Wangli came from Golok to Sertal on business, with his nephew Lodar. Lama Sangngak Drupchok, Supreme Accomplishment of Secret Mantra, gave sound advice entrusting me to them. As I went eastward with them toward Golok, we reached the trailhead to the mountain pass of the local god, Tak-yak of Mar. At that point, we encountered a bridal procession on their ascent. The people escorting the procession dismounted from their horses and poured two cups of alcohol. I thought, "To have something like this drink appear here in the grove of the local god—this must be a very auspicious connection!" Considering this, I became elated.

That night, a girl saying she was Dakini Zulé Men, Zulé Medicine Goddess, sang to me,

> Ah Ho! Do you understand today's signs?
> The maiden with beautiful attire and ornaments
> You met climbing upward on your ascent
> Was an omen of you meeting a qualified consort of awareness.
>
> Without a qualified consort of awareness,
> Your channel of sublime insight will not open.
> Should that channel not open,
> The expansive treasury of wisdom mind won't overflow.
> As a result, many writings of others
> Are inconsistent with the tantras.
>
> You were served nectar alcohol,
> A positive omen and auspicious connection
> Indicating that the phenomena of your impure residue
> Will shift into its pristine essence.

This chief local god known as Tak-yak
Is a portent that both Za, Planetary Lord, and Nöjin Shenpa, Noxious
    Spirit Butcher,
Will protect your doctrine.

This region's contaminating pollution will afflict you,
And your health will be compromised for one month.
However, gradually like the sun and moon
Breaking free from clouds, it will dissipate.

"Today, the local god served you that alcohol. Since that forms your initial connection, it is very auspicious. You've mounted the threshold of rising above the black headed people [i.e., Tibetans]." Then she vanished.

My patron Wangli had a nephew, a simple monk named Ngawang Gyatso, Ocean of Masterful Speech. I taught him the text outlining the means of accomplishment related to Dorjé Drolö and gave him its scriptural transmission. Then someone named Kyatsé Dön asked me to do a scriptural reading and recitation. I went there and after one month, a woman saying she was Dakini Ging Chungma, Little Ging Spirit, approached me and sang,

Kyé! Mother's young child, listen to me!
Do not stay in this household!
King Bénak, lord of wealth,
Will come after a while in order to kill.
This patron is narrow-minded—
Look at the small offering he's made you for this reading!

As for your patrons, the Gili family,
You are connected to their household for the time being
By the force of your aspirations.

Rely upon Ngawang Gyatso,
An emanation of the Shübu Palgyi Sengé, Glorious Lion of Shübu,
As your inseparable companion.

You have an exceptional former connection
With the supreme deity, great glorious Dorjé Drolö.
Take him as your sublime chosen deity,
And practice at Mardo Tashi Kyil.
An adept of utmost mastery will appear
From whom you should receive that deity's empowerment and
   transmission.
Once again, not long after that,
When you encounter another old adept
Who has completed the recitation practice five times over,
Request the complete empowerment and transmission as you did
   before.
Always endeavor in this practice!
Yet again after a few years,
You will meet
The last of the seven embodiments
Of Jétsun Drolwé Gönpo, Exalted Liberating Lord [i.e., Taranata].
Take the complete empowerment and transmission once more
From that holy supreme emanation.

In the tenth month,
Focus on completing a sealed month-long retreat.
You will gain some minor spiritual attainment.
A wisdom dakini of basic space
Will feed you with a skull-cup of nectar.
This is an indication of supreme attainment.
Do you understand? Don't forget! Keep this in mind.

"Do not stay in this place—leave! This patron's family will offer you one sheep skin and three or four containers of butter. Apart from just that, they will definitely give you nothing else." Then she vanished without a trace.

Bring Forth the Treasure

IN THE YEAR I TURNED TWENTY-FOUR [1858], at night on the tenth day of the first spring month, I met the great Bodhisattva Tukjé Chenpo, Supreme Compassion. He conferred upon me the complete empowerment and scriptural transmission for the text outlining the means of accomplishment called "The Gathered Peaceful Deities' Naturally Liberated Wisdom Mind." "My child, if you are able to transcribe this, it's possible it will be of some help to others. Keep that in mind." Then he vanished.

After our encounter, I began to write the practice out in words, but the symbols were blocked and I was incapable of decoding them.

That same year, at night on the twenty-fifth day of the first summer month, I met the Indian awareness holder Supreme Hungkara. He revealed the symbolic letters from the palm of his hand and told me, "Child, if you can transcribe these, it will be like an arrow of vajra lightning that subdues enemies of the doctrine. For that purpose, you need the Nöjin Shenpa Marnak tantra. I'll give it to you." He bestowed upon me the complete empowerment and transmission for the tantra called *Heart-Extracting Butcher*. Then he vanished.

Furthermore, as I began to transcribe those letters, a lesser lama named Répön, Cotton-Clad Practitioner, came to Golok from the Horkok area. He told me, "All these treasure teachings are definitely corrupt tenets." His words caused the auspicious connection to go amiss. I even made a wrongful aspiration toward that composition and burned what I had written.

LATER THAT YEAR, when the fifteenth day of the first winter month arrived, my companion Ngawang Gyatso and I began a Dorjé Drolö retreat. On the tenth day in the middle winter month, a white dakini approached me and sang,

> É Ma! Wondrous! Spiritual hero, regarding your close companions,
> Ngawang, Masterful Speech, is like a snow lion.
> Tashi, Auspicious One, is like an Indian tiger.
> Palden, Fortunate One, has entered the vajra womb.

Kili, Dagger, will be a lord of beings if he turns out well;
If he goes bad he will sink like a stone to the depths of cyclic existence.
The force of their aspirations
Leads them gradually to your circle:
They will significantly serve the doctrine.
From now on, for the next fifteen years,
Apart from emanations of the king and his subjects,
It's impossible for ordinary sentient beings to gather around you.
Do not forget these things—instill them in your mind!

A life force–[stealing] ogress lives in the east.
A demon will deceptively appear as a god called Virya, Diligence.
There will be another of low education called Shri, Fortunate One.
In the south, there will be a collector of undeserved offerings called
     Dharma, Doctrine.
In the west will be someone with fine knowledge named Rikpa,
     Awareness.
Moreover, seventeen will arise who revile you
And make corrupt aspirations.
Don't say anything positive or negative to them.
The karmic ripening of legal complaints and lawsuits will assail at you.
Twenty-eight demonic manifestations who steal offerings will appear.
As for guardians of the doctrine,
Keep them as allies and you will not lose or be found at fault.
Do not forget this! Keep it in mind
And all three—beginning, end, and middle—will be virtuous!

"My child, a Hor monk named Puntsok Tashi, Auspicious Excellence, will arrive here to become your student. All life long, never separate from him but employ him as your scribe. This will be greatly beneficial for beings!" Then she vanished without a trace.

That same year in the last winter month, that very monk from Hor arrived in my area. Relying on him as a close companion, I appointed him as my scribe.

IN THE YEAR I TURNED TWENTY-FIVE [1859], I went to meet some students in the Hor region. I did some meditation practices and recitations for a few patrons; on that occasion I saw a great host of spiritual heroes and dakinis gathered within the sacred circle. The practices proved to be helpful for many sick people.

THAT SAME YEAR on the tenth day of the first summer month, I performed one hundred vajra feast and fulfillment offerings. That night, a red dakini wearing a white cotton skirt sang,

> The stores of merit and power of aspirations
> From past lifetimes throughout many previous aeons have converged in
>   you, my child.
> Your sole father, Pema Jungné, Lotus-Born,
> Has made you leader of his enlightened activities and chief of his
>   profound treasures.
> At the red cliff of Upper Mar you'll find something that looks like a
>   small box.
> At a place called Baté in the local dialect,
> Vairotsana's walking staff is concealed as a treasure,
> With representations of wisdom body, speech, and mind
> And the locations of both your prophetic list and a supplementary list.
> Now is the time! Rush to claim your father's wealth.

I replied to her by singing this:

> Kyé! My sister, queen with a lovely face,
> I am a beggar with no one to rely upon.
> At an outer level, I lack the education of knowledge.
> At an inner level, I lack the qualities of meditation.
> I have no wealth, possessions, or resources.
> Above, I am without the haven of a refuge.
> Below, I am without anyone to support me.
> Around me, I have no close family.
>
> Apart from people who insult me out of jealousy,
> I don't have helpful friends who serve and praise me.
> For this exhausted powerless beggar,
> Even if I did have the fortune of possessing a treasure,

I doubt it would help anyone.
Pondering my own future, I wonder,
"Will I become of an outstanding beggar adept without fear?"
May the lama consider me and [and help me] accomplish my
    aspirations!

She answered,

Kyé! My child, don't let your high spirits wane—
Your disciples will appear like constellations [around you].
Though at first you are humble, without a haven,
In the end you will be more exalted than others.
Everyone will praise and serve you.
You will help the disciples with whom you have a karmic connection
And lead them to the path of freedom—this is certain.

Do exactly as I've commanded!
This is the starting point of your happiness.
Your wealth will grow like the waxing moon.
The deities and protectors will accomplish your wishes.
Mamo wrathful goddesses and dakinis will be your companions.
Keep that in mind, fortunate child!

"In this manner, at the site known as the Ba Treasure of Mar's box-shaped cliff, you'll find Saraha's rosary and a clay statue of Drolma made from capillary wormwood, along with your prophetic list. Make haste in going there without delay!"

Just as her prophecy foretold, on the tenth day of the last summer month, I went to the grove at Ba Treasure Cliff. When I arrived there, a piece of rock broke away, merely a span wide, and round in shape. I looked at the gap it left and inside stood a clay Drolma statue, a wax container, and an ancient, ugly rosary sitting in a heap of charcoal. I took them out. The container held a roll of paper. When I looked at its surface I saw this inscribed there: "At the neck of the cliff shaped like a garuda, called Silver Buzzard, you will find your prophetic list."

I went to that place. As soon as I arrived, the sun, clouds, and rain mingled together and a dense lattice of rainbow light emerged. At its center a black man with a lion head sat astride a black horse with white socks around its hooves. Wielding a bannered lance, he struck the cliff face, instantly opening a fissure. Inside sat a roll of paper. Looking at it, I saw that written on its surface were [instructions detailing] the time to bring forth treasure from the Vajra Cliff in Sermé—namely, the Female Earth Sheep Year, on the tenth day of the middle winter month—and the necessity to install a treasure replacement, give thanksgiving tormas to the protectors, and make offerings and vajra feasts to the spiritual heroes and dakinis.

As it described, during the first winter month, I returned to my homeland. On the ninth day of the middle winter month, I went with a friend named Déchen, Great Bliss, into the presence of Lama Tsenzang. I beseeched him, "Would you kindly give me a fine treasure vase to offer as a treasure replacement?" The lama assembled everything to make the treasure vase. He presented it to me with a blue silk ribbon tied around it.

The next day was the morning of the tenth day, and I went to collect the treasures. When I saw the flank of the Ngala Taktsé Mountain in Sermé, all the cliffs, hills, and forests were entirely cloaked in rainbows. The earth, rocks, and trees didn't appear to have any substantial nature. I became immeasurably delighted and continued on. When I drew near a place called Shadrak Dorjé, I saw a musk deer caught in a trap. I opened the trap and let it go.

Déchen asked, "What sort of connection is this? What does that omen indicate?"

I answered, "This is a fine auspicious connection: In the future, fortunate disciples will be like wild animals freed from a trap. It is an omen that they will be drawn away from cyclic existence and the abodes of the lower realms. Therefore, my treasure teachings will greatly benefit beings—this is certain."

We performed one hundred vajra feast and fulfillment offerings, and recited as many offerings and supplications as we could. After that, I had Déchen stay at the base of the cliff. "Continuously recite 'The Seven-Line Prayer!'" I commanded him. As soon as I turned my awareness to basic space, something like the door to a house appeared in the rock. Though I couldn't see anyone, a woman's delicate, melodic voice intoned,

> É É Ma! Wondrous!
> He's arrived, arrived—the guest has arrived!
> To give, to give—I have something to give you!
> If you're skilled in the method of travel

Used by deer and wild goats that go straight up slopes,
Never meeting anyone along the way,
You will have superbly positive auspicious connections.
When you go from the pass down to the valley,
If you meet someone with a harelip,
That's an omen that a dispute will occur.

For a treasure revealer who doesn't understand the view,
It's rarely possible for auspicious connections to align.
Although many treasures lie hidden
At the Vajra Cliff of Sermé,
Due to the shortcoming of not having a consort,
I will give you no more than half.
Carry away just that half
And conceal an excellent replacement for the treasures.

Then the sound faded away.

Déchen said, "I just heard a woman's voice reverberating. What was that?"

"I was singing a song to myself," I told him.

I gradually climbed up a stone stairway. With the sense of an easy and gentle ascent, I reached a place five fathoms [about thirty feet] in height, where there was a half-moon–shaped gap in the rock. When I struck it with a chisel, it opened. I saw numerous charcoal mounds inside. In their midst was juniper and birch bark, among which lay many boxes. The prophetic list stated that it was inappropriate to take objects from there more than three times. As instructed, after making three retrievals, I had seven boxes in hand. Although I also saw many sacred representations of wisdom body, speech, and mind, because I lacked a doctrine custodian and a consort, I couldn't take them out. After that, I left the treasure replacement inside and restored the seal of concealment just as it was before.

When I reached the base of the cliff, I looked around and the stairway I just used had disappeared. My friend Déchen asked me to place the treasures upon his head and make an aspiration prayer, which I did.

As we returned, along the way we met someone with a harelip. Déchen asked, "What sort of coincidence is this?"

I said, "It seems to be an omen that the two of us will soon be confronted with a dispute."

That night, a dakini adorned with the six bone ornaments appeared before me. I asked, "Who are you?"

She replied, "I am the dakini of Cool Grove [Charnel Ground] known as Kun Gyuma, Maiden Who Travels Everywhere. What are you pondering?"

I said, "Yesterday I met someone with a harelip. I'm wondering what that concerns."

The dakini told me:

> Yé! That person you saw riding a very fast horse
> Is an omen that you will traverse the swift path to great bliss.
> That person carrying a load of medicine on his back
> Is a sign that you will dispel the chronic disease of cyclic existence.
> For all fortunate beings connected to you through their aspirations,
> That name is maintained as an omen of liberation.[10]
> The fact that a youthful friend accompanied you
> Is a sign that you will meet a companion of awareness.
> That person with a harelip
> Is an omen of karma ripening as a dispute.
> This isn't a negative coincidence—it's an excellent auspicious connection.
> This excellence is just slightly marred by fault
> It's been spoiled by your pessimistic assumptions.
> Doesn't this indicate that you still adhere to lower views?
> In the great emptiness of cyclic existence and enlightenment,
> Magical projections of illusory phenomena arise.
> If you understand the meaning of that, what harm can there be?
> Know that, and keep it in mind as essential.

Then she vanished without a trace.

Around that time, [a local leader named] Abo Chung Yö said, "Everyone, lay and ordained, reports that during the Sheep Month in winter, all the mountains and plains were filled with rainbows. Seeing that, it's certain that you've done something very detrimental to our local god. Therefore, if you don't me give all the treasures you removed, I swear I will lead an army against you!" When I heard that, I quoted Guru Rinpoche:

When a destined individual encounters my treasures,
The ferocious gods and demons of China and Tibet all converge,
Seeming to rush after the treasure with the piercing cry of *ki*!

"It's certainly just as Guru Rinpoche stated. All of you can go ahead and lead your army! I have my own effective methods." Saying that, since I stood my ground, the army never even appeared and the dispute vanished on its own.

After that, I went eastward across to the region of Golok. The custodians of my teachings, Puntsok Tashi and Ngawang Gyatso, both said, "Now is the time to fashion a definitive version of these treasure teachings."

I told them, "We have to seal them until six years have passed," so we didn't commit the yellow parchment to writing for some time.

Great Perfection

In the year I turned twenty-six [1860], I received numerous dakini prophecies when I went to look for provisions in Buchung Tashul. Not even one of them missed the mark. On one occasion, the dakini Kuntu Nangjéma, All-Illuminating, said,

> The thing untamed by Guru Rinpoche,
> A foul demon lord of bad karma
> Called Sépung Nakpo, Black Thorn Heap, will emerge.
> He will gather Hor under his rule,
> And take control of many passes and valleys.

> With wicked intent,
> Filled with corrupt aspirations,
> Someone called Barnang Lokma Trin, Sky Lightning-Cloud, will rise up.
> During a challenge at Mardo Ser,
> White snow will descend like arrows from above.
> A blue lake will surge upward from below.
> The demons' black rock will be smashed from its foundation.
> Unlock the way to journey to both upper and lower areas.

And she departed.

The year I turned twenty-seven [1861], at night on the tenth day of the Miracle Month, a yellow dakini with round eyes like the eye of a peacock feather approached me. She held a cane in her right hand and a lacquered bowl in her left, and asked me, "My child, do you want to go south together to the Grove of Gathering?"

"Let's go! Let's go!"

As soon as I answered, we went straight there. Light and rainbow designs entirely covered and suffused the ground. Patterns and lattices of light and rainbows were visible in the sky. A gentle rain of myriad flowers fell from the surrounding space. In this splendid grove sat individuals presented as the thousand buddhas of this fortunate aeon, each seated upon a high jeweled throne. Possessing the attributes of the Teacher, who is the manifest body of enlightenment, they each displayed a gesture indicative of one of the five buddha families. They sat there unattended in the midst of five-colored rainbow light. When I encountered them they spoke in unison: "My child, listen to this transmission!" With a thundering resonance, they each gave the scriptural transmission from the text in their left hand. "We've completed our entire canon with nothing left out. For the welfare of disciples, you should trust in that and put into writing the pith instructions that capture the inner essence of our teachings. Now the nature of reality's space treasury will overflow from the expanse of wisdom mind." Then the buddhas and the pure land all dissolved into me and disappeared.

From that time forth, like planets and stars shimmering on the surface of the ocean, I recognized that all phenomena—both that of cyclic existence and enlightenment—are a perfectly contained, self-manifest display within supreme basic space. Further, merely by focusing my mind's intent on any subject, whatever teachings I needed would flow forth [in my mind's eye] as if a precise copy had been made.

THAT SAME YEAR at night on the seventeenth day of the middle summer month, a red woman wearing a blue cape approached me in a dream. She said, "Let's go, my child!" We went together and arrived in a place so delightful it made my heart ache. Someone saying he was Pakpa Ludrup, Nagarjuna, appeared as a monk with an extremely handsome face and form. Thirteen hundred monks encircled him; they all held texts and sang,

> Kyé Ho! Fortunate child of our spiritual family,
> This place is the Vajra Seat of India [Bodhgaya].
> We are the victors' sublime heirs,
> You are the victors' regent.
> Of everything that comprised the five sensory pleasures
> Throughout your lifetimes without beginning,
> Don't grasp onto a single thing for yourself.
> Sweep it all together with you mind
> And make offerings for the teachings.
> The inexhaustible trove of your mental wealth and enjoyments
> Is the supreme, unsurpassable mandala offering.

I asked, "What words should I use to offer this mandala?"
They answered with this four-line verse:

> Om Ah Hung! In order to complete the two stores of merit and
>   wisdom,
> I offer to the three jewels absolutely everything that manifests in all my
>   lifetimes,
> This priceless gem of body and mind,
> And this array of the possessions and enjoyments of gods, nagas, and
>   humans.
> Tram Guru Ratna Mandala Pudza Megha Samudra Saparana Samaya
>   Ah Hung

As instructed, I repeated the words and presented that offering.
Once again they spoke to me. "Listen now!" Intoning all at once, they
each gave the scriptural transmissions for their volumes. At the end, the central figure himself spoke these verses:

> This is the complete transmission with nothing left out.
> In brief, all the canon's texts and treatises, however many there are,
> Are synthesized in *The Perfection of Sublime Insight Sutra.*
> To attain manifest awakening, many skillful gateways
> To the creation and completion phases have been taught.
> For example, no matter which path you take from any direction
> Toward a large, sprawling city,
> You will still arrive in that great city.
> Likewise, since all phenomena are synthesized within the sole nature of
>   reality,
> The nature of reality is known as "the inexhaustible treasury of space."
> Therefore, the doctrine that delivers all beings to liberation
> Is Great Perfection, the unsurpassable result.

> As for the profound skillful means of the swift path of Mahayoga,
> Just as many springs and rivers in all directions
> Merge as one taste in the vast ocean,
> Likewise, all teachings without exception can be grouped as relative or
>   ultimate truth.

The two truths inseparable are fused within Great Perfection.
If you understand the meaning of Great Perfection, you see the truth of
   the nature of reality.
Connection to its vital instructions will carry you to the level of
   awareness holder.
Teach its meaning:
Nothing is more truly effective than this to help beings. Know that!

As soon as he spoke, everything vanished as if I had woken up into basic space from a dream.

Following this, the expanse of the space treasury of the nature of reality welled forth, and I comprehended the phases of the paths of creation and completion exactly as they are.

How Should I Conduct Myself?

I TURNED TWENTY-EIGHT in the Dog Year [1862]. Someone saying she was Dakini Méri Dzinjé, Holding a Fiery Mountain, told me, "If you enter retreat at Dröpuk, Cave of Escape, the dakinis' assembly hall, your wealth and power will increase during the latter part of your life."

Ah Ho! Listen, individual of excellent fortune!
Dröpuk is the land where dakinis gather.
The site where vajra dakinis converge
Is a source of happiness
And an excellent place to accomplish pacifying activity.
When you've done retreat there,
The qualities of meditative experience and realization will be born in
    you.
It is the tantric practice place for awareness holders
Who indivisibly unite skillful means and sublime insight.
[The area] is like a regal queen on her throne
Surrounded by subjects in all directions.
[Practicing here] is an auspicious connection for your disciples to gather
    around you.

If you rely upon Durtrö Lhamo Sonam, Meritorious Charnel-Ground
    Goddess,
From time to time as a consort,
It's possible that you will have a holy sublime son
Like a white snow lion,
Supreme among beasts.

Likewise, that lion's companion,
Another son like a striped Indian tiger,
Will come, carried by the Rabbit Year.

If you rely on a worldly wrathful dakini,
Draktsün, Cliff Queen, as your activity consort,
The young dawning sun,
Supremely dazzling like a god,
White in color like Venus,
Will appear as another son, a doctrine-holder.

If you befriend Norgyün Bumo, Stream of Wealth Maiden,
A yellow stupa of gold,
A conch moon, white and waxing,
And a blazing meteorite vajra
Will hold the life force of the doctrine.
Like wish-fulfilling jewels,
It's possible they will grant sublime food of one hundred flavors
To satisfy guests from all directions.

Furthermore, the great garuda
That cuts through the heights of space
As an heir to your doctrine
Will go to unfixed mountain locales
And impartially serve beings in the future.

Do not forget these symbolic words
Spoken by me, your mother.
Keep them in mind and both your spiritual and worldly power will
    increase.

Then she vanished without a trace.

As advised in the prophecy, I went to Dröpuk one morning in the first spring month. After staying in retreat for just one month, many excellent portents of astounding virtue and good fortune appeared: At night on the seventh day of my retreat, a subterranean goddess named Tinglo Men, Medicine Bowl, sang this song:

Kyé Ho! I, the grandmother of existence
Known as Tinglo Men
Hold the northern area of Tingru.

In a previous lifetime, an individual from the Drokmi clan
Was Khyé-u Chung Lotsawa—that's you!

Dig in that fissured rock above
And find the ritual of the black sa-tsa[11]—
A profound method using substances
To avert danger from hail.
Next year, when you return to this place,
Food for your retreat will appear.
During the summer you can beg for dairy provisions
And during the winter you can beg for grain, but other than that,
Don't constantly go looking for payments for religious services.

These days, at the end of the era,
Mobs of unruly people
Self-glorify and pretend to be treasure revealers.
Spending their entire life roaming after such payments,
They don't even stay three months in retreat!

Having rejected that sort of poor conduct,
Guru Rinpoche's regents
Are the great treasure revealers who preceded you.
They prepared to work for the welfare of beings
And were diligent in the essential practices.
They spurned seeking gain from collecting payments for services
And gave themselves over to teaching and writing.
When they arrived at the latter part of life,
Their power increased without effort.
Their fortunate disciples
Swelled to magnificent gatherings of men and women.
You, as well, will gradually do as they did.
Put this into practice with that same approach
And it's certain you will accomplish what is deeply meaningful for this
    life and the next.

Then she vanished.

FURTHER, ONE NIGHT in the third week of that retreat, from amid a densely gathered canopy of light and rainbow clouds, Orgyen, king of the doctrine, appeared in space before me. "Child of my spiritual family, it's very important for you to exert yourself in vajra feast and fulfillment offerings, to offer copious tormas to the formidable doctrine guardians, and to complete an uninterrupted month-long sealed retreat every year without fail. Take these as the three key instructions. Consume this holy accomplishment substance without leaving anything behind."

He handed me a skull-cup filled with nectar. When I drank it all, an inconceivable experience of bliss blazed within me and right away I beseeched him, "Supreme precious refuge, perfected essence of the entire body, speech, mind, qualities, and activities of the three times' victors with their heirs, I bow to you and take refuge. Exactly how should I conduct myself?"

"Kyé! Magnificent individual, you should behave as you have in the past—as someone who doesn't 'keep face,' as would a madman. Constantly sustain that conduct and when you are reverentially served, treat everyone with equanimity, in a peaceful and disciplined manner. Maintain harmony. Teach the sacred instructions. Do whatever you can to help beings!" When he finished speaking, he vanished into basic space.

THE EVENING WE ARRIVED for the "receiving spiritual attainments" sections [at the conclusion] of a great accomplishment ceremony, Awareness Holder Dudul Dorjé appeared and poured alcohol into a bell metal bowl. The alphabet rose upon its surface like a vivid reflection, with a swirling rainbow vapor of five colors. He handed me the bowl saying, "You are my emanation; we are indivisible. My child, because Dakini Dorjé Pakmo, Vajra Sow, has given this to you, touch it to your forehead, throat, and heart." He dissolved into me, and when I drank the nectar, an acute experience of realization surged in my mindstream.

AT NIGHT ON THE TENTH DAY of the first summer month, a blue dakini wearing a white silk cloak like a sheepskin asked me, "My child, do you want to go see a spectacle at the place called Source of Pure Wishes?" I went with her to a very delightful land, a pleasure garden with every variety of desirable enjoyment drifting like a naturally arisen thick mist. At its center loomed a celestial palace of the five wisdoms, blazing like the sun; its light glowed with sheens of white, yellow, red, green, and blue. In its midst stood a jeweled throne, and upon a seat made of a lotus, moon, and sun sat the king of awareness holders, Supreme Hungkara, with a white body and a lustrous red glow. One could gaze at his face and form forever and never be satisfied.

He told me, "Previously, [when you stayed in retreat] at that place called Dröpuk, where vajra dakinis gather, your qualities of experience and realization naturally arose. Therefore, make that place your residence from time to time, and strive in the essential practices there. After a year has passed, go east to Sergyi Dzichen Shé and do two one-month retreats. During those retreats, if you perform two thousand vajra feast and fulfillment offerings, the fruition of their merit will increase and ripen, like sprouts flourishing in the rain. When you reach Dröpuk, the superb place where dakinis gather, a few of your karmically endowed disciples will appear. Confer the sacred teachings according to each one's specific capacity, and it's certain you will guide them to the city of supreme freedom."

I replied, "Lama, I don't know how to teach even a shred of the essential teachings! It's like this:"

> I am an infant without refuge or guardian.
> Above, there is no one to shelter or protect me.
> Below, there is no one to support me.
> Beside me, not a single person props me up.
>
> Although I've taught others
> As my self-manifest teachers ordered,
> No one is interested in me
> Except as an object of universal criticism.
>
> I'm fortunate enough to bring forth profound treasures,
> Yet during the final days of this degenerate evil era,
> An arable field of disciples hasn't appeared.
>
> Even though I express the truth without deception,
> Everyone will sing out that what I say are lies.
> I don't imagine that I'll have disciples
> Who are faithful, with conviction.

Sole father who knows all,
Bless me right now
So my mindstream fully matures!
Bless this humble beggar
Right now
With the great assurance of fearlessness.

He answered:

Even if the Buddha himself appears
Directly in front of those who apply themselves to practice
If they're deficient in karma and fortune
He cannot help their minds.

So it was that Buddha Shakya Wangpo, Might of the Shakyas,
Appeared in this world,
Yet was unable to dredge the depths of beings' realms.

By the force of your aspirations,
You're setting out to serve beings.
There are a few fortunate disciples
Connected to you through past karma.
Due to the forceful momentum of each one's karma,
A few remain.
The time has come for you to guide them!

Just one hundred years from now
Non-Buddhist barbarian border people
Will cause not even a murmur of the teachings to endure.
Since we've reached a dark era,
Transcribing many lengthy texts
Will only cause you fatigue.
Therefore, you must transcribe into words and spread
The innermost pith of all your sacred teachings,
And it's possible you can help those fortunate individuals.
Stretch your mind to its utmost limit
And you will accomplish the supreme purpose of this life and the next.

"My enlightened vision will shift to your mindstream—the sacred pith instructions will overflow like a river." With that, I woke from the dream into the basic space of awareness.

As BEFORE, I went to the nomad pastures in the Hor area. I practiced many of the Dorjé Drolö practices that originated from my pure-vision cycle. In the middle summer month, someone named Anam Wangchen, Anam of Great Power, came and told me, "I lack trust and confidence because these days so many people claim to be treasure revealers and accomplished adepts. However, Jawa Alak advised, 'You should sponsor Gili Tertön to do a recitation ritual for you. If he's not an emanation of Supreme Orgyen, I've deceived you!' Since I heeded his advice, I'm inviting you to come." I went to his place and performed the Dorjé Drolö practice from my treasure revelations. Furthermore, the individual referred to as "Jawa Alak" is Tulku Jawa Rinpoche, whose name is Do-ngak Gyatso, Ocean of Sutras and Tantras. He is a lord among scholars.

An Authentic Treasure Revealer

IN THE LAST SUMMER MONTH, I went to the Gili homestead. Someone called Kéla Chöpak arrived there and said, "If you are an unerring treasure revealer, I will act as your doctrine custodian. You must write out for me a means of accomplishment related to Tamdrin, Horse Neck."

I wrote a definitive version of a text outlining the means of accomplishment related to Tamdrin from my cycle called The Profound Doctrine Overflowing into the Expanse of Wisdom Mind. When I granted him the empowerment and scriptural transmission, he still harbored doubts. On that occasion, Tulku Chaktsa came from Katok Monastery in order to continue teachings for a monastic center in Golok and to collect offerings. He stayed where we were living, and Kéla Chöpak placed the text under his pillow, telling the lama, "Tonight I placed a new treasure teaching beneath your pillow. What is it like? It would be so kind of you to determine whether it's good or bad, and say something about this tomorrow morning."

The next morning he asked, "What did you decide about this thing I requested of you last night?"

The lama replied, "I dreamt last night of an excellent field with six large fruits. Though only slightly ripened, they were harvested before they were ready. Based on that dream, it's premature to spread these treasures. If copious vajra feasts aren't offered, the dakinis won't be happy. If they aren't pleased, I wonder if many extra or missing marks might appear among the symbolic letters [of the root treasure text]. He seems to be an authentic treasure revealer."

Then Kéla Chöpak once more implored [Tulku Chaktsa] Kyilung Tukchok Dorjé, Sublime Wisdom Mind Vajra of Kyilung, "You must decide on the quality of this treasure teaching and make a statement."

He replied, "If one is to examine whether or not he is an authentic treasure revealer, it will become clear in the end: Like the sun breaking free from the clouds, if he becomes ever-brilliant and ever-exalted, he is excellent; otherwise, the end result of being a fake treasure-revealer can only be gradual dissipation of [his fame and followers], and nothing else."

On another occasion, I transcribed a practice for Charity of the Body [from my treasure cycle]. Someone else showed it to a man named Ré-ön, who scoffed, "This text states, 'The dakini of the natural radiance of the movement of mind.' Such dakinis can only be like female demons! Other than that, if it is the radiance of movement, it's impossible for them to be wisdom dakinis. Ha ha to that! I've come to a conclusion based on this single phrase."

After that, Ré-ön asked Katok Tulku [Chaktsa], "Tulku, is it true or not that you've said this Gili Tertön is an authentic treasure revealer?"

"My dream portent was extremely auspicious," he replied.

Ré-ön countered, "If you look at how he states, 'The dakini of the natural radiance of the movement of mind,' you get some idea."

Tulku replied, "If there is fault in that, even Dodrubchen states, 'Mental consciousness's liberation or delusion is the miraculous illusory dance of circulating energy's movement.' What he stated is equivalent to what Gili Tertön said, therefore, is he also wrong, or not?"

Ré-ön mumbled, "If he said something like that . . ." and bowing his head, amid a crowd of many gathered people, he didn't say anything more.

When I heard about that incident, I performed a declaration of truth incantation and sent him a curse. I burnt his name [placard] in the fire and from then on Ré-ön gradually incurred legal complaints, and lawsuits and many other misfortunes ensued. At a certain point, an army brought him to ruin, destroyed his possessions, and wounded him with weapons. In the end, his home and surroundings were turned upside down.

In the last autumn month, someone called Chö-nyön Drakpa, Renowned Madman Severance Practitioner, offered me a drum, a hand drum, a thighbone trumpet, and a pair of volumes of [Jikmé Lingpa's] Heart Essence of the Vast Expanse. He asked, "Transcribe a text from The Secret Treasury of the Dakinis, and I will do that practice."

That night, a bright blue woman saying she was Dakini Ngadré Gyalmo, Drumbeat Queen, approached me. I asked her, "What is this Chö-nyön Drakpa like? Of what quality is he?"

She answered:

> Hé Hé! That holy hidden adept
> Is an incarnation of the great Sakya Kunga Gyaltsen, Ever-Joyful Victory
>   Banner of the Sakyas,
> And the hidden adept Kong-nyön, Madman from Kongpo.

In order to purify his remaining obscurations,
He's taken on a body like this for now.
The auspicious connections of his meeting with your treasures
Are that he's given you this drum and bell
As a portent [that your treasure teachings] will be as acclaimed as the
    profound Heart Essence teachings;
As an indication of Severance practice, he's given you this hand drum;
These are signs that your name will be renowned.
Excellent omens like these are so rare!

The next night, when I saw images of Awareness Holder Jikmé Lingpa, Longchen Rabjam, and Pema Jungné fused together in a single coemergent form, the trio placed upon my head the two volumes Chö-nyön Drakpa had given me. They declared, "We grant you empowerment and transmission of what words can express; the empowerment and transmission of the inexpressible meaning; and the close-lineage empowerment and transmission that is complete in itself. May you receive them! May they be complete!" Having said that, their form appeared to vibrate and quiver. I exclaimed, "Those earthen images are astonishing. They are really amazing!"

At that, an old man jeered, "I laugh at your impure eyes! Seeing even these illusory wisdom forms as earthen images—what is that all about?" As soon as he said that, I woke up.

When I transcribed a practice from The Secret Treasury of the Dakinis, I felt confident, and spectacular good omens arose. A dense canopy of rainbow light emerged, while simultaneously a small flock of vultures descended; delightful aromas wafted in mists, and a naturally arisen symphony resounded.

Further, on the tenth day of the first winter month, someone named Gyalwa Tsultrim, Moral Discipline of the Victors, offered me a well-formed skull-cup. He implored, "Please give me a short, concise sacred practice of 'Severance of Evil Forces.'" I transcribed it and gave him the scriptural transmission.

THE YEAR I TURNED TWENTY-NINE [1863], I went to Drӧpuk on the first day of the middle winter month. From the tenth day onward, I stayed in retreat for one year,[12] together with two of my students cultivating my experience in circulating energy, fierce inner heat, and the exercises from the Heart Essence of the Vast Expanse. This resulted in signs of heat, and our vase breathing becoming visible, like a vase. Even during winter, the heat's fire blazed in my body and I was able to wear just cotton. Moreover, I had visionary experiences akin to seeing smoke, optical illusions, stars, and apparent clear light. Relying upon the inconceivable symbolic appearances of clear light, the irreversible, absolutely faultless wisdom of awareness rose in my mindstream.

On the fifteenth day of the middle winter month, I returned to my homeland. On the first day of the following month I went into retreat for two months together with my retreat companions, Kyenrab, Omniscience; Karma Konchok, Precious Activity; Lama Ten, Lama Steadfast; and Rikchok, Sublime Awareness, utilizing a Dorjé Drolö practice ritual from Dudul Dorjé's treasure revelations. During that time, a hostile ruler demon afflicted the monk Kyenrab with disease.

This is how I bound the ruler sorcerer-demon under oath and freed Kyenrab from the disease: After seven days in retreat, I dreamt that three women came to my door. As I meditated on the absorption of fire, they cried out, "Ouch! Ouch!" loudly, and ran away. Later, during the night of the twenty-first day, a red cat appeared in my retreat cabin. I pinned it down with a stick. Since I knew it to be the ruler demon's miraculous projection, I stuck my right hand in its mouth. When it scratched me, its ferocity made me panic. I brought to mind my creation-phase practice of Dorjé Drolö—I clutched its neck with my left hand and squeezed tightly. Suddenly, the cat became a monk wearing ragged clothes. He pleaded, "Brother, don't wring my neck! I have something good to tell you."

I countered, "We don't need to talk. You have to make me a promise."

"Tell me what I need to promise!"

"Promise that, henceforth, you won't cause any harm."

"I swear I won't cause harm to you or those around you. As for this monk Kyenrab, I won't let him go until I've had a few words with him. I swear that I'll free him. I promise!"

Then I laid my hand on his head and poured nectar in his mouth. I placed him under oath and sent him away.

Three days after we reached the end of the retreat, the ruler demon possessed that monk. He recounted the story in detail and talked about various other things. Then every sort of disturbance vanished without a trace.

To conclude [the retreat], we performed two thousand vajra feast and fulfillment offerings to our chosen deity, and we received the spiritual attainment [substances]. Excellent signs, truly virtuous in nature, appeared, including a white rainbow extending into the roof of our residence and snow falling continuously in the form of flowers.

A Hidden Adept

THE YEAR I TURNED THIRTY, I returned to Dröpuk. During my stay, a dakini appeared during the night of the eighteenth day of the first summer month. Her body was light blue on the right side, red on the left side and bright yellow in the middle. She wore a belt of yellow gold threads, red copper threads, and black iron threads wound around her waist, and a skirt of five-colored silks. She approached me and asked, "My child, do you have the signs and qualities of accomplishment or not? If you do, then tell me about them!"

I replied, "Who are you? Supreme Orgyen told me it's not right to divulge my signs of accomplishment and miraculous displays to anyone. 'For a while, if you live as a hidden adept, you won't experience obstacles to your practice, nor will you succumb to the sway of the eight worldly concerns. This is crucial advice.' Therefore, I won't say anything."

"I am lady of the secret treasury of the sixty-four hundred thousand Great Perfection tantras. Longyang Men, Vast Expanse Medicine Woman, is my name. If you didn't previously boast to humans, there's no fault in telling me, because I'm a nonhuman dakini. So tell me," she implored.

I thought to myself, "This is true," and relented, "Ah, fine then! When I was sixteen, I went to the Gönten family, my patron's home, to recite texts. My patron told me, 'Previously I stayed for one year alongside a spring, which was my summer place adjacent to Sera Monastery. It was located below the Döndrup homestead, and that spring dried up. Since then, there's been no water for five years; living there is unfeasible. This is a great loss, yet there's nothing to be done about it. Now you—you're not like other old monks. Given that you exhibit clairvoyance, if you have a way to make this spring overflow, it will surely be a sign of your accomplishment.'

"I wondered, 'Can I fulfill that wish? I have to examine my dreams.' I fell asleep and brought that spring to mind. I dreamt that inside a dilapidated house lay a black snake, dried up from the neck down and exhausted. All around sprawled a multitude of fish and frogs with withered limbs. They didn't exhale, though their inner breath was not quite spent. When I came upon them I thought, 'These wretched sentient beings—how pitiable! Why are they having this experience?'

"The snake recounted, 'I am the naga woman Nordzinma, Wealth Holder. In the past my residence was a golden fortress with turquoise pillars; as for me, I was endowed with the glory of power and luxury. However, lots of women washed their hands and feet in this spring, and the filthy run-off made my power entirely decline. Bereft of possessions, my fortress home destroyed, I suffer terribly in fear of the scorching sun and sand—I'm miserable! If an accomplished adept were to make water offerings, it would likely be helpful, yet no one sees my suffering. Now what can I do?'

"When I related the dream to my patron, he said, 'I'm certain you aren't mistaken, and it will help.'

"I went to the site of the spring and made abundant water offerings. I meditated that Bodhisattva Tukjé Chenpo, Supreme Compassion, appeared in the sky before me. Streams of nectar flowed from his body and cured the nagas' sicknesses, revitalized them, and restored their fortress abodes and luxuries to a level many times greater than before. Visualizing that, I made hundreds of thousands of water offerings. Upon their completion, a beautiful woman actually appeared and bowed before me. 'You are a holy accomplished adept of immense kindness to us. We will definitely send some harm in retaliation to the women who inflicted such damage on us. I swear we will!'

I insisted, 'Don't kill them, and don't torment them.'

The woman said, 'You've revived the dying, cured our ailments, increased the glory of our riches many times over, and our fortresses have become quite fabulous. If we gave you naga livestock in payment for your kindness, [in your world] they would become insects. Even if we offered you wealth, it would become rocks, trees, and so forth. Therefore, in Sergyi Traklung lives a naga woman called Serdangma, Golden Glow. She has a poisonous snakes egg. I've offered that to you. Keep it safe, and if it stays clean, you will become a wealthy man with marvelous riches. I won't transgress your command. I won't attack human lives or any people.' She flew into the sky and at the same moment, a wisp broke away from a black cloud and grew larger.

"When I told my patron how things had transpired, he said, 'If you don't recite [*The Perfection of Sublime Insight in One Hundred Thousand Verses*], their retribution will certainly be sent to strike us.' As soon as I did what he asked, for some time, fierce wind raged and hail fell. Simultaneously, lightning struck, killing a female yak and her four calves, and a massive river flooded.

"Are those signs of accomplishment?

"Moreover, a cow-yak hybrid belonging to my patron's family died. I recited a declaration of truth incantation and repeated aloud the naga wom-an's vows; this caused the animal to stand up and walk away. Further, in my patron Gönten's home, a weasel was laughing raucously. This frightened all the horses, cattle, and sheep, and they bolted. At that time, I recited a declara-tion of truth incantation and repeated her vows aloud. Immediately, without seeing any form, I heard an audible voice intone, 'Don't say things like that! We've taken twenty-one horses and livestock, but apart from just five, we're giving the rest to you as your share.' Everyone in the family heard what was said.

"Are those signs of accomplishment?

"A previous year, I received the empowerments and scriptural transmis-sions for Awareness Holder Dudul Dorjé's treasure revelation cycle from Katok Chaktsa Tulku. One day at a vajra feast, a woman told me, 'Don't stay here. Leave!' That infuriated me, and at that same moment, a lama of the Hor family, whose home I was staying in, became a ruler demon. When I went to the house, a friend had the key, so I had no way to open the door. I stood in front of the door, and, without thinking of being on the other side, I ran straight through into the house and found myself inside.

"Is that a sign of accomplishment?

"As soon as I arrived inside the house, that ruler demon, in a miraculous apparition as an old monk, came up behind me and bound my arms and legs saying, 'Now what strength do you have?'

"'I have this strength, and I will defeat you!' I vowed. Feeling terrified, I immediately meditated on my body as Guru Drakpo, fierce and dark red, and I clearly visualized a blazing inferno. He exclaimed, 'Ouch!' and fell to the ground. I seized his right leg and whirled him around above me three times. When he struck the ground, he turned into a rabbit pellet. I stuffed it into a bag, tied the bag's mouth shut, and concealed it under my bed.

"After twenty-one days passed, that old monk said, 'Let me go, and with [Katok Lama] Drimé Shingkyong Gönpo, Stainless Pure Land Protector, as my witness, I won't harm your retinue and subjects.'

"I asked, 'You who have broken vows, will you take an oath?'

"'Oh misery! I swear I won't hurt anyone.' I took him out [of the bag], and once released, he was very wretched.

"He swore, 'I will do whatever I can to harm the people in the house below here—Kyaka Lama, a brother and sister, and Taktsal Lama.'

"As he prepared to leave, I asked him where he was going. 'I'm going to Lama Orgyen Gyatso's, Ocean of Orgyen's, place in Lho,' he said, and departed.

"During the twenty-one days [of the spirit's confinement], the lama recovered from his illness. Regarding that experience, that night I dreamt the ruler demon said, 'For twenty-one days a ruthless, cruel monk kept me in prison; I was tormented by hunger and thirst. Finally after enduring all that suffering, now I've arrived here.' The next day, the [Hor family lama's] sickness got even worse and he died.

"Is even that a sign of accomplishment?

"The next day, Kyaka Lama's sister went mad. I advised the lama, 'Hold a public gathering, and leave in secret during the recitation of the vajra feast offering: Run away quickly and stay in Dorjé Phurba, Vajra Dagger, retreat for one month.' Despite my advice, he didn't do as I said. Instead, he left after the vajra feast was distributed and died the next month.

"I told Taktsal Lama, 'You have to make a great burnt offering with all the remainders of your food and drink, and repeat the name of the Hor lama three times. At the end, without anyone noticing, escape covertly. If you do this, apart from that, nothing bad will happen. If you don't do that, you will surely perish in an accident.' Although I warned him, he didn't heed the things I said, and he went home. After staying home for three days, he rode to Marta Mé on a yak; the yak startled, and that's how he was killed."

The dakini said, "You don't need clairvoyance and miracles greater than those. At the same time, if you keep them a firmly sealed secret from others and remain a hidden adept, that's excellent: You will be free from obstacles, and hindering conditions won't arise in your spiritual practice. That's crucial advice. Now that you've finished telling me your secrets, here is my counsel:"

> Hé Hé! Celestial mother's young child,
> The pure essence of your impure body
> Is the heart jewel. From its center
> Rises the trunk, the supreme channel.
> The fruition of the pure essence is the eyes, which are the seer
> Of the outer element, the five lights of basic space,
> And the inner element, luminous orbs.
> The basis for their unfolding is self-arisen sublime insight.
> Though fully present within all sentient beings,
> By the force of their not having made this apparent,

They go astray in cyclic existence.
This aeon of impure karmic [embodiment]
Collapses into the pristine basic space of purity—clear light.
Settle in its play, the nature of reality.
Without searching,
The qualities of the paths and stages will naturally arise.
You've directly seen Cutting Through—
The truth of the nature of reality.
Put into practice these sacred instructions
Of the swift path of supreme transference,
And I will miraculously manifest
As the purity of pristine clear light:
Mother and child [luminosity] will indivisibly merge in a single taste.

When she dissolved into my heart, the authentic key instructions of the swift path of Direct Crossing were pointed out to me directly.

Compelled by necessity, or for whatever reason made sense,
A nonhuman, embodied wisdom dakini
In the manner of an ordinary person, insisted on answers to her
    questions.
I gave transparent answers based on my experience, without
    concealment.
With her melodious speech, she granted me confirmation.
Pointing out to me the innate, self-arising channel and luminous orbs,
She gave me these profound pith instructions:
Regarding the meaning of the outer and inner symbols,
In order to illustrate that clear light is primordially inseparable,
The same moment she dissolved as one taste with me,
I realized correctly the key instructions of the secret swift path.

Traversing the Swift Path

FROM THAT TIME FORTH, relying on the clear-light path of Direct Crossing, I gazed through the skylight of my house and settled my mind in evenness, in one-pointed meditative concentration. I saw vast domains of inconceivable pure lands. I saw scenes such as Sangyé Yeshe Nyima, Buddha Wisdom Sun, teaching the doctrine to an entourage of eighty million, and Sangyé Mingyur, Buddha Immutable, teaching to one billion disciples. Unimaginable appearances arose.

One day in the year I turned thirty-one [1865], someone appeared in the space right in front of me saying he was Sangyé Dön Mizawé Gyalpo, Buddha Undoubtable King. He was adorned by the myriad ornaments of the enjoyment body of enlightenment (sambhogakaya). His body's ornaments, garlands, and long necklace were composed of seeds; inside every seed appeared a pure land of the buddhas. Further, inside each of those buddhas' ornaments, I could see many more buddha pure lands. Each panorama unfolded successively into the next, and immediately the inconceivable clear light of awareness was fully present. These appearances didn't cease for seven days, so my attendants, consorts, and disciples all wondered if my state was an omen of impending death. Their minds heavy, they were miserable. At that time, a tiny red bird arrived exclaiming,

> Kyé! Inconceivable Khyé-u Chung,
> I am Dakini Garab Tso, Lake of Utmost Joy,
> Of the exalted land [India].
> Look at how all the appearances of this life
> Are unstable and don't endure,
> Like magical illusions or dreams,
> And remember you must act for your own benefit [by attaining
>   realization].
>
> Look at the phenomena of diverse appearances
> With the eyes of sublime insight—
> Everything has the nature of space.

The basis of everything that apppears is space.
Having familiarized yourself with that fully evident state,
You are an individual who has attained supreme confidence.

Not far off is this, the certain direct path
To self-awakening within you.
Within this fully manifest indwelling state,
Don't search—settle on your ground
And you will achieve the citadel of Kuntuzangpo, Ever-Excellent.

She flew away. Another bird, glowing red, told me,

É! Khyé-u Chung endowed with skylike mind,
Listen to me without distraction!
Look at how the illusory city of cyclic existence
Has no essence,
And how each individual doesn't see
Any cessation to their own suffering.

Awareness of all phenomena of cyclic existence and enlightenment
As the supreme nature of reality
Is the contemplative practice of the space of the nature of reality.

Happy, magnificent individual
Traversing the swift path—it's not far
To the level of Kuntuzangpo.

My child, for the benefit of beings,
You were commissioned by Orgyen Kunzang Pema, Ever-Excellent
    Lotus,
As a guide and teacher and an envoy of his activity.
Therefore, be responsible for the welfare of others.

As for the supremely profound path of Direct Crossing,
For now, just leave it as it is and nurture your disciples!
Do you understand?

After I repeated that aloud, one of my attendants, an older woman named Yeshe Drön, Lamp of Wisdom, said, "I just heard this lovely birdsong that lasted quite a long time. I never heard anything sounding like that—it was really amazing, like a mute person singing a song."

In that way, during the experience of the manifest presence of the nature of reality, the energy of the vase empowerment struck the solidity of my body, thus ripening my body into the vajra body. The energy of the secret empowerment entered my speech, ripening it as the expression of vajra speech. The sublime insight empowerment struck my mind, ripening it into the wisdom of sublime insight: the expanse of the space treasury of the nature of reality overflowed. The word empowerment struck apparent reality, causing all appearances to shift into the play of rainbows and drops of light. All these signs were fully apparent.

At that time someone appeared saying he was Rikzin Garab Dorjé, Awareness Holder Vajra of Utmost Joy, naked under a white silk skirt. He told me,

All phenomena of cyclic existence and enlightenment
Are just like magical illusions and dreams—
The supreme state without a basis and foundation.

Self-manifest reality lacks any intrinsic nature,
Yet primary causes and conditions definitely arise interdependently.
Your awareness is rootless and baseless—
Panoramic sky in an encompassing expanse.
Your basis of being is free from elaboration,
Definitely objectless and wide open.

Primordial purity is the supreme encompassing expanse.
From its unveiled natural radiance in pristine clarity
Emerges the spontaneously present display
Of the treasure trove of enlightenment's wisdoms and qualities.

Displays of pure lands and wisdom bodies
Do not depend on the labor of effort.
Hold to your own ground within this fully manifest state
And you will come to buddhahood within yourself.

Thus he spoke, and I replied:

> Kyé! Universal embodiment of the three times' victors,
> Teacher of beings, listen to me!
> I was born in this degenerate era
> By the force of vile karma.
> I'm not of a lowly family,
> Yet my intractable ancestor
> Powerful in black incantations,
> Has challenged and threatened me
> With curses, binding hexes, and disease.
> Since he brought all that together,
> Future and far-flung generations of my children
> Will be humble and weak, with diminished wealth.
> If there is a means to recover from this,
> When the Heart Essence of the Awareness-Holding Dakini [earth-
>   treasure cycle]
> Has moved to the vault of my heart,
> I will surely hold it as vital collateral.
> Bless me right now
> To have fortune equal to yours—
> [May I receive] the blessings of the lama
> Which lead to attaining enlightenment in this very life.

I uttered that and he vanished into the sphere of space like a rainbow.

ON ANOTHER OCCASION, a dark red adept saying he was Vajra Master Supreme Hungkara appeared in an expanse of rainbows and drops of light. He wore heruka attributes and said to me,

> Kyé! Do you recognize me?
> I am king of awareness holders,
> That entity called Supreme Hungkara.
> My child, you are at the stage of the increase of the visions of
>   meditative experience:
> Appearances of deities and pure lands
> Arise as ornaments to apparent reality.

Although they appear in diverse and unpredictable ways,
By coming to a definite conclusion
That these are the appearances of illusory meditative experiences,
You will be freed from the narrow passageway of errors and deviation
    in your understanding.
If you practice for seven years
Without a single interruption,
You will attain enlightenment as the supreme rainbow body.
To claim your father's inheritance,
Take responsibility for the welfare of others!

I responded:

King of awareness holders, listen to me!
In this dark thicket of Mar-yul,
I have no context in which to help beings.
With no thought for anything other than spiritual practice,
I strive for my own benefit, [attaining realization].
Under the sway of craving food and clothing,
I have no choice but to go off seeking provisions,
Because, by nature, this is what sentient beings do.
Lama, grant your blessing
That conducive conditions will effortlessly arise.

The lama answered,

Kyé! Inconceivable Khyé-u Chung,
When you encounter Pema's treasures
It's certain you will rely upon a consort of sublime insight.
If you rely on a consort as a companion,
There's some suspicion you will turn to the maintenance of cyclic
    existence.
Therefore, at times like that,
Throughout this lifetime don't lose yourself to undeserved payments.
For the rest of your human life
Devote yourself to spiritual practice—focus on that!
Many individuals will appear

Who are incapable of experiential cultivation [in meditation].
When they espose their own belief systems,
Put aside their piles of treatises—
Let go entirely into the basic space of reality,
The actualized presence [of the nature of reality].

Then he vanished into basic space.

Glorious Copper-Colored Mountain

IN THE YEAR I TURNED THIRTY-TWO, in a dream on the first night of the first month, a little child with white skin who was wearing a white silk skirt approached me. "Great individual, what is it that you want?"

I answered, "In this world, the sublime teaching of the Profound Domain of Severance of Evil Forces is rare. I wish for this teaching in relation to Great Perfection. Do you know this or not?"

"I don't know that teaching, although in a place called Joyful Grove resides someone named Lama Jamyang. This superb guide teaches whatever is wished for to his self-manifest magical-projection entourage. Since he's giving these teachings to help his disciples, do you want to go there?"

I said that I would, and we went there, crossing over many lands. In a joyful grove of utmost felicity, a rainbow lattice with many openings arose as an immense, spacious enclosure. At its center, upon a very high, jeweled throne, sat my very own lama, his physical aspect similar to when he had lived previously in the human world. Wearing silk and jewel adornments, he appeared seated. Immediately upon arriving in his presence, within a state of deep respect and faith, I offered prostrations and touched the crown of my head to his feet: I made many aspirations. As soon as I settled myself in front of him, the child said, "Lama, this individual said that he wishes for the profound sacred instructions of Severance of Evil Forces. Would you please teach as he requested?"

My sublime lama didn't speak for a moment, and sat gazing into space. At one point, this is what he said: "Kyé Ho! Child of the lineage, what we call 'Severance' is the pith instruction to destroy self-clinging. It is the sacred instruction that kills the four evil forces in their own beds. Among everything you can learn; it is supreme. It dispels hindrances to every meditation. It is the innermost pith of all Buddhist teachings. It is the excellent path of every sacred practice. It provides the framework for every swift path to attaining omniscience. It is the sacred instruction that directly pinions negative circumstances and cuts through them. It is the pith instruction for considering bad omens as your own good fortune. It is the profound teaching for taking sickness as the path. It is the supreme method for harnessing gods and demons as your allies. It is the skillful means for coming to a definite conclusion that cyclic existence and transcendence are self-manifest. The transference of consciousness practice is "Opening the Door to the Sky." Direct Crossing severs the phenomena of the intermediate state into basic space. It is the excellent path of freedom, unique within yourself: Listen now as I explain its meaning."

He taught extensively and concluded by saying, "Keep in mind everything that I explained. Teach these things to others and by the force of "Opening the Door to the Sky,", many fortunate disciples will attain transcendence in the basic space of the nature of reality, beyond cause and result!" Then it seemed as if the surrounding environment and everything within it dissolved into me.

At night on the seventh day of the middle spring month, a bright blue woman appeared, naked without attire or ornaments. Saying she was Dakini Dorjé Chammo, Vajra Wife, she asked, "My child, do you want to go and see Glorious Copper-Colored Mountain on Tail-Fan Island?"

I said I did. She held me by the fingers of my right hand and we went to a place where I saw an immense black mountain peak rising to the midheavens. As soon as we reached its summit, the dakini said, "My child, stretch your arms into the realm of space and draw out your body's strength. Take that stance; because your dream body is intrinsically nonexistent, you will fly unhindered."

I did what she told me and soared through space like the king of birds. I traversed 165 greater continents and crossed over seventeen oceans. When I finally reached the far shore, the dakini told me, "This is called Lower Lanka, a continent where ogres eat humans as food. There are eighteen Lanka regions across this great ocean. We've reached the border of a series of those outlying oceans."

"Where is Glorious Copper-Colored Mountain?" I asked.

"It's quite close."

"Must we travel over the eighteen greater continents of ogre lands?"

"No. What is known as Glorious Copper-Colored Mountain lies at the heart of the great ocean, therefore these bordering oceans surround it."

Then we traveled just a short time and I saw a colossal mountain, blue at the base, white in the middle, and red at the top. Immediately I asked, "What's that peak over there?"

"It's called Glorious Copper-Colored Mountain."

When we reached the hillside and looked at it from a facing mountain surrounded by a huge ocean, I saw on Copper-Colored Mountain's right slope a dense billowing cloud of rainbows. In that expanse, no one's body was visible, but I saw eighty-eight persons from the neck up. Their heads were either covered by scholar's hats, hair drawn up in topknots, or various other headdresses.

They smiled and gazed at me with entirely loving expressions. Since I didn't know them, I asked the dakini, "Who are those people over there?"

"You are being watched by the eighty great accomplished masters and the eight supreme awareness holders." I offered prostrations; when I prayed to them, a lama wearing a hat shaped like a heart vase appeared from amid the clouds. He placed both hands upon my head and stated, "I am called Awareness Holder Supreme Hungkara. You are my activity emanation. May you attain the complete vase empowerment of the unchanging wisdom body. May you attain the complete secret empowerment of unimpeded wisdom speech. May you attain the complete sublime insight–wisdom empowerment of enlightened mind free from delusion. May you attain the complete spontaneously accomplished great bliss empowerment that is free from words and characteristics. Henceforth from today, may you attain the holy empowerment of you and I indivisible." He then dissolved into me.

A dakini then approached me saying she was Nyi Öbarma, Blazing Sunlight. Her body was white and she wore a red silk skirt. Holding a sunbeam in her right hand and a divination mirror in her left hand, she told me,

> Holy being, peer into this.
> Do you understand these symbols? Examine them well—
> They forecast whether your future will be good or grim.
> If you don't understand, I will show you.

I told her, "I don't understand these symbols," so she decoded them, and explained them accordingly.

Four ogresses with red hair and round eyes arrived, holding up a silk palanquin's four corners. "Sit on this!" they ordered. I did so and immediately we moved through the arena of space and arrived at the far peak, [Copper-Colored Mountain]. Where the mountain's slope met the shoreline, red cliffs rose in the form of blazing arrows, lances, swords, three-pronged staffs, and tridents, forming a continuous ring. In a gap in the circling cliffs, I saw a passage to a dock and an iron ladder.

A great plain circled the base of the mountain. At its center loomed silver fortresses, and in similar fashion, fortresses made of gold, copper, and iron. Incalculable numbers of these fortresses, up to nine stories in height, stretched all the way around the mountain. Inside the structures, inconceivable hosts of seers and awareness holders congregated. In the center of all these fortresses, at the topmost level of a nine-story stronghold made of dry and bloody human skulls, sat the ogre king called Raksha Tötreng, Skull Garlanded Ogre, a black wrathful deity with nine heads and eighteen arms. His ogress consort was red, fearsome, and impossible to look at directly. The pair were surrounded by their ministers—black ogres, ogres who savor blood, those that steal beings' breath, powerful ogres, ogres that move in the daytime and those that move at night, general husbands of ogresses, and those that move in ogress towns, ogres with power over Lower Lanka, ogres who hold Lower Lanka, ogres who travel through human regions, ogres who have power over human regions, demons who [devour] any humans, and so forth. That thousand-fold retinue of ogres served as their attendants and minions. They dwelled in the east and ruled the eastern continent.

In the south stood a silk-white conch fortress. Within it sat the ogre king called Dorjé Draktsal, Vajra Wrathful Force, a fearsome white wrathful deity, surrounded by a retinue of one thousand. They ruled over the southern continent.

In the west stood a black iron fortress. Within it sat the ogre king called Raksha Dongdruk, Six-Faced Ogre, a fearsome dark yellow wrathful deity, surrounded by a retinue of five thousand. They ruled over the western continent.

In the north stood a wide and high fortress made from precious lapis lazuli. Within it sat the ogre king called Draktrö Tötreng, Skull-Garlanded Fierce Wrath, a terrifying blue-green wrathful deity, surrounded by a retinue of eight thousand. They ruled over the southern northern continent.

All these kings and their consorts possessed peaceful wisdom minds, which never strayed from the basic space of phenomena, yet their wisdom forms bristled with utterly terrifying, fierce, and majestic attributes.

I asked the blue dakini, "What is this place?"

She replied, "This is a pure land of the manifest body of enlightenment, a celestial realm on earth: When one abandons the ten nonvirtuous acts, cultivates stores of merit and wisdom, and makes significant aspirations, one will be born here. In every direction, inside palaces made from precious crystal stand golden thrones swathed in silks, seats for all those who attain such rebirths."

We journeyed one league in space above that royal mountain. The entire terrain was filled with rainbow designs, like outspread brocade. Delicious aromatic mists wafted from grassy knolls of medicinal plants. Myriad five-colored flowers covered the ground, which was springy and rose up to the touch. When the sole of my foot grazed that earth's surface, my body, speech, and mind became intoxicated with pleasure.

The landscape was immeasurable, and within it loomed a celestial palace made of five kinds of gems, perfect in all its attributes. Inside, throngs of spiritual heroes and dakinis danced. Countless offering goddesses continuously sent forth oceanic clouds of offerings. At the center, in the midst of seas of awareness holders and accomplished adepts, stood a wide and high throne made of various jewels, upon which sat Supreme Orgyen Pema Jungné, Lotus-Born. You could gaze at his face and body forever and never be satisfied. Garab Dorjé was on his right; Vimalamitra on his left; King [Trisong Deutsen], the twenty-five subjects, and others were in front. All the awareness holders and accomplished adepts of India and Tibet were present there, inconceivable in number.

Further, the intermediate level above the ground story contained an immense celestial palace made of precious crystal. Inside its spacious expanse, upon a seat made of a lotus, sun, and moon, sat the one known as Pema Jikten Sumgön, Lotus Protector of the Three Worlds. His body was bright white; he had one face and four arms. Beautified by the buddhas' marks and signs of physical perfection, you could gaze upon him forever and never be satisfied. He taught the doctrine to an oceanlike retinue of bodhisattvas around him.

The topmost story contained a wide celestial palace made of lapis lazuli. Inside, upon a ruby throne, on a lotus and moon seat, sat the one known as Pema Drimé Ö Nang, Stainless Lotus Light Illumination. His body was red, adorned with the buddhas' marks and signs of physical perfection. He sat there teaching through symbolic means to his retinue, the self-manifest expression of his awareness.

I offered prostrations to those teachers, who personified the three bodies of enlightenment. I circumambulated them and made sweeping aspirations. In response, their empowerments and sacred teachings ripened my mindstream.

At that mountain's midsection grew something called a mabuna tree. Bells and small chimes sprouted from it as if they were flowers and fruit, making a profuse symphony. Moreover, many other trees constantly produced the other offerings of daily use, in infinite numbers.

In the east stood a mountain called Luminous, white and vivid; a multitude of sensory pleasures of form emerged from its mirrorlike pristine crystal. At its summit was Orgyen Dukngal Ngésel, Definite Alleviator of Suffering, surrounded by an inconceivable retinue.

In the south stood a mountain made of gold called Desirable. It radiated like mist all things desirable and marvelous. At its summit was Orgyen Rinchen Gyalpo, Jewel King, surrounded by a retinue of eighty thousand.

In the west stood a red copper mountain. A cloud of various delicious aromas wafted from its slope, which rose into the midheavens. At its summit was Pema Dewé Jungné, Born of a Blissful Lotus, surrounded by an immeasurable retinue.

In the north stood a mountain called Piercing made of precious gems. It emitted various kinds of food and clothing, filling space. At its summit was Orgyen Yul Lé Nampar Gyalwa, Victorious In Battles, surrounded by a billionfold retinue.

From those hills, myriad offering clouds of sensory pleasures streamed forth, covering the central area of Glorious Copper-Colored Mountain. A large plain circled the outer ocean, itself surrounded by slate and forested mountains. Beyond these lay numerous plains, valleys, and ravines, regions that held innumerable ogre cities. Whenever an ogre or ogress spied any type of living being, they would quickly seize it and devour it alive like jackals. They also ate the fruit of the rakshi lila trees and the fruit of the bulang kappa they planted. These were their most prized foods.

Immersed in such inconceivable pure visions, I offered prostrations at the feet of Supreme Orgyen, then touched them to my head. "Glorious Orgyen, Buddhist king, heed me! Hold me with your compassion, I pray! Confer empowerments upon me, I pray! Grant me blessings, I pray! Give me prophecies, I pray!"

He then placed his hands upon my head, saying, "My child, may you fully attain the supreme holy empowerments that bring maturation. May you fully attain the blessings and sacred spiritual accomplishments of the body, speech, mind, qualities, and activities of the victors of the three times with their spiritual heirs. May your ordinary body, speech, and mind shift to become the display of the three vajras—enlightened body, speech, and mind—and once you reach spiritual maturity and are liberated, may you gain mastery as a

Buddhist king of the three realms. May any connection with you have the power to bring beings to the paths and stages of liberation.

"Now sit here and listen well! These days, we've arrived at an evil era when the five forms of degeneration are rampant. Therefore, teach the innermost essence of the sacred pith instructions to individuals connected to you through their aspirations and karma, and give all the empowerments and transmissions of the profound teachings in their entirety. To establish the basis of your spiritual practice, come to a conclusion having penetrated the depths of the view of Cutting Through. As the path, fully understand the meaning of the key instructions of Direct Crossing and all the qualities of the signs of progress along that path.

"Teach the sacred instructions that directly pinion negative circumstances and cut through them according to the profound practice of dispelling hindrances through Severance of Evil Forces, which is related to the path of the great approach. Severance constitutes the pith instructions for considering bad omens as your own good fortune and accepting the upheavals of sickness as the path. It is especially profound. In the past, people knew the full import of these vital instructions, but now no one does. These days, the decline of the Secret Mantra's supreme approach is entirely due to the weakness of sentient beings' [positive] karma and merit: Their teachers delight in, consider best, and teach to others the paths of lesser spiritual approaches, in which the concepts of the rational, intellectual mind are valued with attachment. Disciples with little merit meet only such teachers. Therefore, I will reveal to you the profound teachings of Great Perfection, the excellent path to enlightenment in one lifetime."

He then proclaimed the great tantra of supreme mystery, *Self-Liberation of Dualistic Fixation,* like a scriptural transmission. It was as if a precise copy of this, clear and stable, appeared in my mindstream. Guru Rinpoche told me, "Cultivate your experience of the superb path of Great Perfection, the swift path to manifest enlightenment in this lifetime. Teach it correctly to others."

After he had spoken, I asked once again, "Universal embodiment of all victors and their heirs, precious lord refuge of all beings, I beseech you: Reveal to me what will be the state of the doctrine and beings during my lifetime."

Supreme Orgyen said, "Child of my spiritual family, these days we've arrived at an evil era of degeneration. The status of demons with corrupt aspirations has been elevated to prominence. Under the sway of [that outlook], there is little that's good and much that's wrong.

"In this first part of your life, major disasters won't occur in your area. During the latter part of your life, due to the incursion of border people's power substances and incantations, irresolvable calamities—disease, war, and famine—will spread; fear and turmoil will erupt. Nevertheless, until your life ends, the doctrine of sutra and mantra definitely won't be lost to demons on a corrupt path. Later, after some time, not even a spark of the doctrine of sutra and mantra will remain in your region; demonic creeds will spread and there won't be even a sesame seed's worth of a chance for happiness.

"During the latter part of your life, your gathering [of disciples] will grow, and likewise, your doctrine will increase and flourish. I sent you into the world as executor of my activity, so that my remaining disciples, many karmically destined individuals, can reach the state of freedom in this lifetime. Remember this and do as much as you can to help others. Carry this out without woe and weariness!"

Then the dakini from earlier said, "Now we'll go." As I prepared to leave, she intoned:

> Kyé Ho! Fortunate child of the lineage,
> In the false outlines of this dreamscape's appearances,
> There is no such thing as either going or staying.
> Appearances change right where they are:
> Focus on basic space and awaken into basic space.
> Do you understand?

She then dissolved into me. I turned my attention to the basic space of awareness, then woke up.

Dynamic Dance of the Mamos and Dakinis

THAT SAME YEAR, one night in the last autumn month, a yellow dakini arrived. She wore a green striped cape and blazed with a sheen like pure gold. "Do you want to go see the spectacle at the summit of a mountain called Sharp Snowless Peak?" she asked. As soon as I said yes, she grabbed the fingers of my right hand and we flew upward seven leagues into space, until we reached the summit of a huge mountain, its immensity so wide and high it was impossible to measure. I looked around and saw an inferno to the northwest. It thundered at a pitch that made the three planes of existence quake. I asked the dakini, "What is this place?"

"It's said to be a naturally arisen charnel ground of Orgyen. Do you want to go there?" I said yes, so off we went. Dried bones in towering heaps circled the terrain. At the center stretched an enormous plain of bloody human skins, immeasurable in breadth and width. Adjacent to and surrounding the plain, all the grass and trees were groves of arrows, clubs, and swords. Blood, pus, and mucus rained down; dark red tongues of flames billowed in clouds. Seas of blood encircled the ground, covered with human corpses strewn about. Droves of power substances and weapons whirled around as in a hailstorm. All sounds reverberated as the din of "Phat! Pem! Jyo! Dok!" like the roar of a thousand dragons. The growls of myriad hostile carnivorous animals thundered as they raced and leapt about.

This terrifying place made my skin crawl. In its midst loomed a vast and wide celestial palace on an immense plain. Its cornices were made of dried human skulls; its walls, old skulls; its foundation, bloody skulls. At the center, upon a tiered throne composed of a pile of many fresh and withered human corpses, on a lotus and moon seat, stood a dark blue dakini, wrathful and fierce, said to be Wisdom Dakini Dorjé Pakmo, Vajra Sow. A black pig's head squealed upward at the crown of her head; that sound overwhelmed all the spiritual heroes and dakinis. Her right hand held aloft a curved knife into space and her left carried a skull-cup of blood at her heart. Her body was naked, with a necklace made of a garland of skulls. She was terrifying and unbearable to look at directly.

To her right stood Dakini Yeshe Tsogyal. Her body was dark red, and she had an intensely wrathful demeanor. She held a hook in her right hand and a skull-cup in her left. To Dorjé Pakmo's left was the Nepali Shakya Devi, a wrathful black female deity, brandishing a skull club and skull-cup of blood. Around them thronged the five classes of dakinis of basic space, wrathful and wild with fearsome attributes. They were in turn surrounded by billions of dakinis. Some were light blue. Some were white. Some were yellow. Some were red. Some were green. Some were dark blue and other shades, with a diverse array of colors and attributes as the dynamic dancing display of their myriad emanations.

I prostrated respectfully to those dakinis, joined my hands in prayer and beseeched them,

> Kyé! I respectfully pay homage to the chief dakini, the exalted deity
> With whom I have a prior karmic link.
> Bless my mindstream, I pray!
> Reveal to me the profound creation and completion phases
> Outlining the means of accompishment related to the wisdom dakinis,
>   I pray!

In response to this appeal, the three central dakinis spoke to me, their wisdom minds and voices in unison:

> Kyé Ho! Fortunate child of my spiritual family,
> These days in the world, in the land of Tibet,
> Many claim to be treasure revealers:
> Arrogantly considering themselves lofty, look at how their
> Thoughts, deeds, and the many texts they write are forged out of
>   deceit.
> Look at how they set aside altruistic endeavors
> And how they delude themselves.
> Some are blessed by corrupt demons.
> Some are deceived by meditative experiences that result from clinging
>   to ordinary mind.
> Some think themselves lofty, and say anything that comes to mind.
> There's no need to transcribe their "treasure teachings."

The border people have intruded into the center of the country:
Look at how the clouds of their corrupt dogmas
Veil the sun of the holy Buddhist doctrine.
Abandon useless, tiresome effort.
Other than gathering your remaining disciples [from past lives]
Don't develop a long-term vision,
Thinking the doctrine will long endure.

From a red monkey clapping its hands,
A rain of red blood will fall.
The flapping of a fire garuda's wings
Will stir the formation of blue steeds.
The golden dogs let out a yellow howl
That makes the underground gophers tremble.
When the golden pig ruts the earth,
The poisonous black snake rises from its bed.

When they finished speaking about this and many other things, they
recited *The Tantra of the Gathered Dakinis' Blazing Curved Knife* and "Opening the Door [to the Sky] Unhindered," [the Transference of Consciousness
practice] of Severance of Evil Forces. They told me, "My child, you will have
sixteen supreme disciples with favorable karma and hundreds of lesser disciples. You will sow the seed of liberation in 1,035 individuals. The treasure
teachings won't long remain, so teach them to your karmically destined disciples and order them to practice! At present, barbarian dogmas have arrived as
welcome guests. Since we've reached the time when they will seize this land,
don't make long-range plans! The difficulty of doing the work of revealing
and transcribing treasure texts is nothing more than child's play." They told
me,

Kyé! Your mind undistracted, turn awareness to basic space.
In the great-bliss mansion of spontaneously present basic space
Look at the play of the mamos and dakinis' dynamic dance
And the delighted laughing faces of the five glorious wisdom family
    deities.
The mother dakinis accompany you;
You've reached a place secluded from existence.

Those who lack similar fortune
Plummet to the ranks of demons and ogres:
Look at how their entry to the path of freedom is blocked.
Therefore don't delay—
Swiftly reach the expanse of the Original Lord Protector.
Phat! Phat! Phat!

That keen sound woke me.

IN THE YEAR I TURNED THIRTY-THREE [1868], at night on the seventh day
of the second month, I dreamt of a monk so fearsome I couldn't look at him
directly. He plunged the sharp tip of a blade into my heart, saying, "Tonight,
the time has come for me to kill you."

I told him, "Kill me and I will meditate on compassion for you."

He countered:

Compassion is something found in the minds of animals.
They have compassion for their offspring,
Then the child kills its mother.
You have compassion for me,
Yet our compassion is mutual.
Come here, charming shapely girl,
And consume the flesh and blood of this compassionate man.

As soon as he voiced this song, a woman with large eyes, red hair, and
very long teeth appeared and slung her breasts onto my shoulders. Her teeth
plunged into my brain, at which point I became terrified and panicked. After
a moment, I recognized these events as a dream and sang this song:

Hé Hé! Listen to me, malicious monk demon,
And this ugly female minion you brought along,
You are the delusory impressions of a dream:
In this body of space, a form without an I,
Where can be found a killer and his victim?
Both you and I are of a single taste,
Like a face and its reflection in a mirror.
Although we appear, this appearance has no creator—

> Everything has the nature of emptiness.
> It's empty: You cannot kill emptiness.
> Kill me and you both die.
> Death doesn't exist—merely its appearance.
> The sky's design of a rainbow
> Vanishes into the space of the sky itself.
> Now, let you and me inseparable
> Blend in the supreme indwelling pervasive evenness
> Within the pure, unformulated sky of basic space. Ah! Ah! *Phat!*

That said, the demon uttered, "This wicked man talking about meditation pains my heart. Now let's go! Let's go!" With that they vanished.

Symbolic of Your Disciples

THAT SAME YEAR on the twenty-first day of the first autumn month, a glowing red bird sang to me.

Ah Ho! Listen my child:
Many holy sublime individuals
Have advanced into unmanifest basic space,
Leaving behind their orphan disciples of this degenerate era:
Nothing lasts forever.

The medicinal ha-lo flowers have withered,
Leaving behind the green grassy plains.
In the bitter cold of the winter months,
Nothing lasts forever.

The king, a mighty human sovereign,
Has passed beyond this life,
Leaving behind his orphaned royal children.
Nothing lasts forever.

Flocks of garudas have flown away,
Leaving behind their helpless little chicks.
Nothing lasts forever.

Many majestic wild animals have departed,
Leaving behind the [lowly] weasel.
Nothing lasts forever.

All supreme practitioners have departed,
Leaving behind false lamas mired in the eight worldly concerns.
Nothing lasts forever.

The king's treasury is spent,
Leaving behind his subjects who have some wealth.
Nothing lasts forever.

The sumptuous fruits have all vanished,
Leaving behind the stockpiles of field mice.
Nothing lasts forever.

The green grasses of summer have dried up,
Leaving behind gray grass corpses.
Nothing lasts forever.

Most lamas and tulkus, attached to cyclic existence,
Conduct funeral ceremonies [to receive payments],
And although they're adept at pointless hoarding,
Nothing lasts forever.

Prominent leaders, violent and greedy,
Create stringent laws,
Yet when they meet the burden of their ripened karma,
Nothing lasts forever.

Wealthy people with riches and possessions
Who pass their time in the delight of gain and profit
Live as in a dream or magical illusions.
Nothing lasts forever.

When you've gained a pure human body,
Don't put your hopes in the activities of your mouth and hands—
Rely upon the profound instructions of liberation
Directly within your own mind.

Don't anticipate the liberation you desire
When your mouth and eyes are wandering.
Don't expect wordy education with no basis in realization
To be useful to you in your next life.

Don't expect the liberation you want
To stem from knowledge without meditation.

Having come, having come from the basic space of the nature of reality,
Going there, going there, to there I fly!

Then it flew off.

THAT SAME YEAR, on the tenth day of the middle winter month, while I rested
in the basic space of the clear light of Direct Crossing, a small bird came down
before me and sang,

Kyé Kyé! The grassy meadows of the northern steppes
Are not the ideal place for every living creature,
Yet they are the home of the white-faced wild ass.
Do you know the mothers are giving birth?

The dark clay mountains
Are not the ideal place for every living creature,
Yet they are the fierce dré yak and female yak's abode.
Are you aware of the hundred mothers and their hundred offspring?

The high and severe rocky cliff
Is not the ideal place for every living creature,
Yet it is the habitat of the vulture, king of birds.
Are you aware of the white vultures, mother and child?

The secluded mountains in unfixed locales,
Are not places where every person can live,
Yet they are the abode of supreme individuals who abandon all activity.
Are you aware of the disciples gathered around you?

Many constellations shine in the sky,
Yet both the sun and moon are rare.
On the ground grow many flowers,
Yet an udumbara lotus is rare.

Many trees and forests grow,
Yet a wish-fulfilling tree is rare.
Though there are copious herds of wild animals,
A white lioness is rare.
Many attain a human body,
Yet a meaningful life is rare.
Many people are called lamas
Yet authentic teachers are rare.
Many assume the guise of noble monks,
Yet those who uphold moral discipline are rare.
Though countless people are skilled in speech,
It's rare for anyone to apply [the meaning] to their minds.
Many are called great meditators,
Yet those who realize emptiness are rare.
Many are called accomplished adepts;
Ultimately, genuinely accomplished ones are rare.
Many are referred to as treasure revealers,
Yet those who aren't frauds are rare.

Are you truly a treasure revealer? I don't know!
Excellent, holy being
Imbued with superb fortune, karma, and aspirations—listen to me!
Cultivate wholeheartedly your experience
Of self-manifest pristine clear light,
The profound path of supreme transference,
And you are certain to gain liberation in this very life!

Though you have many disciples,
Those able to stay in mountain retreat will be rare.
Many claim they will be custodians of your doctrine,
Yet those with the capacity to teach and spread
The three cycles of your profound teachings' innermost essence will be
    rare.
Plenty of people listen to and request teachings,
Yet those who practice will be rare.

Ingrain in your mind these things I've described—
Hold to the unassailable ground within yourself
And incidentally it's possible you may help others.
The basis of your own being is the capital city
Of the pervasive lord Kuntuzangpo, Ever-Excellent.
Do you understand? Are you aware of that, my friend?

Are you aware of the scale of the northern steppes?
Do you know how vast is the expanse of space?
This little bird prepares to go there.
On the wide plain of the basic space of phenomena,
How happy are this little bird, mother and child,
Who delight in the treasury of space!

Then it flew away.

In the year I turned thirty-four [1868], on the twenty-fifth day of the
first month, as I was making the offering of a vajra feast based on the practice
cycle of Dakini Tröma Nakmo, a dense lattice of rainbow light coalesced. A
small flock of vultures, the king of birds, descended. Everyone gathered there
heard exquisitely sweet melodies of flutes and lutes coming from intangible
empty space. That night, an older adept appeared before me with long white
hair, seated on a silk palanquin conveyed by four dakinis, white, yellow, red,
and green in color. He wore maroon brocade with a pattern of clouds and
dragons. I was fascinated at the sight of a beautiful knife slung at his waist.
The ornaments around his waist were made of silver and he blazed with
intensely dazzling masses of light. He held a dark blue dakini by the hand. As
soon as they approached me, the adept sang,

You are powerful, having trained for many lifetimes.
You unlock the door of profound treasures,
And are capable of guiding to freedom anyone connected to you:
To you I've come to beg for a body.
Previously, in the Male Wood Mouse Year,
My son, Puntsok Jungné, Magnificient Source,
Entrusted to you

A white crystal stupa
Emanated as Dakini Yeshe Tsogyal.
In this lineage of accomplished masters,
To avoid the burden of a womb-[birth's] flawed impurities,
He was born as your son, just as I had told him to do.
Likewise, to be born as your son
I must come to this human land
To nurture and assemble my remaining disciples.
Therefore, I'm here today in your garden to see you.
I am the Buddhist king, Trisong Deutsen.
I am also Khyentsé Yeshe Dorjé, Wisdom Vajra of Omniscience and
   Love:
Do away with your doubts, superb individual!
Ultimately the father and son, inseparable,
Will gain the glory of Great Bliss Pure Land.

Having said that, he took a golden vajra from his pocket. He placed it, with the hat he was carrying, at the bottom of my tantric shawl. I told him, "Don't do that! Don't put your insignia and hat below my clothing."

He replied, "The two of us are one, indivisible, so there is no fault," and dissolved into me.

AT NIGHT ON THE FIFTH DAY of the fourth month, I arrived in an area with a large, sprawling city. In that place scores of spiritual heroes and dakinis had converged at an immense vajra feast gathering. Various musical sounds welled forth and their voices sang,

Lamas and awareness holders, come to this gathering!
Peaceful and wrathful chosen deities, come to this gathering!
Mamos and dakinis, come to this gathering!
Doctrine guardians and protectors of the teachings, come to this
   gathering!
Dza Hung Bam Ho! Samaya! Hé Yé Pem Pem!

Ocean of lamas, enjoy this vajra feast!
Ocean of chosen deities, enjoy this vajra feast!
Mamos and dakinis, enjoy this vajra feast!

Doctrine guardians and protectors of the teachings, enjoy this vajra
feast!

As they sang, I couldn't identify what the feast offering substances were
made from, nor could I discern their colors. They blazed with light. Shaped
like the snout of a pig, they were spread out like a riverbank—so immeasurable it covered the entire land. Ritual vases, vajras, daggers, mirrors, and
a copious assortment of other things were also arrayed there. I asked, "To
whom do these belong and what are they?"

A black woman told me, "These are your subjects."

A blue woman said, "These are symbolic of your disciples." Then everything vanished into basic space.

IN A DREAMSCAPE at night on the third day of the fifth month, an incalculable assembly of spiritual heroes and dakinis came from the arena of space.
They were ruby red and blazed with light. Everyone played a thundering
symphony of various musical instruments. I asked one girl, "Who are they?"

She answered, "They are going to meet an adept named Rangdrol of
Sermo Jong in Repkong. Tonight he must pass away."

"To which pure land are they going?" I asked.

"That pure land yonder," she said, pointing her finger. When I looked
over there, the ground was festooned with red flowers. There stood a dense
forest of wish-fulfilling trees, within which blazed a mass of red light like
the sun, suffusing every direction. When I saw that, my mind was filled with
intense yearning. Gazing upon a vibrant pleasure grove, I felt irresistible
attachment to that place.

I said to that dakini, "That tremendously happy place is so captivating—
what is it?"

"That land over there is called Great Bliss: That luminosity is the sheen
from Buddha Ö Tayé's, Infinite Illuminator's, light rays. If you make aspirations, in the future you too will go to that place." Just as she counseled, I made
prostrations and aspirations.

When I finished, I told the girl who knows all, "It's been said that something called 'Great Bliss Pure Land' exists. I had come to a definite conclusion
that it didn't exist, apart from merely my own perception, yet here it is! It's
surely not only self-manifest—it has an independent existence. That is astonishing!"

She chided, "Ha ha! Something apart from one's own perception, something that exists independently—I've never seen such a thing before, and it's impossible for me to see such a thing in the future. Even now, your thought that this dreamscape isn't self-manifest—that is more astonishing!" Her words woke me from sleep.

AT NIGHT ON THE EIGHTEENTH DAY of the first winter month, as soon as I arrived in front of Sengé Dongpa, Lion-Faced Dakini, she gave me a turquoise lotus bowl and lapis boxes, and said, "My child, swallow these three things and my meditation and recitation practice will become clear in your mind. You have so many obstructing conditions. Keep in mind the fourteen-syllable mantra of the black life force essence of the dakinis' pure heart blood. If you always recite that mantra and endeavor in rituals to turn back [threats], you will dispel all negative, adverse conditions. This is certain."

The dakinis of the four classes intoned the keen sound of, "Ah Ri Li Hé Ha!" and its resonance woke me up.

Direct Confrontation

IN THE YEAR I TURNED THIRTY-FIVE [1869], in a dream at night on the fifteenth day of the fifth month, a girl saying she was Dakini Sertreng, Golden Garland, told me, "Do you want to go see what will happen in the future?" I went with her and arrived in a land I didn't recognize. On the flank of a large mountain stood a stupa held up by four supports. Beneath this stood a stone fence like a box, within which sat many series of seven bowls, in excess of one hundred altogether.

The dakini told me to take these containers, and I responded, "There are more than one hundred unbroken containers. There are also many broken ones—I don't need those. The intact ones definitely belong to someone. I don't want to take what hasn't been given to me." The dakini said, "They don't belong to anyone! The broken ones are individuals with damaged tantric commitments or persons who are unsuitable recipients for the teachings. However, the ones that aren't broken represent disciples who are worthy vessels, so take them and fulfill an excellent purpose of auspicious connections." As instructed, I put all the intact bowls in my pocket.

As I backed out, I looked around, and saw seven stupas made of stone that were caked with earth. Some were coated with dung. I asked that girl, "If you're so skilled in auspicious connections, what is the meaning of these stupas covered with earth and dung?"

"They symbolize the religious institutions polluted by undeserved payments [for religious services]. Those sets of seven bowls are the disciples associated with you and your sons. Now let's go!"

Then I entered into a rough and narrow ravine through which I had to pass. On the way a terrifying man with a black complexion and a red beard seized my right arm. When he took my hand in his mouth, unbearable panic immediately flared within me. Finally, I remembered the "direct confrontation" of Severance practice, then told him, "Now it eat! Carry it away!" I stuffed my fist into his mouth and he vanished without a trace.

The woman said, "Through direct confrontation you've vanquished the king of undeserved payments. Now you'll gain control of a Buddhist monastery. Look up at the sky!"

I looked up: Hail rained down from black clouds. I heard the deep roar of thunder and asked, "What's that?"

"It's a portent of barbarians pouring into the center of the country."

When we went on one league further, a striped tiger appeared, impossible to look at directly. As it growled, "Hor! Hor!" loudly, the roar woke me from sleep.

THAT SAME YEAR, in a dream at night on the nineteenth day of the last winter month, a green woman the color of turquoise calling herself Dakini Palgyi Gyéde-mo, Chief of Glorious Delight, appeared. She came alongside me singing,

> Listen now, holy sublime being!
> Tomorrow in the afternoon
> A hostile ruler demon will overcome
> The mind of a holder of monastic discipline.
> He will go mad and prepare to take his own life.
> To subdue that spirit,
> Use the supremely profound essential instructions
> Of Severance of Evil Forces practice.
> Beat him, strike him, destroy his cycle of delusion;
> Once you've launched his consciousness into basic space,
> Make a feast offering with his flesh and blood.
> If you heed these key instructions, you will subdue that spirit.
> However, if you don't directly cut through this upheaval,
> It will descend upon you: This matter holds great profit or grave peril.
> A portent of this will occur tonight—look at it!
> Sever self-clinging, fortunate child.
> Whatever good or bad omens and signs arise,
> Cut through attachment to clinging to them with hope and fear.
> Know the key instructions for how to practice ultimate profound
>   Severance,
> And make them familiar in your mind.

Then she vanished, and just a moment later, an old monk grabbed me by the collar with his left hand. With his right hand, he stuck a knife's very sharp tip into my heart, saying, "Now you brutal, dastardly man, I swear I will kill you!"

I was terrified; I took the knife at my waist and struck him on the head, splitting it open. He collapsed, but at the same time my knife broke. I picked up his knife and cut his body into pieces. A drop of his blood splattered onto my heart, and I experienced a sensation of contamination.

The next day, a man named Ling Lhachok, Sublime Deity of Ling, told me, "A monk near me called Ngoli has gone mad. You really must come to help."

"I had a really dire dream, so I'm not going."

He said, "If you don't come, it's as if you're killing me. That's the reason I'm lying prostrate in front of you."

Unable to turn him away, I went along. We arrived where the mad monk was staying, and as soon as I thrashed him forcefully with a human skin, it split at the waist. I recalled last night's dream—uncontrollable trepidation welled in me.

The next day, the mad monk was free from sickness. My heart began throbbing and I couldn't sleep, so I performed ransom distributions, vajra feasts, and fulfillment offerings, yet nothing helped. Then, while meditating on being joyful if I'm sick and happy if I die, I went to a forest grove on an incredibly fearsome and wild cliff. I put a rope around my neck. By giving myself over to that experience, the malady subsided without a trace.

IN THE YEAR I TURNED THIRTY-SIX [1870], in a dream at night on the ninth day of the seventh month, a black man appeared, too terrible to look at. He put his hand in my pocket and said, "I'm Gurgyi Gönpo's high minister. He sent me to fetch your lungs and heart."

As I dwelled in the meditative concentration of the all-encompassing nature of cyclic existence and transcendence as the display of emptiness, he sneered, "I can't get to him, so I'll go after his disciples—ya ya!" and clenched his teeth in a menacing expression. When he turned his head, I flashed the knife hanging at my waist and struck his head. His body split like bamboo, dropping to the right and left.

At that time, Lama Tsangpa was using black magic to delay something vital to a man named Ling Lhapa, Deity of Ling. To remedy that situation, someone went to do a recitation of White Parasol practice, but went mad. He came to see me, and I relied once again on the profound instructions of Severance to release him from the illness.

ONE NIGHT during the tenth month, a terrifying ruler demon appeared, accompanied by seven women, black in color. He seized my left leg tightly; as his strength grew, I grabbed his hair, drew my knife and told him, "I'm going to kill you!"

He said, "Don't kill me and whatever you command, I will do."

"Do not harm a single being. Make that promise!" I ordered.

He responded, "I can't do that: All we do is cause death with famine. Give me another command and I'll adhere to it."

"If that's the case, don't harm my lineage of disciples. Make that promise!"

"I swear I won't harm anyone who becomes your disciple." Once he made that pledge, he departed.

ON THE TENTH DAY of the eleventh month, I began the practice of Nordak Chenpo Apara, Great Wealth Lord Apara, for one month. At night on the fifth day of the following month the great wealth god revealed his face to me and said, "For the last nine years, I haven't given you any riches. Henceforth, I will give you whatever you desire.

"Next year, regarding your eldest son, if you return him to his owner, he will help the doctrine and beings. As for your middle son, if you give him away as well, it's fine; if you don't, that's fine too. Don't give your youngest son to anyone: It's possible you will motivate him to greatly serve the doctrine. You will have either five or six more sons who will aid the doctrine and sentient beings. They will all be like sovereign wish-fulfilling jewels that alleviate decline, poverty, and destitution. They will be born by the force of positive aspirations.

"Your students will equal the stars in the night. In particular, seventeen will shine like the sun, moon, and major stars. They will be of immense aid to the doctrine. They should live in the mountains in unfixed locations and persevere in the essential practices. Each year they must be diligent in the longevity practice of immortality—this is of utmost import. Using the profound instructions of Severance of Evil Forces, they should give up clinging to their cherished bodies: Making a feast offering of their flesh and blood is the supreme vital instruction to dispel all obstacles.

"Don't forget! Keep what I've said in mind, and I will do whatever I can to promote supportive conditions for you, the lama, and all your students." Then he vanished without a trace.

AT NIGHT ON THE THIRD DAY of the twelfth month, a red woman appeared. Saying she was Dakini Wangyi Gyalmo, Powerful Queen, she sang,

> Kyé! You are someone with excellent fortune.
> This place is the abode of vajra dakinis—
> Equal to Orgyen Duma Tala—
> An Unsurpassable Pure Land appearing on this earth:
> It is the natural birthplace of meditative concentration.
> Now you should depart from this place;
> As much as you move, you will attain different forms of
>   accomplishment.
> Stay for a while in a lesser valley called Nyamang;
> If you exert yourself in direct wrathful conduct,
> You will subdue an enemy of the doctrine.
> The pass at Puklung Gékyi Latok
> Is a power spot of the spirit of the Great Noxious Spirit [Butcher]:
> You will gain renown for wrathful power [by practicing there].
> Make that your dwelling place for a while.
> Some of your excellent students will gather there.
> Without much delay, go there!

Then she vanished.

I TURNED THIRTY-SEVEN in the Metal Sheep Year [1871]. I went to Lower Nyamang Valley on the first day of the first month, and stayed there performing the practice of Lhachen Wangchuk Chenpo, Magnificent Ruler Deity. I remained in sealed retreat from the fifteenth day of the first month through the fifteenth day of the second month. During that period, Lhachen openly gave me a five-syllable mantra that, when recited, was a sharp iron hook incantation capable of extracting eyes. By reciting it for ten days with the practical instructions, that [unnamed] enemy of the doctrine became blind. I gained renown for that power.

IN THE LAST SPRING MONTH, I prepared to build a house on top of Puklung Gékyi Latok. During that time, at night on the tenth day, an elderly woman appeared saying she was Dakini Kuntu Gyuwa Rikdenma, Noblewoman Who Travels Everywhere. She counseled me,

Sublime being, listen to me!
On the third day of the middle autumn month
The stars and planets will be well aligned for building your home.
Until that time,
The time isn't right for construction.
Until then, stay here!
Neither good nor bad circumstances will arise.

I answered,

Supreme grandmother of existence,
How long will my doctrine endure
Here, at the pass of Puklung Gékyi Latok?
Mother, I implore you to show me!

In reply, she sang,

When the thoughtless dreamer is destroyed,
You will clearly see interdependent connections and signs—
I have nothing to tell you today.

Listen to what I have to say!
Quarrels with foes will descend like snow;
Consider this to be your past karma.
Supreme Orgyen stated,
"When you encounter my treasures,
The gods and demons of India and Tibet, out of jealousy,
Will reveal myriad dancing forms, angelic and nefarious.
They shriek *ki!* and rush about.
At that time, my superb children,
If you don't entertain anxiety or fear,
How can there be an avenue for demons to enter?"
Remember his strict command!

She then vanished into emptiness.

WHEN THE THIRD DAY arrived of the first autumn month, I assembled scores of workers and we went about laying the foundation for my home. While we dug the foundation for the protector temple, we found a trio of precious gold, turquoise, and conch; a trio of copper, silver, and iron, as well as agate, rubies, lapis, coral, and more. Some jewels we could identify and some we didn't recognize. Their sum overflowed from a small trough. I understood this to be an auspicious connection indicating the increase of our merit and wealth.

Under the foundation for the storehouse we found three human skeletons of different sizes and pearl garlands strung together with copper wire. Although the interdependent indications for the protector temple were excellent, it wasn't in line with the edge of the house. Since this wasn't good, I didn't build it there.

When the house was complete, a mad monk arrived. To examine the portents, I ordered him, "Go to the Mar River, find an unusual stone, and bring it back to me." He left and and returned that night carrying a maroon river stone shaped like a human ear.

My students asked, "What sort of portent is that?"

I told them, "This is a sure sign that I won't be able to stay here very long: One hears with the ear, so I must go to a far-off place."[13]

ON THE THIRD DAY of the first winter month, a yellow girl appeared in space before me. Saying she was Dakini Lékyi Wangmo Ché, Supreme Queen of Activity, she told me, "This month, from the tenth day until the fifteenth day, perform numerous vajra feasts and make offerings, and this monastery will be a Buddhist center for two generations. Although you don't have the fortune to stay here for very long, what you've done will not become meaningless. It has some purpose." Then she vanished. Just as she advised me, I made extensive vajra feast and fulfillment offerings based on the Dorjé Drolö practice from Awareness Holder Dudul Dorjé's treasure revelation called Heart Essence of the Manifest Embodiment.

When I Reign with Four Cycles

AT DAWN ON THE TENTH DAY of the middle winter month, a disciple named Dharmapa, Doctrine, insistently implored me, "Transcribe the text outlining the means of accomplishment related to Dakini Tröma Nakmo for me; I will definitely endeavor in that practice as much as possible."

I began with the text's title and preamble, and then decided to set it aside for a while and examine my dreams. That night Dakini Yeshe Tsogyal appeared saying, "I am Dakini Yeshe Tsogyal. What are you doing?"

"A disciple of mine insistently requested, 'I need a means of accomplishment related to Tröma Nakmo, Wrathful Black Goddess.' Therefore, I prepared to transcribe that text and began the task. Is this good or not?" I asked.

The dakini sang to me,

> Presently, this disciple of yours
> Is [a reincarnation] of Sengé Gyatso, Oceanic Lion,
> A student of the great treasure revealer, Shérab Özer, Light Rays of
>   Sublime Insight.
> Although he has the momentum of his lama's aspirations,
> As repayment for previous karma,
> In this life he was born into an evil family.
> If a corrupt demon alters his mind,
> He will turn against you: Under another's control,
> He won't help your doctrine.
> If he isn't beguiled by that demon,
> He will become a supreme lord of the doctrine and beings,
> And thus will be greatly beneficial to your teachings.
> If he doesn't fall under the demon's sway,
> And engages in the practice of clear light Direct Crossing,
> He will attain vajra rainbow body.

When she told me that, I beseeched her, "Compassionate mother, if he turns against me and relies on other masters, can he attain rainbow body?"

She replied, "In the past, when you were Dudul Dorjé, he was a student of yours called Pema Özer, Lotus Light Rays. Dudul Dorjé said, 'In the future, having taken the body of Chakmo Dudjom Lingpa, when I reign with four cycles of profound treasures, you will be my subject. May you apply yourself to these profound practices and become enlightened in the rainbow body of supreme transference!' He has the force of that aspiration, yet if he doesn't rely on you, he will be left an ordinary person at death; that will be the extent of his path to freedom.

"If he turns away from the demonic path, once he's proficiently trained and comes to a definite conclusion in the view of Cutting Through, and then relies on the final path of Direct Crossing, it's possible he will attain liberation. If he falls under the influence of another teacher and fears his own meditative experiences, he won't have the opportunity to practice and will be misled by demons and dakinis.

"Furthermore, if you transcribed this profound teaching, that would be excellent: Even if he doesn't do the practice, there are many custodians of these teachings who are suitable recipients—they will have the fortune of gaining liberation through these instructions. Therefore don't shrink from hardship. Transcribe it quickly and an auspicious omen of its spread every-where will also occur. A portent of spiritual accomplishment will definitely appear to one superb student." Then she disappeared.

THE NEXT MONTH in a dream at night on the eighth day, I found myself in a wide and vast region of the northern steppes. In a pleasure grove blanketed with meadow flowers stood a large dark blue silk tent, in which rose a jeweled throne with a seat of many silk brocade cushions. Here sat my own Lama Jamyang, his wisdom form apparent as if he were actually present. As soon as I saw him, immeasurable faith, respect, and joyful yearning welled up within me. Tears overflowing from my eyes, I said, "You are my lord protector eternally throughout my lifetimes. Many years have gone by without a suitable opportunity for us to meet. Today I have the providence to meet you! Where is this place in which you reside?"

The lama said, "Previously, I aspired to be reborn in the western pure land Great Bliss. Though I focused my intention there, because I didn't fulfill the essential points of meditation and recitation associated with that place, the phenomena of that pure land didn't unfold. Since I had completed the meditation and recitation of Vajrasattva, in the first stage of the intermediate state, when I brought to mind Vajrasattva's eastern pure land Manifest Joy, its phenomena unfurled. This is where I am. These treasure teachings you've received are really amazing! Tell me exactly how they came to you."

I answered as he requested. "Compassionate lama, you are a supreme bodhisattva who has mastered the pure lands endowed with the five certainties, thus you surely already know my situation. However, since there must be some great purpose for you to have asked, I will explain.

"In the past, when I was twenty-three years old, one night in a dream a white man with a gold topknot appeared saying he was Lord Protector Chenrézi, All-Seeing Eyes. He told me, 'My child, by the force of excellent karma and merit, and by the might of pure aspirations throughout many previous lifetimes, you are a fortunate individual who has perfected the qualities of the stages and paths of awakening. In the present you have the good karma to bring some benefit to beings and the doctrine. Therefore, eat this box.' It was a thumb-sized crystal box. Upon its surface the letters *Om Hung Tram Hri Ah* shone in five colors, like a reflection appearing in a mirror. As soon as he handed it to me, I swallowed it.

"The exalted bodhisattva proclaimed, 'This is called The Profound Doctrine Overflowing into the Expanse of Wisdom Mind.' Then he dissolved into me.

"After that, for a while I stayed in retreat relying on the meditation and recitation practice of Jampal Mawé Sengé, Gentle Splendor Lion of Speech. One afternoon my house filled with a delicious aroma. At that time I actually saw the deity. He gave me a golden box the size of a small bird's egg and told me to eat it. Immediately I swallowed it, and he said, 'This is called Wisdom's Infinite Matrix of Pure Phenomena.' Then he dissolved into me.

"On another occasion I saw a great wrathful deity who said he was Great Glorious Chana Dorjé, Vajra-in-Hand. He was impossible to look upon; I was incredibly frightened when I met him. The Lord of Secrets said, 'Great one, listen to me without dread, panic, or fright. I am called Great Glorious Chana Dorjé: I am the essence of the fusion of the might and power of all victors of the past, present, and future; I am the source of all arrogant guardians of the doctrine. You, as well, are my wisdom mind emanation. I acclaim you as my emissary who enacts the benefit of beings.' He had a thumb-sized turquoise stupa, within which arose the images of the Sanskrit alphabet's vowels and consonants and the 'Heart of Interdependent Origination' formula. He handed it to me, and told me to eat it. When I placed it in my mouth as instructed, it became insubstantial but I made the motion of swallowing it anyway.

"He said, 'This is called The Space Treasury of the Nature of Reality,' and then dissolved into me. From that time forth, the three cycles of pure vision arose in my mind as if a precise copy had been made there.

"Futhermore, when I met glorious Orgyen Tsokyé Dorjé, Lake-Born Vajra, he gave me the entire set of empowerments that bring about spiritual maturity, the sacred instructions that liberate, and the supportive scriptural transmissions of an ocean of discourses, mantras, and tantras. When I encountered Mother Yeshe Tsogyal, she introduced me to cyclic existence and transcendence as supreme emptiness. Realization was born within me.

"In the meantime, I met hosts of awareness-holding lamas and myriad transcendent victors with their spiritual heirs. I received their nectar speech and they blessed my mindstream.

"I received the prophetic lists for [the earth treasure] The Profound Doctrine of the Heart Essence of the Dakinis in this way: From within the sites Ba Treasure Cliff of Mar, Tsunmo Ngulgö Cliff, Margyi Potsong Stupa, Gyédrö Stupa, Tashi Gomang, and Chak Ri-chen, I retrieved prophetic lists, supplementary lists, and the like in boxes made from rock, bamboo, earth, wax, and wood. I also found them written on parchment without a container, as well as within a pile of charcoal. That's how I obtained them."

My lama said, "Those profound teachings, your three cycles of pure vision, are tangible manifestations of the exalted lord protectors of the three kinds of beings. Given that the Buddhist doctrine will only endure for a short time, its complete potency has come together all at once in your doctrine, so it contains very great blessings, which are swiftly delivered. Individuals who put into practice these teachings will quickly gain liberation without much delay. Have no doubt!"

I said to my lama, "What can be done about the doctrine lasting only a short time?"

He gave many prophecies related to future events and then vanished into basic space.

> The body, speech, and mind of the lord protectors of the three kinds of beings
> Embody all victors' omniscience, love, and capability:
> Their miraculous manifestations appear as whatever is suitable to guide beings.
> This celebration—these three profound teaching cycles—

Issues from the site of those bodhisattvas' inconceivable vajra symbols
    and words.
This amazing font that grants everything desirable—what is it?
Whatever it is, whoever has the karma to chance upon it,
Is fortunate: This is their final worldly existence.
Other people whose minds are frenzied with their own idiocy or
    arrogance
Speak ill of these teachings out of jealousy. No matter what they say,
This old man who has gained confidence is happy.

Not a Single Lama in This World

I TURNED THIRTY-EIGHT in the Water Monkey Year [1872]. While I was transcribing the practice cycle of Dakini Tröma, a great whirlwind emerged, carrying the written pages away in every direction. I understood this as an omen that these texts would reach absolutely everywhere in every land. All the mountains and plains filled with vultures, the king of birds. Small feathers from their wings, talismans of the dakinis' spirits, showered down.

My student Pema Tashi, Auspicious Lotus, made a vow to do this practice and then began to transcribe the text into words. That day a stream of milk imbued with flavors, vitality, and nutritive qualities flowed from the sphere of empty space until it just filled a cup. When he drank it, for three days his body and mind were suffused with bliss and new realization was born within him. In the end, Pema Tashi gained distinctive realization superior to anyone else and became quite learned. Having undertaken the essential practices in unfixed mountain locales, he gained mastery on the swift path to authentic, complete enlightenment.

> A flowing stream of ambrosia milk—utterly substantial—
> Materialized from intangible, unimpeded space.
> If you rely upon this means of accomplishment's truly profound pith
>   instructions,
> In the essence of empty basic space of sublime insight
> Pakmo's blessings appear as skillful means,
> A sign that the two accomplishments will effortlessly come to pass:
> When a lama with realization and a student
> Suffused with blessings and the utmost fortune of receiving profound
>   instructions
> Meet, even supreme spiritual accomplishment
> Is achieved without difficulty. That's the nature of such auspicious
>   connections.

Compelled by joy, my student Tsé-chu, Tenth Day, asked me for something to practice. When I transcribed a text for him, a rainbow stretched out

like five silk ribbons shone above my house, a portent of his impending liberation in the illusory rainbow body. At the end of his life in Lhasa, when
he passed away, exceptional canopies of rainbow light and other signs and
indications appeared. Everyone in Central and Western Tibet was amazed.

During the middle winter month I practiced Dakini Tröma during a
month-long retreat. On that occasion I was accompanied by my supreme disciples Tsé-chu, Pema Tashi, and Orgyen. There was no one else apart from
this trio. I came to the firm conclusion that they upheld their tantric commitments. At that time, a rain of small feathers from vultures, the king of birds,
fell; the house was infused with a sweet aroma; and other fantastic signs and
omens appeared.

IN THE PAST, while staying at the Hor family's homestead, Lama Kyenrab,
Omniscience, from Nuzok [Monastery] requested me to transcribe a Jampal,
Gentle Splendor, tantra. Accordingly, when I began that task on the tenth
day of the middle winter month, thunder roared from the heavens and small
hailstones fell erratically. I considered that to be indicative of a favorable coincidence, the thought of which made me quite delighted and happy, so I told
the lama about it. He said, "During the winter, isn't the sound of thunder
something disastrous?" He made this and other pessimistic comments; I saw
there wasn't going to be much of a good connection. I ceased writing after five
pages and set it aside without transcribing anything more.

IN THE YEAR I TURNED THIRTY-NINE [1873], at night on the ninth day of the
middle summer month, a dakini appeared saying, "Here is something you
need." She gave me an extremely beautiful and fascinating iron ritual dagger
wrapped in black silk; attached to the silk was an unsightly stone ritual dagger.
"My child, I'm giving this to you. As a sign that this has come through the hands
of a foolish lama, it has a black silk wrapping. The stone dagger connected to it
will be of scant help to anyone else: It will likely accomplish its own purpose."

Early the next morning on the tenth day, Dorjé Zangpo, Excellent Vajra,
from Chutsang and a sculptor named Dorjé, Vajra, arrived together. We
offered a vajra feast celebration. That night a dakini appeared telling me,
"This Dorjé Zangpo is an emanation of Dakini Yeshe Tsogyal, therefore
reveal to him the innermost pith of your profound teachings. There is grave
danger that his mind will be altered by a corrupt scriptural transmission: If
that change doesn't occur and if he listens to your advice, he will have count-

less disciples and establish them on the path to freedom. At the end of his life, he will attain liberation in the light-mass rainbow body."

I asked, "Dakini who knows all, if his mind is altered by another's corrupt teachings and transmissions, what will become of him?"

"He will become like a garuda plummeting into a poison lake: His life will be short and throughout this lifetime, he won't even be helpful to others. As for Dorjé, his companion, he won't be of service to others, but he will accomplish his own purpose [by attaining realization]. They must both stay in mountain hermitages, wandering to unfixed locales. This is of utmost importance!" Then she vanished without a trace.

AT NIGHT ON THE EIGHTH DAY of the first winter month, a woman calling herself Dakini Gekdzéma, Goddess of Charm and Beauty, told me, "Next year an enemy will rise up against you, for which you should use Great Wild Za, Planetary Lord, as an antidote. Before the year ends, it's extremely important for you to complete the requisite number of petition and offering practices to Za, Planetary Lord."

> Éma! Wondrous! Listen now, my fortunate child!
> The nature of this earth is space:
> Space appears as earth.
> The nature of all water is space:
> Space appears as water.
> The nature of all fire is space:
> Space appears as fire.
> Even the nature of air is space:
> Space appears as air.
> The nature of rainbows is space:
> Space appears as rainbows.
> The nature of the self's appearance is space:
> Space appears as a self.
> The nature of environments and inhabitants is space:
> Space appears as the display of environments and inhabitants.
>
> Look at the example of appearances in dreams.
> When dream appearances unfold,
> They manifest in forms both solid and tangible,

Yet they don't show up in daytime.
When daytime appearances unfold, environments and inhabitants
Manifest in forms both solid and tangible.
Yet when dream appearances unfold,
Daytime appearances don't appear; they can't!

If you examine things based on this explanation,
Even oneself and others are space:
Space is pristine, clear, and unobscured;
Space is free from arising or cessation;
All phenomena are unsullied space.
Space is not inert—all phenomena arise.
Space is the nature of reality, free from elaboration or extremes.
The totality of phenomena, pure and impure,
Are the display of equal purity within space itself.
Once you've realized the nature of space,
To have space made apparent
Is the Great Perfection, the supreme path of freedom.
There is nothing to do other than the Great Perfection.
Everything is emptiness; this realization of indwelling space
Is the view of emptiness.
There is nothing to do apart from emptiness.
This meaning was spoken by the Transcendent Conqueror
And he extolled this as the supreme path of absolute liberation.
Teach it! Explain it! Trust in it!

Then she dissolved into me.

I TURNED FORTY the next year. In a dream at night on the third day of the second month, the sun dawned in the east and the young moon rose, visible through the skylight. In the south the major stars glowed, and comets streaked in the north. As I dreamed, Dakini Yeshe Wangmo, Wisdom Queen, appeared. I asked her, "All these planetary bodies appear simultaneously. What kind of sign is this?" She sang,

Kyé! Individual blessed with good fortune, listen now!
The dawning of the young sun in the east

Is Nöjin Shenpa Marnak, Dark Red Noxious Spirit Butcher.
This sunlight covering the earth
Is a sign of him impartially guarding your lineage holders.
That moon rising in the skylight
Is Lhachen Wangchuk Chenpo, Magnificent Ruler Deity.
That moonlight covering the ground
Is a sign of Supreme Deity Lhachen's love for the strict doctrine.
The appearance of major stars in the south
Is a sign of the mamos protecting your doctrine.
Comets emerging in the north
Are a sign of Za, Planetary Lord, performing enlightened activity.
Understanding those signs' meanings, endeavor in [these protectors']
    fulfillment offerings and petition practices.
The cloudless sky
Is a portent that you will have realized disciples.
Know this to be so, child of the lineage!

Then she vanished.

THAT SAME YEAR at night on the fifteenth day of the first summer month, an adept saying he was the superb scholar Vimalamitra approached me. I asked, "Why have you come here?" He answered,

I have many things to ask you!
I have no reason apart from that.
Who were you in the past?
Who were you in the era of Lord [Trisong Deutsen] and his subjects?
Tell me both those things!

I replied, "In my past life I was called Dudul Rolpa Tsal. Before that I was called Dudul Dorjé. Among the lord and his subjects, I was the great adept Drokben Khyé-u Chung Lotsawa. Since then, I have taken rebirth as ten different treasure revealers."
Once again he asked, "Where were you born?"
"I was born in the Sertal province."
"Why did you come to Golok?"
"I didn't have any provisions, so I came here seeking such things."

"What divine encounters and prophecies have you had?"

"I've had many of those, most of which I've forgotten. Since they're so numerous, I can't relate them all."

"Which lamas have introduced you to the view and meditation?"

"Not a single human lama in this world has introduced me to the view and meditation. Sometimes I realize them through my own inner strength; on some occasions, in dreams and meditative experiences, awareness-holding lamas and hosts of mamos and wisdom dakinis repeatedly give me pointing-out instructions. Therefore, I recognize, just as it is, cyclic existence and transcendence as the constant nature of great perfection.

He told me, "I will teach you the sacred instructions of the all-embracing consummation of cyclic existence and transcendence. So listen to what I say!" Thus he gave me the sacred instructions of the all-embracing consummation of cyclic existence and transcendence. He had me understand everything he had taught and then said, "After you die, at the moment of transference, may you be led to me, your lord protector. Therefore, bring me and my pure land intently to mind."

I responded, "I want to go to Great Bliss, a pure land of great assurance [of enlightenment]. Among such pure lands, this is the one of never returning, therefore I've focused my intention and aspiration prayers there."

Once I voiced that, the sound of his laughter woke me up.

The Ancestor of the World

THAT SAME YEAR in a dream at night on the ninth day of the first winter month, I arrived in a region I didn't recognize, where a forest of juniper and many different kinds of trees had grown. There, at the base of a rock, I encountered an old man whose hair, beard, and eyebrows were completely white. His skin was black in color; droplets of silver fell from the folds of his wrinkles. In his hand he held a staff. I asked him, "Who are you?"

He told me, "I am a long-lived man called Lekpé Lodrö, Good Intelligence. Who are you?"

"I am called the Gili Tertön, Treasure Revealer of the Gili [family]. That's who I am."

"Why are you called a treasure revealer? Many are said to be treasure revealers, although it's probably not possible for there to be a faultless treasure revealer. Isn't that so?"

I countered, "Old man, even if I explain to you the history of the treasures, you won't understand, so it would be pointless."

"Ha ha! I am the ancestor of the world: I know the story of this world's creation and absolutely everything concerning the world's eventual aeon of destruction. Tell me your story in detail!"

"Well, if you know so much, then what are those people who claim to be treasure revealers like?"

"Well then—some people desire women, so they say they are treasure revealers and then write down whatever comes to their minds. Some are of low standing and yearn after high stature, so they do the same. Some despair over becoming destitute and are fed up, so they do the same. Even if they become treasure revealers, what do they need a woman for? Women don't know Buddhist doctrine. Even if people like that become treasure revealers, what can high position and power do? Treasure revealers don't amass followers that way—[that's not the point of revealing treasure,] right? Even if people like that become treasure revealers, why do they lose themselves seeking payments for religious services their whole life long? Treasure revealers aren't messengers of deception intent on gaining payments, right? Even if people like that become treasure revealers, why do they flounder, without a

bit of leisure, in worldly bustle? Treasure revealers aren't servants to shep-
herds, right?"

I became furious. "Who appointed you to say things like that? What's the
point of talking about whether or not we are treasure revealers?"

He responded, "Hé hé! Don't get angry! I have something nice to say.

"You think that others are great meditators: I've definitely concluded they
aren't meditators. I'm not criticizing you alone, but those I'm certain are not
treasure revealers. This old man is using them to take a measure of you. What
are you like? I'm looking at that.

"Some of them have things resembling treasure revelations, so it's possible, instead of being humans, they are miraculous manifestations of demons.
Some even invent [texts] through the strength of their familiarization with
extensive scholastic understanding and learning. Some even meditate a lot and
[invent texts] from the emergence of their meditative experiences' dynamic
expression. Some even force awareness into a turmoil with their coarse minds,
so various things arise that way. Some experience fabricated mental concepts
and it's possible they write these down.

"What treasure revelations do you have? Where are your treasure sites?"

I replied, "I have an earth-treasure cycle of revelations called The Profound Doctrine of the Heart Essence of the Dakinis. The treasure sites were
Ba Treasure Cliff of Mar, Ngulgö, and Sermé Ngala Taktsé. I have been
blessed by the lord protectors of the three kinds of beings, and Guru Rinpoche
accepted me as his disciple. Awareness-holding accomplished adepts have
given me their seal of entrustment, aspirations, and empowerments. Thus I
have an inconceivable array of teachings, such as those from the three cycles of
pure vision, and yet, I've been unable to transcribe all of them."

He said, "If you're unable to write them out, then from the start, what's the
point of receiving treasure revelations? Are your treasure teachings imbued
with power, efficacy, and signs of blessings, or not? Tell me in detail and this
old man will be happy to listen! What do old people like? They like idle talk.
What do young people like? They like other young people. That's how the
saying goes. I like talk."

"I haven't heard of signs of heat [signaling progress in meditation] arising
for those who practice the chosen deities from my treasure revelations. I don't
know why that is. As for those who practice the arrogant doctrine guardians
for merely one month, or two or three, I've never heard of signs not appearing for them. Once I've given instruction in the completion phase, signs and

indications of enlightenment's stages and paths arise to those who practice wholeheartedly. In particular, for those individuals who cultivate their experience of Direct Crossing for eight months, I've never heard of anyone failing to reach the first stage of an awareness holder.

"On the subject of stories of sorcery, in general, everyone who opposed me, in no more than nine years, has been defeated, destroyed, and then disappeared. It's impossible that these three things haven't befallen them. In particular, I'll tell you an abbreviated story. Last year a dakini advised me, 'You will have an enemy appear. Address petitions to Za, Planetary Lord.' Relying on my treasure treatise entitled 'The Sharp Striped Lightning Arrow of Za, Planetary Lord,' I recited petitions and made offerings.

"A trio named Pöso, Chöshul Dorli, and Chöshul Wangpo stole the horses, with bridles and saddles, belonging to my disciple Dorjé Zangpo and his student. They visited me at dusk saying, 'Both our horses and saddles from below have been carried off. You've surely gained mastery in the activity of overt wrathful conduct. We've heard that other great treasure revealers of the past were like that, so we beg you—demonstrate signs of your virtuosity to those enemies tonight!'

"Right away I convened my students and we performed one thousand petitions to Za, Planetary Lord, concluding with an exhortation. Then I dispatched him, and the following ensued: At night on the twenty-ninth day of the middle winter month, all at once a furious windstorm raged, large hailstones fell, and fierce thunder roared. Za rained down upon those thieves. The one named Chöshul Dorli had his mouth seize up, so he couldn't put any food in it. Wangpo vomited heart blood and died. The horses were sent back.

"Thereafter, in the winter of the following year, Pöso said, 'What sorcery does he have? I'm going to steal from the Gili family again,' and he stole three unbroken horses belonging to them. Of those, two of the horses pulled against the rope and he lost hold of them. On the twenty-ninth day, I visualized the horse thief and then stabbed a sharp hex torma on his rope. The next day at dawn, a dead marmot lay at the bottom of the rope: 'That's an omen that a monk will die,' I surmised. The robber's younger brother had recovered from smallpox, but when he contracted it again, he perished. Having that and various other unwelcome things assail him, the robber had no chance for happiness.

"I finished building my house. While building the temple someone named Kyimo Lhabum had his winter residence seized. He said 'That was a terrible

trespass,' and conflict flared. Because of this, I dispatched Nöjin Shenpa Marnak, Dark Red Noxious Spirit Butcher. The thief died and his wealth was
destroyed. Furthermore, there was a powerful female governor in Golok who
had opposed me. She went blind, lost her authority, and then died. In that
way, my treasure revelations's protector practices are unrivaled by any other."

He replied, "What can words do? By examining the blessings and the efficacy of a practice, you undoubtedly know [its value]. As for the chosen deity
practices, in the creation phase of practice one must not misstep by thinking
the deity has an autonomous existence; one must recognize its essence as the
lama and maintain stable vajra pride [of oneself as the deity]: If these are missing, it's not possible to accomplish the deity. If you're a Severance practitioner,
have you experienced things like upheavals?"

"In the past there was someone named Nang Bari Gyagar whose son
drowned. When I went to perform transference of conciousness for the son, I
was struck by a violent illness. Since no remedy helped, that night I did a final
entrustment visualization, which caused a black man with red hair and a red
beard to appear. He said, 'I'm the one called Dzayul Sertrab, Golden Armor-
Clad Being of Dzayul. That's me. I'm going to suck out your sickness. Will
you give me many tormas?'

"'I will definitely offer tormas to you.' Once I replied, he put his mouth
over my kidney area and inhaled, by which I had the experience of all my
internal organs being drawn out. Early the next morning my illness entirely
vanished on its own and I was restored. I can't relate all the experiences like
that exactly as they've unfolded. In two hundred incidents, I've faced the trio
of resolution, upheaval, and Severance. Now those things don't happen anymore. Old man, do you believe me?"

The old man replied, "I believe you! I believe you! Now listen to this
song:"

> In the fullness of autumn, those green meadows
> Are resplendent and profuse,
> Yet with the queen of winter approaching
> The era of abundance won't last for many months.
> Old people, past the early part of life,
> Can vainly swell with greatness, stature, and profit.
> However much they've done, bravely undergoing hardship,

They'll soon set out for the lord of death's abode,
And can't stay here for long—look at them!

Treasure revealers of this degenerate era
Have no leisure in body and mind.
They doggedly toil to transcribe treasure teachings
Hoping their doctrine will long endure,
Yet barbarian creeds have already arrived—look at that!

I, the old man born at the same time as the world,
Am accustomed to mundane activity,
Yet telling my experiences to others is pointless.
They can't live very long—
Look at how their youth fades!

If I criticize you, how does that harm you?
That will cause you no injury.
Even if I believe you, how does that help?
That won't be even a hair's breadth of help to you.
Even when others say one hundred foul things against you,
Cut through your outbursts of anger and hatred.
Even when they heap praise and compliments upon you,
That doesn't serve you a great deal.
Don't be pleased and attached to praise.

Within the pure space of the view
Settle in meditation without meddling or alteration.
Settle uncontrived and unmoving
Within conduct, free from adopting or abanonding.
If any fortunate disciples appear,
Teach them the liberating sacred instructions.
When the period of your youth has lapsed,
Give up the tasks of seeking provisions and amassing religious
    payments.
When the lord of death arrives to welcome you,
Concentrate on making your mind happy.

I, the old man Lekpé Lodrö,
Won't be bested by others! I'm going into the rocks.
Even you will egress from this dream city
To the wide region of daytime appearances.

Then he dissolved into the rocks, and immediately I woke up.

The Spectacle of Potala Mountain

THAT SAME YEAR, on the first day of the middle winter month, I began a one-month retreat based on the Dorjé Drolö practice from Dudul Dorjé's treasure revelation. From the fifth day until the fifteenth day of the last winter month I stayed in retreat relying on the deity Tröma, Wrathful Goddess.

IN THE YEAR I TURNED FORTY-ONE [1875], at night on the eighteenth day of the fifth month, a woman saying she was Dakini Sangdzö Dakmo, Keeper of the Secret Treasury, told me, "You should go alms-begging for dairy products in the summer. In the winter don't go out begging—concentrate on staying in retreat."

"Fine, but if I don't find anything to eat, I will have to go."

The woman replied, "Acquire seeds to cultivate the field here at this pass and that's what you will eat." She also sang this song:

> When the manifestations of vow-violation spirits attack,
> Those spirits will take something.
> Due to that event,
> The glory of your wealth will be challenged by demons
> And you'll have an upheaval of sorrow's acute pain.
> Don't stay here when that happens.
> The place to go is the southwest.
> If you live from time to time
> In the Yarchenla Valley, virtue and excellence will ensue.
> Foster the splendor of fame and fortune,
> And many lucky disciples will appear.
> Don't forget this! Keep it in mind.

Then she vanished.

IN A DREAM one night in the last summer month, a black cloud hung high in the sky, unbearable to look at and extremely dark and dense. It was surrounded by dark red clouds. From within their billowing mass a fear-

some tiger fell onto a pile of ashes in front of me. After a moment the tiger
began vomiting and an old woman tumbled from his mouth. A moment
later, a child was born to that old woman and she took him onto her lap.
Then the child rose and stood on the ground, saying, "Ya! Mother, what
is this place called? Whose monastery is this? Who built it?" The mother
replied,

> My beloved child, listen to me!
> If you don't recognize this place,
> It's Driyul, a land of ferocious sorcerers.
> If you don't recognize these local people,
> These are the evil townfolk of Golok.
> If you don't know which monastery this is,
> This is the place that took form last night.
> The man who made it is Dudjom Dorjé.
> This place is a town of illusion.
> These people are visitors to a marketplace.
> This monastery is a way station for travelers.

The child said, "Mother, tell me the history of how this aeon formed and
how sentient beings and the doctrine came about!" She responded by recounting in detail the history of how this aeon came into being.

Once again the child insisted, "Tell me what will happen in the future!"
Just as he asked, she told him in detail and although I listened, I haven't
included it here for fear of writing too much.

Then the child asked, "Where are we, mother and child, going?"

The old woman replied, "We're not staying here. We're going to the
unimpeded city." Then she swallowed her son and said, "Alas! Dudjom, you
don't have the providence to remain here in this place for very long." As soon
as she uttered that, the tiger swallowed the old woman and told me, "The
time of the non-Asian[14] foreigners' demonic dogma is imminent." Merging
with the clouds, the tiger vanished.

IN THE YEAR I TURNED FORTY-TWO [1876], on the first day of the third month,
I cultivated the field at Puklung Gékyi Latok by sowing two bags of barley
seeds. Once autumn arrived, fifty-one bags of barley had ripened.

In a dream at night on the tenth day of the first autumn month, a dakini saying she was Kunsal Gyalmo, All-Illuminating Queen, approached me directly. Coming close to me, she said:

> É É!
> The corrupt aspirations of wild southern demons
> Result in this region's misery
> And draw hordes of upper obstructing spirits as guests.
> The blue naga prepares to cut his braids,
> And the elements at the base of Supreme Mountain mobilize as an
>   army.
> The wild borderlanders are led into the center of the country.
> Those events crush the happiness of beings and the doctrine.
> Venomous manifestations emerge in these lands.
> The black bear craves flesh:
> Its resounding snarl
> Causes the white snow lioness unbearable distress.
> When armies of packs of tigers and leopards amass,
> They turn the land into a ghost town.
> For that reason, when the dragon arrives,
> Make haste for the land of Karnaka.
> For a while the sun of happiness will faintly shine.

Then she vanished.

On the fifteenth day of the third month, someone called Chökor Lharo stole one of my cow-yak hybrids. Many people told me that I should use sorcery on him, but I didn't listen—it seemed possible this could come to an end by itself. Saying, "There is no way this won't be the cause of misery for the thief," I didn't do anything.

At night on the fifth day of the eighth month, a yellow dakini blazing gold in color wearing a white silk skirt approached, coming close by me. She asked, "Do you want to go south to see the spectacle of Potala Mountain?"

"Who are you?"

She answered, "I am the dakini called Norsung Chétsik Chémo, Great

Wealth Protectress with Bared Teeth, who resides in that place. We have a karmic connection from the past. Moreover, since your consort is my emanation, I've come to invite you there."

We went flying together into space, over a vast and wide ocean, unfathomably deep and dark blue in color. At its far banks, to the east, south, west, north, and every direction in between, scores of valleys encircled the entire vista, from which rivers flowed into the ocean. All the water pooled together, and at its center stretched an infinitely wide, grassy plain. In its midst stood an immense fissure. The midpoint of the evenly split gap was surrounded by a lake [in which sat an island] with geese, cranes, and seagulls. The white birds were like conch, the yellow birds like gold, the red birds like coral, the green birds like turquoise, and the multicolored birds like brocade. Those and others amounted to an unimaginable array of birds living there, small, medium, and large in size. Yellow and red flowers blanketed the area. On the banks of that lake were many naga, scent-eater, and other nonhuman boys and girls listening to Buddhist teachings from a white crane that knew how to speak human language.

I asked the dakini, "What is that crane over there?"

She told me, "It's said to be a seer named Lekpar Mawa, Excellent Speech. Those children are naga, scent-eater, and nonhuman boys and girls."

"How is it that they're listening to teachings from this bird?"

"These are not beings who have failed to cultivate enough stores [of merit and wisdom]. In human lands, they made supplications with faith and respect to the exalted bodhisattva, Chenrézi, All-Seeing Eyes. Because they aspired [to be reborn] in his pure land, they recited many hundreds of millions of the six-syllable mantra. Unable to actually take rebirth in that pure land, they were born here. They listen to teachings and cultivate the accumulations, and finally, they gain the eyes of wisdom, which are the cause for their rebirth in the city of the exalted one's pure land."

The lakes lay like a ring of iron mountains, and at their center stretched an immense plain. At the plain's midpoint loomed Supreme Mountain; summer and winter, it was entirely covered with white flowers. Its middle peak spiraled high. When we reached its summit, I saw masses of white light diffusing outward in the form of a foundation one league above us. At the center of that ground of light rose a wide celestial palace made of myriad jewels, which held an oceanlike gathering of spiritual heroes and heroines. In their midst was the sublime exalted Tukjé Chenpo, Supreme Compassion. He had one face and four arms and sat on a jeweled throne with his legs in cross-legged vajra posture. Splendidly adorned with the attributes of the utter enjoyment body of enlightenment, he reveled in union, entwined indivisibly with his consort, red Kachö Wangmo, Queen of the Celestial Enjoyment Realms.

As soon as I saw him, I offered prostrations. I made supplications, beseeching him, "Grant me sacred instructions for liberation in this very lifetime, I pray!"

The exalted one revealed to me a paragraph of words on his hand. "Look at these sacred instructions that will definitely dispel suffering." As soon as he spoke, it was as if they were firmly imprinted in my mindstream. "Now I will give you the empowerment, scriptural transmission, and blessings [for] my own means of accomplishishment." Upon finishing, he said, "Oh! May the vase empowerment ripen your body into the vajra body. May the secret empowerment ripen your speech into vajra speech. May the wisdom empowerment ripen your mind into vajra mind. May the force of the word empowerment cause appearances and your mind to shift to the display of enlightenment's bodies and wisdoms. May you reach spiritual maturity and be liberated!"

When he concluded, he told me, "Child of my spiritual family, at present we've reached the five-hundred-year era of degeneration. It is rare indeed for people to have confidence in the ultimate teachings. Because of the strength of my aspirations, there isn't any being who isn't my disciple. Rely on the text outlining my own means of accomplishment, keep it in mind, and persevere in reciting the six-syllable mantra. Seal your practice at its conclusion with prayers of dedication and aspiration. Those who always aspire to be born in my pure land will be reborn here. Therefore, the cultivation of merit is a sacred key instruction.

"Whenever there's a favorable occasion, it's very important for you to make the offering of a vajra feast. As for all your students, if they are able to stay in mountain retreats, many will attain a rainbow body. That is my prophecy." Thus he spoke.

The girl insisted, "Let's go," and when she pulled me by the hand, I woke up. After that, I entered into retreat for the three winter months and maintained strictly sealed boundaries, practicing the meditation and recitation of my chosen deity, [Chenrézi].

In the Presence of Patrul Rinpoche

IN THE YEAR I TURNED FORTY-THREE [1877], at night on the tenth day of
the fourth month, someone saying she was Dakini Kunsal Mikdenma, All-
Illuminating Eyes, sang to me,

> My child, listen to what I have to say!
> You went as the southern messenger directed,
> And now that the lion cub has reached the glacial summit, Kangtsé,
> His turquoise mane will flourish.
>
> Stay in this mountain's rocky fortress.
> Although this is the home of the human-devouring red sorcerers,
> Dakini Dewé Jungné, Source of Bliss, resides here,
> Surrounded by ten million dakinis.
> Except for individuals with damaged tantric commitments,
> Connections made by practicing in that place
> Produce for everyone the possibility of gaining some degree of spiritual
>   attainment.
> Don't forget that—recall it, fortunate child!

Then she vanished.

ON THE FIRST DAY of the middle summer month, I embarked on a journey
during which my son Khyentsé Nyugu was granted investiture on the throne
of the Dö Tsangchen Monastery. We then continued on to Nuzok Monastery
where he was once again granted investiture on the throne. Finally, in the
middle autumn month, we returned to my own monastery.

THAT SAME YEAR, throughout the three winter months, I stayed in retreat performing practice related to my chosen deity. During that time, many dakinis
offered me an array of food, wealth, clothing, and other magnificent riches.
Then, on three occasions during my meditative experiences and dreams, they
made aspiration prayers for me and gave me empowerments.

IN THE YEAR I TURNED FORTY-FOUR [1878], at night on the tenth day of the first month, a green woman the color of turquoise appeared, adorned with the six bone ornaments. Saying she was Dakini Nangsi Wangmo, Queen of Appearing Existence, she sang:

> Listen now, individual endowed with the power
> Of many aeons' good karma, aspirations, and auspicious
>   connections:
> What you've been encouraged to do by the messenger is meaningful;
> It has quite a significant purpose.
> Therefore journey to the near flank of the [mountain god] Dzagyal
>   Pawo, Hero of the Dzagyal Region,
> And stay there for a while.
> Magyal Pomra will give you wealth;
> Dagyal Pawo, Victorious Moon Hero, will serve you.
> Then, during the Snake Year,
> Travel to Serlung.
> Your gathering of students will increase
> And you will know the glory of fame and renown.
>
> If you stay here too long,
> Grave danger will suddenly befall you,
> Therefore understand the meaning of what I'm telling you.
> After this year ends, in the next,
> You will acquire a black donkey of existence
> From a confrontation with dark demons
> Who will scramble after your livestock.
> Dispatch as an emissary the great black demon Za, Planetary Lord,
> To crush the demon hordes.
> You will gain timely profit through these dire circumstances.

Then she vanished.

ON THE FIRST DAY of the middle summer month, we set off north on the path by the river Dzachuka. As we journeyed, three hundred wild yaks appeared at Matö. They came with us for three days. During the day they walked in front of us and at night they stayed close by. I understood this to be a welcome from [the mountain god] Magyal Pomra.

Further, one night in a dream, the field guardian Kunga Zhonnü, Youthful Ever-Joyful, told me, "I'm going ahead of you; then I will announce your pending arrival to Tsamtrul. I have to borrow a place for you to stay." Then he departed.

Tsamtrul told me about that same night [the next day]: "Last night a black man with a lion face appeared. He was wearing a black cloak and riding a black horse with rings of white hair above its hooves. He struck my house with a club and told me, 'Clear out of this house!' Then he left. Therefore I said, 'It's likely that Tertön Rinpoche and his disciples are going to arrive tomorrow, so stash all these things away in the yak-hair tents.' Then the house was cleared out."

That day we stopped at a rest area in Mamö Drilkar. A welcome party had been sent from Dzagyal Monastery and we met them there. The next day when we arrived at Dzagyal Monastery, we were welcomed by a line of monks and even Tsamtrul with his two students came out to greet us. We met all of them, and my youngest son was granted investiture on the throne: They made us a residence in in Tsamtrul Rinpoche's own home and we stayed there.

One night after a week there had passed, I met Longchen Dorjé Ziji, Dazzling Vajra of the Great Expanse [Longchenpa]. He bestowed upon me the absolutely complete sacred instructions of Great Perfection. He fully entrusted me with the doctrine and then said, "This son of yours is my emanation, known as Rikzin Jikmé Lingpa. If he is diligent in retreat, he will arrive at the very highest degree of realization. Have him do that, and I think he will be of some benefit to the doctrine and beings." Then he vanished without a trace.

AT NIGHT ON THE NINTH DAY of the last summer month, a dakini appeared and told me, "Tomorrow take your youngest son to meet Patrul Rinpoche. If you request some scriptural transmissions from him, you will receive them." On the tenth day, when we arrived in the presence of Patrul Rinpoche, they were performing a vajra feast offering and had just reached the point of receiving spiritual-attainment substances. The lama said, "Since this auspicious connection is incredibly excellent, give that feast offering to these two." As he said, Khyentrul and I both received the consecrated food and were overjoyed.

He said, "Tulku, if you sit here, you will receive teachings." As instructed, we sat there and he gave us scriptural transmissions with instruction for *The Way of the Bodhisattva*, *The Ornament of Manifest Realization*, *Entering the Middle Way*, and *The Secret Essence Tantra*. We received those and many more transmissions, then [my son] Khyentrul stayed at that monastery with that spiritual master and his students.

On the third day of the middle winter month when I, the spiritual master, and just four disciples made ready to journey to our homeland, a blizzard fell as we prepared to go. We felt anxious and filled with regret. That night I dreamt that Nöjin Shenpa Marnak, Dark Red Noxious Spirit Butcher, declared, "Have no fear! Don't be sad! I'll stop the snow and aside from what has already fallen, I won't send any more." From that point on no more snow fell that winter.

Renown for My Powers

In the year I turned forty-five [1879], on the fifth day of the second month, Chökor Lhaten, the man who earlier took my horse and saddle, was put in prison and severely punished. Some officials handled that legal case; they resolved the issue and returned to their own area.

On the twelfth day of the last summer month, in retaliation for his injury, [the thief] drove my livestock away. I was out alms-begging for dairy when he fled. Since I wasn't at home when that event took place, I was summoned and returned to my homestead. Everyone insisted, "Now you must use your sorcery."

I explained, "If one applies sorcery during the days of the waxing moon, it's difficult to triumph: You have to dispatch your forces during the waning moon." At the stroke of midnight on the seventeenth day of the month, I performed the Wild Za, Planetary Lord, dispatchment from my own treasure revelation. That night, Za descended on the enemy's home. The next day, on the roof of his yak-hair tent, a black snake as large as a pillar lay coiled. Many of his animals became paralyzed and died. My enemy was put in prison by the local leader and enormous suffering assailed him.

Further, I performed the wrathful fire puja of my chosen deity. When I had completed a hundred thousand mantra recitations, devastating hail fell on my enemy's fields and a large hill collapsed on them. That field, known as Ranyé Field, had cost the price of three silver units of measurement known as "dil". It was covered by a heap of rocks, impossible to clear away. Moreover, throughout that entire region, not even a bushel of the autumn crops could be harvested, so a great famine ensued. My animals were returned to me, and my legal case went well. At the conclusion, my enemy was utterly destroyed; I gained renown for my powers. As the dakini had predicted, I triumphed in the end over the earlier transgressions. Her prophecy had come to pass.

In the year I turned forty-six [1880], I was thinking of going to Lama Rong in Upper Ser. I sent a trio of messengers ahead. At Martö, they were stalled by a small dispute with the [local protector] Yungdrung Chaktsé, Swastika Iron-Peak, and then the horses went to sleep. They were unable to go any further. When the messengers were ready to turn back, the horses got up and they returned home again. Based on that, I presented burnt offerings and many silk banners in front of the local protector. In response, he actually appeared and pleaded with me, "This area is yours and mine—please don't move away!"

"Don't say that! The dakinis prophesied that I must leave."

"In that case, though there's no way I can go this year, next year I must visit the place where you've gone."

I told him, "Next year, in the last summer month, when I call your name, if you're able to make small round hailstones fall from a cloud in the sky, that will be a sign you've arrived. Then I will make offerings and petitions to you."

Then we set off on the thirteenth day of the first summer month. When we reached Serkok, a black man calling himself [the great noxious spirit] Kowa Lé Ziden appeared riding a scrawny, hornless yak. He said, "If you don't stay here, I will carry this off," and then he led away one of my black yaks and fled.

When I prepared to draw in and embed him [into an effigy], Nöjin Chenpo, Great Noxious Spirit, insisted, "Don't do that! Don't do that! I'll let the yak go and everything will be fine," so I didn't continue.

On the third day of the middle summer month, we arrived at Lama Rong in Upper Ser. The malevolent naga that lived in that area emerged riding a naked man. He came before me proclaiming, "It's not right for you to stay here. It's completely detrimental to me."

I replied, "I will offer you a cairn with flags atop a hill and a spirit house so you won't come to any harm." Then a black snake transformed into a riding crop and he struck me. I seized him by the neck. When I squeezed, he grew fearful and panicked, then pleaded, "Let me go and I swear, with you as a witness, I'll not harm you." In response, I released him; he leapt into a spring and disappeared.

I TURNED FORTY-SEVEN THE NEXT YEAR [1881]. On the thirteenth day of the third month, a black woman appeared who had her breasts crossed over her shoulders. Her red hair reached the ground; she was naked without any clothing whatsoever. She told me, "You are cruel, savage, and belligerent. You can't stay here! From Upper Danyi Gongwa down to Lower Litsang, I am she who controls taking the impure life-breath of livestock at their time of death. What do you think? If you can go away, then leave."

She lunged directly at me. As she struck me with a black yak-hair banner, I seized the woman's right arm, took her banner, and made ready to plant a ritual dagger in her heart. At that she cried, "Let me go, you evil ruffian!"

"You must swear not to kill anymore!"

"I swear I won't kill anymore and I won't harm you." That was the witch of the plain of Serlung Dzichen.

On the tenth day of the last summer month, I went to the peak of a high mountain. When I called out, "Yungdrung Chaktsé!" three times, from the cloudless clear blue sky small white hailstones the size of wheat grains fell. Everyone there was amazed.

Before that month, a girl saying she was Dakini Yeshe Tsogyal approached me. She wore a gown of five-colored brocade in horizontal layers and was adorned with ornamental garlands of myriad jewels. "Holy one, in the year you turn forty-eight, there will be a major obstacle to your life. Therefore, it's crucial that you persevere in methods to dispel that hindrance."

When I asked, "What must I do?" she sang,

> Kyé! Child of my spiritual family, listen to me! Hear me!
> A woman of the Dong family
> With a name ending in Drön, Lamp,
> Bears the strength of previous aspirations.
> Therefore, if you rely on her as your consort,
> This will dispel obstacles to your longevity and your wealth will burgeon.
> You will also acquire three gems,
> And your fame and renown will fill the three planes of existence.
> Know this, without mistake or confusion, to be a crucial instruction.
> If you falter, that error will be detrimental.
> If you're able to follow through with that key instruction,
> Your gathering of students will increase.
>
> The fierce power of the border people's curses
> Will damage the longevity of your doctrine's custodians.
> For that, meditate on your chosen deity
> And apply yourself to the vital points of the view and meditation of
>   emptiness.

Eighty years from now [1962],
The nectar of the doctrine will evaporate;
The barbarians' dogma will envelop this earth.
From the next Fire Bird Year [1897] on,
The mindfulness of humans will deteriorate
And they will persist in the toil of turmoil and conflict.
All mountains and valleys will be filled with bandits.
The sun of the happiness of the doctrine and beings will set.

When the black snake coils in the water,
If you reach the border of southern Mön
And open the door to a fierce hidden land,
That's the appropriate time: It's not right to let it slip away.
If you can't carry out that crucial directive,
You have disciples in upper Doyul:
Go to that place.
If you put your trust in Wangchuk Mahadeva, Magnificent Ruler Deity,
It will prove virtuous for a while.
Keep those words in the vault of your heart.

Then she vanished.

ONCE I APPLIED THE PRACTICAL INSTRUCTIONS as she described, I was freed from the imposing passageway of obstacles to my longevity. Just as the dakini had prophesied, in the Water Snake Year, the year I turned fifty-nine [1893], I prepared to go to the place called Pemakö, Lotus Array. However, due to other circumstances, the auspicious connection was blundered, and the opportunity to go didn't come into alignment.

Following that [encounter with Yeshe Tsogyal], I built a residence at Lama Rong. Several demonic emanations of corrupt aspirations created obstacles, then some portents appeared indicating that it wasn't a good place for me to live.

DURING THE WINTER of the year I turned forty-eight [1882], I gave guidance on Severance of Evil Forces and Great Perfection to a gathering of one hundred disciples. At that time, at night on the tenth day of the middle winter month, a woman appeared saying she was Dakini Kuntu Gyuwa Saljéma,

Wandering All-Illuminator, and sang to me,

> Kyé! Listen undistracted to this dakini's speech!
> In this place lives a sublime individual named Pema, Lotus,
> Who will hold your doctrine.
> He should intently apply the key points of practice and travel without a
> set destination.

> A sublime individual named Dönsem, Meaningful Intention,
> Is the destined inheritor of the unobstructed wisdom mind
> Of Great Perfection. He should stay in unfixed mountain retreats.
> If he isn't deceived by demons onto the wrong path,
> He will manifest enlightenment in the supreme rainbow body.

> A superb person named Gyatso, Ocean,
> Should apply himself to the essential practices.
> If he has practiced his whole life long,
> He will attain true and perfect enlightenment.

> A great being whose name ends with Drol, Freedom,
> Will accomplish the illusory form of rainbow body,
> If he doesn't stray into the domain of the eight worldly concerns.

> A superlative individual whose name ends with Rab, Highest,
> Will accomplish the supreme illusory rainbow body
> If he isn't fooled by circumstances involving the eight worldly
> concerns.

> Those are your disciples who are worthy vessels for the teachings:
> In this evil era, if you give the sacred instructions
> To wild and difficult people, the dakinis will lead them astray
> And unwanted disturbances will erupt.
> Therefore, maintain a tight seal of secrecy.

Then she disappeared.

THAT SAME YEAR, on the sixteenth day of the twelfth month, a black woman appeared saying she was Dakini Sangdzö Chenmo, Great Goddess of the Secret Treasury. She sang,

> Kyé! This is the abode of Illustrious Queen Dakini,
> A land where lotus dakinis gather!
> In the midst of that forest over there,
> Is a goddess of the wood element.
> She is a flesh-eating witch who steals life force,
> Accompanied by four other savage witches.
> If you can't subdue them with wrathful activity,
> You won't be able to utilize pacifying activity.
> The correct time will be when the Monkey Year arrives,
> Signifying a test at hand.
> Prepare various methods of direct wrathful conduct.

Then she vanished.

That Dzichen Witch

In the year I turned forty-nine [1884], at night on the sixth day of the third month, a red dakini wearing a red brocade robe appeared. She held my right hand and asked, "Do you want to go see the spectacle of Willow Mountain?" We shot eight leagues into space. As we flew eastward I saw an immense valley. At its lowest point grew a dense forest; the middle section was filled with sandalwood, bamboo, and plants. At the valley's upper level stood an utterly blue mountain. Its light shone a league out into space, touching everything in all directions. As an example, it blazed with the intensity of the sun's light rays.

Completely encircling the mountain's base stretched an unfathomably deep black lake. Upon its banks were mobs of ghouls, zombies, flesh eaters, and breath stealers, ugly in form like ogres, and various creatures with heads not their own. The din of their war cries and resounding laughter subjugated the gods and demons of apparent existence. It seemed that the whole area was filled with creatures like that.

At the mountain's summit loomed an immense celestial palace, made of an enclosure of three kinds of skulls, adhered with meteorite nails and held by molten bronze mortar. At its center sat a throne erected from mounded frogs, large fish, and big snakes. On the throne's lotus and sun seat stood a dark blue wrathful deity, impossible to look at directly, who held an ornamental garland of snakes and human skulls. His face was marked with clumps of human ash, drops of blood, and smears of fat. He appeared like a shimmering reflection on water. With three faces, six arms, and four legs, he blazed within a dark red inferno. Garudas erupted like sparks from the midst of his orange hair that blazed upward. He was encircled by an inconceivable throng of wrathful deities.

I offered prostrations and circumambulated him, and then touched my head to his feet. When I made aspirations, that wrathful deity placed his implements upon my head and declared, "I grant you investiture as the regent of all victors of the past, present, and future. I grant you empowerment to liberate you from the entirety of cyclic existence. I assure you that you will attain freedom in the exalted state of the Buddhist king of the three realms.

My emanation, the great adept Saraha, revealed to you the sacred instructions of the female deity Tröma, Wrathful Goddess. Teach those to your students, and if they diligently cultivate their experience, all obstacles will be cleared away from within."

Then [the dakini and I] flew from that pure land, yet another league up into space. At the center of a perfectly arrayed pure land, in the heart of a spacious celestial palace made of various jewels, stood a jeweled throne. There sat the peaceful form of that deity, dark blue, adorned with all the buddhas' marks and signs of physical perfection. He was bedecked with the ornaments of the utter enjoyment body of enlightenment. When I saw him, with highest respect I offered prostrations, circumambulated him, and then touched my head to his feet. When I made aspirations, he touched his vajra to my head, saying, "May you receive the complete empowerment and scriptural transmission for my means of accomplishment." When he finished speaking, he asked, "Child of my spiritual family, are you transcribing your profound teachings?"

I offered in response, "I have transcribed some teachings. However, erudite, intelligent people have said, 'The canons and treatises of the Buddha and the teachings of the victors of the past suffice.' Since many people have said that, I thought it to be true. So I haven't transcribed very much."

The exalted one said, "Ha ha! Those people aren't so learned and smart! Making an analysis of limitations isn't the same thing as vast knowledge. Due to an excess of lineages throughout many past generations, the impact of discrepancies between the tantric commitments of lamas and disciples has broken the bridge of lineages, as well as the continuity of empowerments and scriptural transmissions. Thinking that the river of blessings would decline, I filled all the earth, rocks, mountains, and cliffs with treasures. Not knowing the significance of that is definitely fools' talk, while at the same time—regarding all the teachings spoken by past victors—the blessings in the teachings haven't declined. However, those blessings don't come forth due to the actions of ordinary beings. Therefore, when the lineage of empowerment and transmission isn't broken, blessings and spiritual attainments are close and swift. You should know that!

"Transcribe the treasure texts into words and promptly teach everything to your students who are worthy vessels. Once they've practiced, have them reach the ground of liberation. The doctrine of non-Buddhist barbarians draws near like dawn approaching. The doctrine will endure for only a very short while: Spread these teachings quickly!

"You and I are indivisible. Always retain my mantra! The empowerments and transmissions are now complete. As for instruction, all phenomena subsumed by appearing existence, and that of cyclic existence and enlightenment, do not transcend the display of emptiness—recognize this indwelling nature just as it is. Emptiness is like space—if you've come to the decisive conclusion that your phenomena and others' phenomena are entirely the play of a single space, that's called 'pure space,' the view. Making that continuous nature a manifest presence is meditation, called 'the vast expanse of space.' Conduct is not going beyond that, called 'having no second thoughts .' Know that!

"Relying on the basis, Cutting Through, the path of Direct Crossing constitutes the sacred instructions for entering the inner core of clear light. These pith instructions are the most effective methods by which even the worst wrongdoer can attain enlightenment. Therefore, you should intently apply these vital instructions until you reach the age of sixty-two. Cultivate your experience! If you practice this way, it's possible you may live until you're eighty years old. If you make mistakes in the vital instructions of this practice, your life span will only be sixty-seven years. This is certain."

When he finished speaking, the woman said, "Now we'll go! Look to the heavens." I looked up and awoke from sleep.

IT WAS [1884], THE YEAR I TURNED FIFTY. In general, once nonhuman beings made promises to me, breaking them was impossible. However, there was that Dzichen witch I mentioned before. She went back on her vows and was extremely wild; therefore she transgressed her promises to me. Further, from the first month of this year until the fourth month, she penetrated the hearts of all my consorts and female helpers. They went insane, had fainting spells, and further maladies, so I exerted myself in peaceful and wrathful methods, but nothing helped. I supplicated the deities, the three roots, and the hosts of spiritual heroes and dakinis, and then I rested. While I slept, I saw my holy lama, Jikmé. He said, "For what purpose have you summoned the deities? Tell me."

Offering prostrations, I respectfully paid homage and then answered, "Compassionate lama, you already know. The women and girls around me have all been struck with the sickness of insanity. Everything I did for them was to no avail. What is this retribution for? What obstacle is this? What can be done to help?"

He replied, "As the dakini previously foretold, you must subdue [the witch] using the activity of direct wrathful conduct. Apart from that, you can perform any amount of ritual service, but it won't help. Now is the time to heed her advice." Then he vanished without a trace.

As he instructed, I went to the forest where the witch resided and scattered power substances. I shot my rifle many times, destroying haunted rocks. I cut down haunted trees and burned incense made from wicked substances. I forcibly liberated three of the retinue witches, but I let one go because another dakini called Mara-chen, Bearded, told me, "One must be subdued by someone called Bensö." When I performed the burning and pouring of the Dakini Tröma burnt-offerings fire ritual, portents of having subdued them became visibly apparent. I planted a cluster of sixty ritual daggers in the main witch's head, and she fled to the place called Labtsé Kardang of Trom. All the sick women were freed from their illnesses.

Signs of the Dakinis' Agitation

DAKINI SANGWÉ DZÖMA, Keeper of the Secret Treasury, told me, "Now go to Dowé Ngangpé Valley." As she instructed, in the middle summer month I went and stayed there; I gave teachings to a gathering of one hundred disciples.

AT NIGHT ON THE TENTH DAY of the eighth month, someone saying she was Dakini Dewé Jungné, Source of Bliss, appeared wearing white garb, brandishing a corpse club in her hand. She sang this to me:

> Kyé! Holy sublime individual, listen to me!
> If you don't recognize me,
> I am Dewé Jungné.
> If you don't know this place,
> It's Great Vajra Cross Fortress in the northern direction.
> If you stay here for a long time,
> Your doctrine will flourish and you will begin to gather disciples;
> That may be of sweeping benefit for the doctrine and beings.
> Through the power of karma and circumstances,
> I haven't seen anyone fortunate enough to reside here for long.
>
> East of here is a place called Tukten Drung,
> Where a goddess called Dungli Men, Medicine Woman of Dungli, lives.
> She holds a treasure trove of Guru Rinpoche's wisdom mind.
> By calling her name three times,
> She will come to grant you the supreme representation of wisdom
>   mind.
>
> Next year Namké Nyingpo, Essence of Space,
> Will arrive as your son—
> He will act for the sake of the doctrine and beings.

A male demon nearby, skilled at abusing others,
Will cause a torrential army and arsenal to rain down.
As a counterforce, send local spirit-lord guardians
And Nöjin Marnak, Dark Red Noxious Spirit.
They will defeat the horde of demons.
Don't forget this! Keep it in the vault of your heart.

Then she vanished.

ON THE TENTH DAY of the ninth month, I traveled east to the place nearby where a salt storehouse stood. I went there and looked around. At the base of a cliff stood a tree trunk, and in front of it I saw blue smoke surging upward. I turned toward it and called out, "Dungli Men!" many times. In response, a woman, blue-green in color, came forth.

"What do you want from me?" Again she spoke saying, "I'm Ah Chang Kuré. Are you Khyé-u Chung Lotsawa?" When I said yes, she replied, "Oh, I knew that already." She was holding a ritual dagger and a box made of birch bark. She gave them both to me and then said, "This is one of the 108 ritual daggers that Guru Rinpoche wore around his neck. He left this with me to give to you. This birch-bark box contains relics, from the seven supreme buddhas, that magically multiply. It was previously meant for Rongtér Déchen Lingpa. I have this and many other things for him; however, when he was alive, he blundered the auspicious connections and couldn't come to retrieve them, so I'm giving them to you."

Furthermore, she explained to me the full qualities of that place and recited aloud a burnt offering ritual for her wisdom body's spirit. She insisted, "Write this down!" and then dissolved back into the tree.

Then many people told me, "You must come back!" They left me with truly earnest promises and formal requests such that it was impossible for me not to return to that place.

IN THE YEAR I TURNED FIFTY-ONE [1885], on the fifteenth day of the third month, we carried our tents and went to live in the lower valley of Takki Drang Ngu. During that time, a man with leprosy arrived from Mongolia. I thought, "I must do something to help him." While I considered that, on the fifteenth day of the first summer month, a Chok-tsang army of one hundred soldiers showed up. They shot my yak-hair tent twenty times with rifles, yet their bullets didn't pierce the surface but dropped to the ground. In response, I struck my treasure container on the earth three times and launched a curse.

When the army turned back, they experienced some bad omens. Among the leaders, there was one dissenter. Without delay, in less than a month, he had died. Many of the generals, other leaders, and soldiers also died before the year was done. Those circumstances made it unfeasible to stay in that place, so I moved nomadically to Lama Rong once again.

THEN FROM THE LAST AUTUMN MONTH until the middle winter month, I stayed in retreat relying on my chosen deity. At that time, the local protector of Chutsang, calling himself Lhalungkar, Naga God of the White Valley, sent twelve horsemen over toward me, shouting war cries of "Kyi! Ha!" When that happened, the guardian of my doctrine, Nöjin Chenpo, Great Noxious Sprit, swung his sword, killing five of the horsemen. The remaining seven, like mice chased by a hawk, fled terrified back to their own area.

THAT SAME YEAR, one morning in the middle summer month, one of my sons was born. Twenty days after his birth he was able to call to his mother and repeat the letters of the alphabet. He was given the name Lhachen Tobkyi Gyalpo, Magnificent Ruler Mighty King.

IN THE YEAR I TURNED FIFTY-TWO [1886], at night on the thirteenth day of the fifth month, a woman white in color appeared, saying she was Dakini Pema-treng, Lotus Garland. She advised me, "If you stop the frost, you will obtain the spiritual attainment of food. In the end, an emanation of the sorcerer Métak Marpo, Red Sparks, will give this spiritual attainment to someone else. Then you'll reach the point of having to kill him with wrathful activity." Futhermore, she spoke of many other prophecies yet to unfold. Then she vanished.

During that period, the provincial leader of Washul told me, "That goddess of Dzichen is the local protector I like most of all, so you should go up and call her."

On the twenty-sixth day of the sixth month, I went with a few friends to a mountain peak in the area where had I liberated the witch. When I called out, "Goddess of the tree of Dzichen, come up here!" three times, there was a loud sound accompanied by a dark whirlwind as a portent that she was coming. It swirled from the arena of the sky and descended down into the forest. Everyone witnessed that.

ON THE TENTH DAY of the ninth month, I rested in evenness within clear light. At that time, in the visual aspect of the meditative experience of clear light, someone said to be Orgyen Térdak Gyalpo, Treasure Lord King, appeared amid a vast, dense lattice of rainbow light. He was yellow in color, brandishing a treasure vase in his right hand and a mongoose in his left hand. He was attired in a brocade cloak and the three Buddhist robes; on his head he wore the lotus crown that grants liberation on sight. Endowed with a smiling peaceful and wrathful demeanor, he looked at me. "My child, what do you need?"

"I want wealth and riches."

The supreme master said, "I thought that's what you desire—that's why I've come here. I've taken the form of a wealth god called Apara-chitta, Chief of Noxious Spirits, not different from Lakna Dorjé, Bodhisattva Vajra Bearer. Therefore, I'm going to teach you my means of accomplishment, so listen well. Remember it." Having said that, he gave me the complete empowerment and scriptural transmission for the text outlining the means of accomplishment related to that deity. It was firmly set in my mind as if a precise copy had been made.

Once again he spoke. "Kyé! Supreme individual, these days people exert themselves only in recitation of mantra, which cannot produce spiritual attainment since they never focus on creation-phase practice. Failing to recognize that, they lose hope in the deity and lama. Don't be that way—cultivate your experience without ever separating meditation and recitation!" Then he vanished without a trace.

IN THE YEAR I TURNED FIFTY-THREE [1887], many signs of the dakinis' agitation emerged when I was about to begin an extensive teaching cycle. While I wondered what was causing that, at night in a dream on the twenty-fourth day of the middle winter month, my lama named Jamyang appeared. I saw him and implored, "Kyé! Lama, you know the past, present, and future. When you were living in this worldly human realm, you didn't express your prophecies or clairvoyance. However, now that you have this illusory wisdom form, what is it that you can't see or don't know? Recently, apart from my teachings, I'm not doing anything to displease the dakinis, yet there are so many signs of the dakinis' agitation. What is causing this?"

The lama said, "It's true that you haven't performed any wrongful teaching activity. However, Great Perfection is the sacred inner essence of the hearts of all mamos and dakinis. If you have made the teachings resound to those with broken tantric commitments, to those who haven't practiced, to those with misapprehension of the meaning, or to those who lack belief, that's the reason for the agitation of the mamos and dakinis. Apart from that, it's characteristic of sentient beings to do evil and nonvirtuous things, so there's no reason to get upset about it. Therefore, it's very important to be diligent in reciting the hundred-syllable mantra [of Vajrasattva], and in doing confession and purification practice. Consider that.

"Now, among your students, the best should stay in unfixed mountain retreats. Your average students should meditate their whole lives in the context of their householder situations. At the very least, they must do a month of meditation [retreat] each year. If they've done that, the teachings by the instructor and the hearing by the listeners will be meaningful." So he spoke.

Then just like that, by persevering in confession and purification, those portents disappeared.

IN THE YEAR I TURNED FIFTY-FOUR [1888], in a dream at night on the tenth day of the fifth month, a blue woman appeared saying she was Dakini Chökyi Chendenma, Endowed with Eyes of the Teachings. Her body was naked and adorned with bone ornaments. She approached me asking, "My child, what are you thinking? What do you want?"

"I beseech you, give me prophecies, good or bad," I requested. She sang,

> My child, listen to my words.
> Travel from here to the highlands,
> And to the north, in an area of Do,
> You will find a field of disciples for you.
> You will even find some glorious wealth,
> And an opportunity for slight happiness.
> Apart from merely those temporary occasions,
> A time to be deeply happy
> Will not occur in this world, the Land of Jambu.
> The power of the non-Buddhist barbarians' substances, incantations,
> Deeds, and trance states has deceived everyone.
> They persist in the dealings of theft, banditry, and conquest,

In every part of the country, both outer and inner.
Great tumult, small commotions, and everything in-between erupt.
Riotous armies dispatch far-reaching arsenals.
A whirlwind of human and livestock disease rages.
Quite soon, border people will pour into the central country.
The doctrine and beings' sun of happiness becomes clouded,
Hence there is no chance for happiness.
If you strive for temporary happiness,
The place to move to is Gardé.
Take that to be the best prophecy.

Then she vanished.

THAT SAME YEAR in the last summer month, from the tenth day onward, I gave teachings in Bochung Tashul's home. During this time I wondered, "Is my homestead well?" Nöjin Shenpa Marnak, Dark Red Noxious Spirit Butcher, appeared in a dream one night. A torrent of hearts and blood rained down throughout the entire span of the sky, horizon, and earth. The clamor of "Ha Hé Kya!" entirely filled middle space. Nöjin Shenpa arrived in front of me proclaiming, "If you have something you don't know or understand, I will tell you all about it."

I asked, "Is my family well?"

He told me, "They are well. This year Palgé Tulku, Glorious Virtue [i.e., Patrul Rinpoche], is going to come again."

I said, "Ah, Palgé Tulku has passed away. He's not here."

"He passed away, and he's not here, while at the same time he will appear once again. In the last autumn month you'll meet him." Further, he told me, "My meat storehouse bank is empty. Look at this." He showed me an empty building, and inside I saw nothing apart from a dessicated and rotten limb.

"What's needed to remedy this situation?" I asked.

"This happened because you didn't give me meat."

"Learned people say that it's inappropriate to use flesh and blood as offering substances. What about that?"

"Ha ha! From Gönpo Lekden, Excellent Lord Protector, above down to the lowliest ash goblin, who isn't pleased by meat? No one! Why is that? Their minds confused by the five poisons, ordinary people's dualistic fixation leads them to practice deities as if the deity exists independent [of themselves].

It's just that way among people who take the five poisons as a given [rather than transforming them into the five wisdoms]. Therefore they crave the food of flesh and blood. They delight solely in the activity of killing: They have been installed as doctrine guardians, ready to butcher the doctrine's enemies. You should know that. After they've subdued enemies of the doctrine, they have high expectations of thanksgiving offerings. You've been born from a human attitude; we also enjoy everything of yours that's suitable to eat or drink. Therefore, it's appropriate to make these offerings." Then he vanished.

> These words the supremely powerful, utterly wrathful Nöjin Chenpo
> Explicitly explained to me are endowed with profound meaning:
> People whose minds are deeply disturbed by the five poisons
> Are attached to the substantiality of dualistically experienced
>   phenomena;
> Thus the deities they practice are worldly arrogant beings.
> Know the pure vision of basic space and wisdom nondual,
> To be the wisdom deity.
> This is a secret vital point of the philosophy of Ati.
> This teaching doesn't fit in common or conceptual minds
> Just as the tiny eye of a needle can't hold the bounds of space.
> Therefore, it is truly precious to search for meaning based on the pith
>   instructions of a lineage-bearing lama,
> To which are added unerring, firsthand inner experiences
> Connected to scriptural authority and reasoning.

Time for Your Eradication

THAT SAME YEAR, in a dream at night on the nineteenth day, an elderly monk weilding a long knife in his hand demanded of me, "What's the purpose of you coming here? I swear I'm going to kill you!" He then jumped and ran at me.

I asked, "What miraculous powers do you have?"

He said, "Is this a miraculous power?" and then flew up into the sky alongside the clouds. Again he said, "Is this one?" and then swam in a big river like a fish. Again he said, "Is this one?" and then stepped inside a red cliff. He burrowed through the rock with his iron fingernail, which stretched one span in length. In conclusion he said, "If you haven't left by tomorrow, I will kill you in the night."

I replied, "I've decided I won't go. You killing me, and being killed by god-demons who have mental forms in dreams—this is something I've never heard of." He clutched my right hand and threw his knife to the ground. Just as he was about to pierce my heart with his fingernail, I struck him in the groin and he fell on his back. His head split into four pieces. After I ate his brain, he implored, "Don't kill me and I swear I won't harm you." Then I did this visualization. I trapped his four limbs with an iron rope made of meteorite vajras; with four meteorite ritual daggers, like black mountains of wind, I nailed him to a vajra cross. I meditated that it was impossible for him to escape, and it became so.

ONCE AGAIN I went to the home of the elder Tashul to prepare consecrated vases. In a dream one night, thick black clouds billowed from the east. From within them a red man with a red horse appeared saying, "You must leave! If you don't, I'll murder you then eat your flesh, drink your blood, and gnaw your bones until there's nothing left."

"Who sent you?" I asked.

"Kalzang Dorjé, Vajra of Excellent Fortune, sent me. The reason I'm here is that this area has a cruel and wild monk who has committed major transgressions. For that reason, I'm not leaving until I've killed him." At that point he drew his arrow. [My protector] Nöjin Chenpo, Great Noxious Spirit, swung his sword, breaking the bow at its midpoint. The red man fell down and I seized him, saying, "As long as you're intent on killing me, I swear I'll kill you!" I plunged my knife into his heart, causing him to exclaim, "Ah Pa Pa! Let me go and I swear I won't harm you."

"You aren't allowed to harm my patrons either—make that promise."

"I swear I won't hurt them for a while."

Then Nöjin Chenpo proclaimed,

> Hé Hé! What descends from the home of the birds above
> Is an omen of you taking control of the gods and protectors of the one
>   who sent the curse.
> If you kill that omen, the curse will disappear without a trace,
> If you let it go, it will come around again three times.
> The time draws near when this region's community will become my
>   citizens:
> That will be truly beneficial.
> If you take control of this area
> For a while, all that is virtuous and excellent will increase.
> As the result of some flawed connections from the past,
> Some of your students will depart into basic space.
> Therefore, everyone should stay here.
> The vital instruction is to enter the enclosure of clear light.

Then he vanished.

The following night, a vulture descended on the storehouse tent, but I wasn't able to alert anyone to kill it. Other people didn't kill it either, so it went free, and the next day it came close to the door. In the end, it disappeared without anyone seeing where it went.

IN THE FIRST AUTUMN MONTH I returned to my home at Lama Rong. In the middle autumn month, I went to preside as vajra master for a great accomplishment ceremony at Zhichen Monastery. During that occasion, in a dream one night an old monk, blind in his right eye, attacked me, grabbing me from behind. "It's time for my food to come from the Zhichen family, so why did you even show up here? Tonight it's time for your eradication."

At that, I mustered my strength and prepared to stand up, but he bound me so I wasn't able to rise. He said, "Relying on what are known to be the vital points of the creation phase of Dorjé Jikjé, Vajra Fear-Inciter, and having recited one hundred million of those mantras, I've actually become Shinjé [Shé], Slayer of the Lord of Death.[15] I've taken the lives of many important lamas and monks. I'm able to do that, and you have terrible karma." As soon as he said that, I merged my mind inseparably with his consciousness. Exclaiming *Phat!* three times, I merged them with the expanse of basic space. Then I relaxed and he vanished.

Furthermore, in that area, many of the demons that manifested said they gained accomplishment in the practice of Dorjé Jikjé, Vajra Fear-Inciter. Due to Nöjin Chenpo's slaying, severing, and wrathful activity, they didn't have an opportunity to vie with me.

I TURNED FIFTY-FIVE in the Ox Year [1889]. In a dream at night on the fourth day of the third month, a black woman wearing a garment of leaves appeared singing:

> Listen to me! Individual of excellent fortune, listen!
> A fearsome ogre of the east
> Has cut the hair of the ogre of the south
> And surfaced as a savage executioner of Buddhists and Bönpos,
> Sent to gather the life force of the great [protector] ogre.
> If you are summoned to the task of turning him back,
> Exert yourself totally in meditation on your chosen deity.
> Using that vital instruction, you will prevent harm coming to you,
> And for a while, avert any harm to your patron as well.

Then she vanished.

Wealth and Livestock

IN THE FIRST AUTUMN MONTH, I received a summons from Golok, so I went there. In the year I turned fifty-six [1890], I built Kalzang Monastery on the Lidar family land.

That same year on the eighth day of the first summer month, Dakini Sangwa Yeshe, Secret Wisdom, turned her face to me, saying, "Sublime individual, your disciple Dampa will be born in the dakini country of Orgyen on the twenty-first night of the Rabbit Month. This is certain. At the end of the Rabbit Year, go to Dodé Kalpa Zangpö Tsalgyi [i.e., Kalzang] Monastery. Stay there and for a while events will unfold virtuously."

That same year on the nineteenth day of the last autumn month, Dakini Yeshe Tsogyal told me, "Next year an emanation of Glorious Chana Dorjé, Vajra-in-Hand, will take rebirth as your son." Further, she related many prophecies concerning that region and time. Then she vanished without a trace.

IN THE YEAR I TURNED FIFTY-SEVEN [1891], on the twenty-first day of the first month, my disciple Dampa passed away.

At night on the fifth day of the second month, a dakini called Zulé Men sang to me,

> Kyé Ho! Listen fortunate individual!
> I am Dakini Zulé Men,
> Come fom Tail-Fan Island.
> In the first autumn month of this year
> Some people will appear from the highlands:
> They will come to invite Palgé Tulku.
> Such envoys will twice arrive—
> Until the Sheep Year is underway
> It's not the time to enthrone him.
> The mamos and dakinis will postpone the event until then.
> Do just as the envoys request.
> Since it is of great significance, don't refuse them.

If there's any way he can be granted investiture on the throne,
He will be capable of working for the welfare of beings.
When you reach the last month of autumn,
Don't stay here. Once you've migrated with your encampment
To the highlands, it will be quite felicitous.

She said that then vanished.

ONE MORNING in the last autumn month, I went to Kalzang Monastery.
While there, on the tenth day in the last winter month, I saw a dakini called
Dorjé Garkenma, Vajra Dancer, who sang,

Kyé Ho! Fortunate child of the lineage,
To settle here in this place,
Assuage the turmoil of the earth spirit-lord.
Complete one hundred thousand Drolma, Liberating Mother, recitations
    and one hundred thousand repetitions of the "Prayer for the
    Spontaneous Fulfillment of Wishes."
Write out many prayer flags; then raise them aloft.
Repeatedly perform the "Guru Siddhi Curse Reversal" and
"Torma Reversal" formulas, over and over.
Each year, it's important to perform a Phurba, Dagger, practice
To repeatedly suppress recurring disasters.
Satisfy the agitation of the mamos and dakinis
And be diligent in confession and purification rituals: This is imperative.
The north is like a passageway for enemies.
Each year make as many sa-tsas as you can;
Futhermore, it's vital that you fill them with mantras.
If you accomplish all of that, things will be virtuous for a while.

Then she vanished.

FURTHER, DAKINI YESHE WANGDENMA, Endowed with Wisdom and Power,
told me,

At Tashi Gakyil in Mardo,
Temporarily form a Buddhist center and stay there.

As in your previous illusory dramatic enactments,
This moving of your residence is a result of auspicious connections.
Aware of that, think about the meaning [of those signs].

Then she vanished.

IN THE YEAR I TURNED FIFTY-EIGHT [1892], at night on the first day of the
first month, I saw Dakini Dorjé Zhi-gyalma, Vajra Pacifying Victor. She said,
"If you are summoned with haste, you should go straightaway without delay.
Once there, you will receive things that you need. Also, one morning in the
first summer month, when a messenger comes with a summons, you should
go where you are called. This year, the time has come for you to accumulate
wealth and livestock." Then she vanished.

In the fourth month, someone did summon me, so I travelled to the
Taktok Kabma residence. I received some offered wealth and livestock, and
returned home.

In the middle summer month, I slept at Tsachu. Once again a messenger
called me to Upper Taktok. I went there and led a great accomplishment
ceremony that lasted eight days. For another eight days I gave teachings,
after which I was offered a great deal of wealth and livestock. When I was
informed that I would be presented with the monks and the monastery [to
thereafter be my responsibility], I decided to examine my dreams. At that
time, a dakini called Yeshe Wangmo, Wisdom Queen, sang this to me:

É É! Individual of great fortune, listen to me.
If you want to rule this place,
Many [locally] powerful people will lose themselves to evil forces
And submit to being led by local ruler demons.
This place is akin to a dreamscape;
The fortress is like a bird's nest in a cliff;
The people are merely visitors at a marketplace;
Those in the guise of [yellow-robed] monks are like yellow-backed
    wolves.
I don't see any providence in living here.
Based on that meaning, keep this in mind.

Finally, she vanished into the sphere of empty sky.

After that, the monks were offered to me. I pretended to be pleased, then returned home once again.

IN A DREAM AT NIGHT on the eighth day of the tenth month, Dakini Pemé Treng-wachen, Lotus Garland, told me, "During this winter, prepare for and concentrate on a month of profound practice. Use its potency to suppress spirits that cause recurring disasters. This is important—be careful!" She went on to express in song many prophecies regarding the place and time for this. Then she vanished without a trace.

THAT SAME MONTH on the tenth day, Dakini Salkyab Wangmo, Queen of Pervasive Clarity, appeared. She immediately asked, "Do you want to go see a spectacle?" and then we flew upward together fifty fathoms into space. We reached an enormous blazing blue-green mountain. In space more than one league above its summit, radiant green light formed an immensely broad foundation, amid which loomed a vast and spacious celestial palace made of sapphire gems. Inside, on a lotus and moon seat, sat noble exalted Drolma, Liberating Mother, her body greenish-blue in color. She held a vase in her right hand and her left hand flourished a blue lotus. She was adorned with the complete regalia of the utter enjoyment body of enlightenment and sat with her legs in a queen's posture of ease amid an expanse of dense rainbows and clusters of light. Her face was exquisitely beautiful and captivating; she bore the youthfulness of an eight-year-old, utterly resplendent with rays of light. She was encircled by twenty goddesses and surrounded by an inconceivable assembly of bodhisattvas.

Seeing her, I respectfully offered prostrations and circumambulated her and then touched my head to her feet. "You are the supreme mother of all buddhas. From now on, for as long as it takes, until I attain the exalted state of omniscient buddhahood, bless me and accept me as your disciple," I beseeched her.

The exalted one spoke. "Bringing me to mind, offer praises to me and concentrate on blending my wisdom mind and your own mind." She also had me repeat these words of praise three times after her: "Om! I pay homage to noble exalted Drolma. Engendering wisdom mind in the presence of all buddhas, you became their mother," after which she made aspiration prayers. She gave me a completely white, clear crystal rosary that lay upon a green lotus, and said, "I'm giving this to you. Put it in your pocket and go." She intoned *Phat!* three times and the sound woke me from sleep.

ON THE NINTH DAY of the eleventh month, Dakini Métreng Denma, Endowed with a Flame Wreath, said, "You should enter retreat relying on the practice of Lhachen Wangchuk Chenpo, Magnificent Ruler Deity. Exerting yourself in that approach and accomplishment practice for one month, you must produce signs [of spiritual attainment]: It's deeply important to do so in order to take care of both the people and the livestock around you."

As she advised, I began a retreat relying on Lhachen, Magnificent Deity. Twenty-one days later, at night in a dreamscape, there stood a celestial palace made of masses of red light. Inside, on an immense and wide ruby throne's lotus, moon, and sun seat stood Lhachen Wangchuk Chenpo, Magnificent Ruler Deity. His body was ruby red and blazed like the fires at the end of an aeon. Endowed with a smiling peaceful and wrathful demeanor, he was encircled by his consort Umadevi, Chief Goddess, the goddesses of the four seasons, and a host of glorious protectors and arrogant spirits. When I faced him he told me, "Although you persevere in my practice and in offerings to me, since your retreat companions aren't good, right now you won't receive spiritual attainment. Later you'll gain a small bit of spiritual attainment." Then he gave me an iron hook and finally vanished without a trace.

Song of Tidings

IN THE YEAR I TURNED FIFTY-NINE [1893], at night on the first day of the first spring month, a red woman appeared, so gorgeous one could gaze at her forever and never be satisfied. Saying she was a lotus dakini of the west, she approached me and said, "I've come from Lotus Light in the west. I neither go nor stay. I appear as the dynamic expression of your sublime insight, as are all the dakinis of any land who have appeared to you and given you prophecies. As for me, the reason I've come here is this—in the past a monk named Délek, Goodness, made corrupt aspirations; with their momentum, the barbarian dogma is going to surge here like the ocean.

"There is a concealed region west of here called Pemakö: Go there this year. In Kongpo Mégya, at a place called Sengdam rises a cliff like a pig's head looking toward the heavens. Inside there you will discover a prophetic list and a key concealed as treasures. Take those and open the door to the secret site, and you'll be able to open the gateway to sixty-nine valleys: It's certain this will be of immense aid to beings. It's unacceptable to let the apt time frame of this year pass by. Put all your attention to this project."

> Hé! From the Wood Sheep Year onward,
> People will go insane from poisoned water.
> Lapses of memory, accidents, and the five poisons will blaze like fire.
> Mountains, valleys, and all around
> Will be rife with bandits and thieves craving action.
> Outer pandemonium, inner turmoil, and conflict will spread;
> Virtuous conduct will be gradually overshadowed.
> Many people and horses will be stabbed to death.
> A range of undetermined diseases will spread.
> The arrogant demigods will cause harm as demons.
> At this point, since there is no opportunity for happiness,
> Make haste—go swiftly to that place.

She sang this, then vanished.

THAT SAME YEAR, at night on the tenth day of the first summer month, my student Ngawang Gyatso appeared adorned with the complete regalia of the utter enjoyment body of enlightenment. From the expanse of intermingled clouds and rainbows, he prostrated to me, saying:

> Namo! Homage! Precious Lama, lord of refuge,
> Having reached the consummation of my life,
> At the edge of fifty-two I passed on:
> I've manifested in Manifest Joy Pure Land.
> All of your karmically destined disciples
> Should utilize the united path of Cutting Through and Direct Crossing.
> Of these karmically destined ones, courageous in practice,
> Some will gain liberation in the supreme rainbow body
> And some will gain liberation in the illusory wisdom [body].
> This year in the middle winter month
> My best friend, Puntsok Tashi,
> Will pass on to the concealed region of Pemakö.
> Taking the form of a magnificent spiritual hero,
> He will serve as the master of a vajra feast of an assembled retinue of a
>   hundred thousand.
> Your disciple Rikzin Gyatso, as well,
> Having arrived at that place will become a spiritual hero.
> We've reached the ground of eternal happiness,
> And I offer you this sweet song.
> May the lama's life be stable!

Then he vanished.

ON THE THIRTEENTH DAY of the first autumn month, my young son Lhatob went to a large monastic community named Taktsé Samdrub Monastery, which upholds the tradition of Pal Gyalwa Katok [Monastery]. He was recognized as a reincarnation of the incomparable Zhichen Tulku Rinpoche and enthroned on a tall golden throne.

When that concluded, I returned home and bestowed, to their completion, many empowerments and scriptural transmissions upon those students of mine who were foretold of in the scriptures of Pema [Guru Rinpoche].

THAT SAME YEAR, at night on the tenth day of the last autumn month, a dakini called Déjé Wangmo, Queen Creator of Bliss, appeared adorned with jewels. She approached me and sang this:

> The time frame for opening the door to the concealed region [of
>   Pemakö] has slipped away.
> Now teach the path of supreme transference
> To your male and female students.
> From the Karmin Kar, Non-White White, group
> Three individuals will accomplish rainbow body.
> From the Gyamin Gya, Non-Chinese Chinese, group
> Two individuals will accomplish supreme transference.
> From the Lamin La, Spiritless Spirit, group
> Three individuals will accomplish rainbow body.
> From the Takmin Tak, Non-Tiger Tiger, group
> Two individuals will accomplish rainbow body.
> From the Tamin Ta, Non-Horse Horse, group
> Five individuals will accomplish rainbow body.
> From the Ahmin Ah, Ah-less Ah, group
> Three individuals will accomplish rainbow body.
> From the Tongmin Tong, Non-Empty Empty, group
> One individual will accomplish rainbow body.
> From the Tukmin Tuk, Shitless Shit, group
> One individual will accomplish rainbow body.
> From the Gémin Gé, Gé-less Gé group
> Four individuals will accomplish rainbow body.
> From the Wangmin Wang, Powerless Power, group
> Two individuals will accomplish rainbow body.
>
> Regarding these and others among your students,
> If they cultivate their experience in the sacred instructions of supreme
>   transference
> In places isolated from the domain of the eight worldly concerns,
> And they surrender wholeheartedly to this essential practice,
> One hundred male and female disciples
> Will surely attain the rainbow body of supreme transference.

How amazing, in this degenerate time,
That in your presence
People are diligent in the teachings and practices
Of the supreme doctrine of Orgyen's wisdom mind.
With great wonderment,
I offer to you this song of tidings.

Then she vanished.

THAT SAME YEAR at night on the twenty-fifth day of the middle winter month, I saw the face of the exalted Jikten Wangchuk, World Sovereign [i.e., Chenrézi]. He said to me, "My child, some spiritual mentors have appeared who criticize and defame your view and meditation, and do what they can to lead people to the lower spiritual approaches. They have become the servants of demons. Give up being angry at them and develop strong compassion!"

Listen to me, sublime being with outstanding fortune.
As for clear light Great Perfection,
Those with lesser fortune don't have the providence to receive this
And lob complaints instead. Do you understand that, my child?
All sentient beings are empowered to partake
Of Great Perfection, Secret Mantra's supreme spiritual approach:
Everything is impartially there, already complete within them.
All individuals who encounter that doctrine and its teacher
Are empowered to partake of it.
Failing to recognize that, some people are blind—
They turn away from that path, and are led downward.
Their nonsense prattle
Contradicts and harms the doctrine of the great spiritual approach.
They serve demons and a misguided path:
Give up attachment and anger toward those sentient beings
Deceived by their bad karma. Uphold your own doctrine.
The sun's face of the supreme spiritual-approach doctrine
Is close to setting: This is the border between twilight and darkness.
Know this to be so! Nurture your disciples.

He said this, then vanished.

THAT SAME YEAR at night on the eighth day in the last winter month, Dakini Labdrön, Lamp of Lab, approached me. She sang,

> Kyé! My child, listen to what your mother has to say!
> The conch arrow, shot westward,
> Landed at the gateway of Pemakö.
> Some people with foul aspirations
> Used turmoil, robbery, conquest, and dispute
> To make the lake of poison boil,
> And the white conch arrow sank there.
> Now for a while you have neither the power nor fortune
> To reach that place.
>
> Black doves, emanations of demons of defeat,
> Call forth in their own language,
> And the actions of many who share the same attitude
> Topple the white snow lion of the glacier peaks.
> The force of its fierce roar
> Makes the jewel on the naga king's crown rise up,
> Such that the boiling poison lake surges to the heavens.
> The naga demon armies, setting out for the highlands [of central
>   Tibet],
> Will force four parts of the doctrine's lamp to wane.
> The breath of the poisonous black snakes
> Erases the potency of healing medicine.
> The spread of barbarian infernos
> Incinerates the doctrine's fields of felicity.
> Now there is no opportunity for happiness.
>
> Urgently devote yourself to the essential practices
> At a site isolated from the eight worldly concerns.
> My child, teach the supreme sacred instructions!
> When some fortunate students appear,
> Connected to you through previous aspirations and karma,
> Grant them their inheritance of the profound, holy pith instructions.
> Although you won't live much longer,

Your life span is as much as there is to the authentic doctrine of Great
   Perfection.
Know that!
Do you understand those symbols, fortunate child?

Then she vanished.

In the year I turned sixty [1894], at night on the fourth day of the first
month, a girl called Dakini Töpé Treng-denma, Skull-Garlanded Maiden,
appeared, greenish-blue in color, wearing a striped yellow silk blouse. She
told me, "From the pure land of the central direction, Spontaneously Present
Array, Lama Jikmé tells you, 'Come here!' Do you want to go?"

When I answered, "Let's go," she held my left hand. We went up into the
eastern sky and immediately arrived at the grove of a beautiful and captivating pure land. A spacious house made of lapis gems stood there, within which
stood a jeweled throne. Upon its lotus and moon seat sat the lama himself,
sitting there as if really present. I offered prostrations, touched my head [to
his feet], and then implored of him, "Grant me profound, supreme empowerment."

The lama conferred upon me the supreme empowerment of the dynamic
expression of awareness. "My child, the nature of mind is pure from the beginning. Make apparent the basic space of pure space and settle in that indwelling state without contriving, marring, adopting or abandoning anything at
all. Develop stability in that." Then he vanished without a trace.

Armies and Major Turmoil

IN A DREAM AT NIGHT on the eighth day of the last winter month, an old man saying he was Menpa Tsojé Zhonnu, Doctor Revitalizing Youth appeared. He had white hair and eyebrows, his face was filled with wrinkles, and he carried a cane. He told me, "This year you've been in a house. You should certainly spend next year in a black yak-hair tent. If you're wondering, 'Will there be a monastery here?' you'll need a retreat space to give teachings and practice meditation. Apart from that, there is scant necessity for a monastic community and something that can be labeled 'monastery.' Although you will have some additional measure of danger from spiteful enemies and thieves, which you don't have with a monastic institution, by the same token, these days we've reached the culmination of the five-hundred-year period of degeneration, so enemies, robbers, and bandits are quite plentiful anyway. As a remedy for that, persist in both the practices of Ngaksung, Mantra Protectress Ekazati, and "The Poisonous Razor of Za Dü, Planetary Lord Demon". Even if you accomplish these, you must still continuously persevere in making fulfillment offerings and petitions. When enemies appear, it's very important to dispatch and invoke those protectors.

"These days, lamas and monks aren't even able to do a month of sealed retreat. They only repeat their daily prayers. There may be some people who perform recitation practice, but it's impossible to accomplish the deity by that alone. Further, as they lose conviction in the deity, and corrupt views toward the text outlining the means of accomplishment arise, they aren't aware that lack of success is their own fault. They pass the blame to others. I think such people are pitiful!

"In the past all of you had power. Now you have none. That is your own karmic retribution returning to you. How astounding that you don't understand that!" he said, sending shame my way.

I responded, "Old man, what are you saying? If this isn't something from the deities, but something I caused, what have I done? If you know, then tell me! If you don't know, what meaning is there in an old man talking a lot?"

"Oh yes, yes! My ample discourse is not aimed at you and [your patron] Tashul in particular. It pertains to the monasteries of this land in general. You don't like it, but what comes to you is not the deities' fault. If you were to ask, how is this your responsibility? When you forcefully dispatched and invoked your deities, when you showed signs of power to your enemies, and when your livestock were returned to you, you happily took them back and enjoyed them. This aggravated the protectors and made it impossible for them carry out their tasks. You lamas and monks of this evil era all have tremendous desire and clinging toward food and wealth. By acting as described, the fierce protectors in the end become infuriated and punish practitioners. It's impossible to retain your powers. Serves you right!"

I replied, "You could be right. I've also thought about things from that perspective. I heard it said that you've become an eminent doctor. These days doctors don't recognize illness and can't really help. Why is that?"

He answered, "Ha ha! In this evil era, during the time of degeneration, comparing the grass of previous excellent aeons to today's six fantastic herbs, the grass of the past had more potency. Comparing the water of the past and the milk of the present, of these two, the water of the past is superior in taste and potency. Likewise, medicine these days doesn't have any effect on sickness. In addition, due to weak efforts, doctors aren't skilled in medical examinations. Also, sicknesses of the past and the present aren't the same. That's why they don't recognize them.

"As for what's been explained by this old man and your unnecessary question, what's the point of asking?"

"I wonder, if I trained in medical examination, could I learn it?"

He told me, "The first part of your life is over and you're at life's tail end. At this time, with merely the moment of the sun peeking between the clouds left to you, even if you trained in medical examination I don't see that you have the time to help either yourself or others." Then he vanished.

IT WAS THE YEAR I TURNED SIXTY-ONE [1895]. From when I was eight years old until I passed my thirtieth year, there was a young child, white in color wearing a white cape, who was always with me in my dreams at night as an inseparable companion. One night at the end of my thirty-third year, he told me, "Well, now you have some slight understanding of the view. Know that that is due to my kindness. I am a child of the gods, Dungi Nawachen, Conch Ears. I was sent as your companion by the utmost exalted Bodhisattva Tukjé Chenpo, Supreme Compassion. We won't meet one another again for some time." Then he vanished.

He appeared that night [when I was sixty-one] and told me, "These days all the qualities of glory and renown have come together for you. I'm happy about that.

"In the second summer month you should set up a yak-hair tent. Live in that tent. What you need for tent-living can be acquired quite easily. Further, you can go anywhere you want without any hardship."

"They say they're going to build a great assembly hall at this monastery. If that's true, I think it would be best if I stayed here."

He replied, "If they build it this year, it will seem like they try and try, but it won't happen. It won't come to fruition for some time.

"Next year there will be reason for you to go to Dzagyal Monastery. I think that armies and major turmoil will come close to this area, although there won't be formidable problems right here."

> É É! Listen to me, your friend
> Who has been with you since you were small.
> All apparent existence, the environment and inhabitants,
> Is a city of illusory dreams—
> There is nothing steadfast. Do you understand?
> All composite phenomena
> Are self-manifest delusory appearances
> That change within themselves. Do you understand?
> Everything you seek out and accumulate
> Is like a child's pointless game.
> Do you understand?
> For the sake of child and wife
> You persist, your whole life long, in negative acts,
> Though each individual bears their own karma's ripening. Do you
>   understand?
> You vainly think you will enjoy your region, home,
> Food, and wealth forever,
> Yet, like waking from a dream,
> Nothing permanently endures. Do you understand?
> Elderly people at the end of their lives
> Prepare to stay around forever
> Although they have no time left to live. Do you understand?
> As for all the tasks you've done and do,

You're always busy and never satisfied,
Yet your work is never finished.
Are you aware that you must leave [this life]?
If there is someone who practices
The methods for liberation from this cyclic existence,
Their life is meaningful. Do you understand?
You accumulate so much virtuous conduct,
With a mouth and hands that have no leisure,
Yet you only add to cyclic existence. Do you understand?
Your own basis of being is Kuntuzangpo, Ever-Excellent—
Panoramic space, free from elaboration.
You must hold to that within yourself. Do you understand?
Once you've grasped this directly within yourself,
You will gain full mastery of the nature of reality,
The holy doctrine. Do you understand?
Apart from the appearances of the basis of being becoming apparent
As the multitude of pure phenomena around you,
There are no pure lands. Do you understand?
To render present the inexpressible, inconceivable nature of reality
Is the utmost summit of all spiritual approaches. Do you understand?
If you understand this, within the state of inactivity,
Turn your attention to the basic space of spontaneous presence—
The aeon of impure karmic [embodiment]
Will shift to the pristine essence of pure basic space.
When it has shifted to the pristine essence of pure basic space,
You will attain manifest, complete buddhahood
As the body of ultimate enlightenment, free from elaboration or extremes.

I'm going to Potala,
I'm going without turning back:
Letting go in the expansive evenness of the indwelling state
Free from going and any place to go.

Then he vanished.

IN THE FIRST AUTUMN MONTH our tent encampment moved to Dzagyal Monastery. I was greeted there by a procession of monks playing musical instruments and then [my son] Palgé Tulku was granted investiture on the throne. I gave teachings from the middle winter month until the middle spring month. At the latter part of the middle spring month, we moved our tent encampment once again, to a valley called Tri-barma.

IN THE YEAR I TURNED SIXTY-TWO [1897], in a dream at night on the eighth day of the fourth month, a girl told me, "I am called Zangpo Kyongma, Excellent Guardian. Do you want to go see the spectacle inside Drong Purple Mountain in Upper Ser?"

I responded, "If it's just a mountain, then there must not be anything to see, right?"

She said, "Outside it's a mountain, but it holds a large province inside."

"There isn't room inside that small mountain to fit a big area."

"The large province of a dreamscape and a city of nonhumans are comparable."

Considering that to be true, I went along with her. When we reached the base of the mountain, I couldn't see a mountain at all. There loomed an immense fortress with a peak that soared into space. Its cornices were made of gold; the middle section was forged from molten bronze; and the lower section and foundation were rendered from turquoise. When we went inside, it was actually a five-story building.

Inconceivable hordes of mamos, flesh eaters, zombies, and goblins thronged in that place. I asked, "What are you all doing gathered here?"

A black man with a beard on the right and left sides of his face said, "We are the legion of Drong Purple Mountain servants."

When we entered the second story it was crowded with a lama on a large throne surrounded by crowds of monks, Mönpas, and scholars. I asked, "Who are all of you?"

"We are the groups that make offerings to the lama."

When we entered the third story it was filled with many structures of meat. Inside them stood a dark blue man with a red beard, a dark red man with a black beard and eyebrows, and a yellow man with a red beard and eyebrows. The trio was hacking at meat with axes; I asked, "Who are you?"

The yellow man said, "We are the custodians of the local spirit's meat."

When we entered the fourth story, scores of doorways stood around in every direction. At the center of the room, upon a tiered throne of various silk brocades, was a blue-green woman resplendent with light. She was adorned with myriad silks and a complete array of jewel ornaments. Many beautiful young maidens were serving her.

I asked, "Who are all of you?"

One girl answered, "I am Yu Chamma, Turquoise Wife, daughter of Shar-nyenpo Yu-tsé, and queen consort of Palden Drak Lhagön, Glorious Cliff Lord Deity, who is none other than the chief of the earth's mighty foundation and the lord of humanity—the exalted sublime bodhisattva Tukjé Chenpo, Supreme Compassion. I am an emanation of Exalted Tro Nyérma, Great Wrathful Frown."

When we entered the fifth story, a blue silk tent hovered in an expanse of dense clouds, mist, and rainbows. At its center stood a jeweled golden throne with brocade cushions stacked high, upon which sat a maroon man with a haughty demeanor, wearing a white silk turban and red and blue silk clothing. The entourage gathered around him was completely indescribable. The man said to me, "Oh! Aren't you Kyé-u Chung Lotsawa?"

I said yes, and he replied, "Have a seat and let's talk." Then Gélek Rabten, Supremely Stable Felicitous Virtue, laid out a cushion and a silk brocade seat for me. The great man told me, "Sit here for a while." Once I sat down he said, "It's said that you're a treasure revealer. Is that so?"

"Yes, that's true."

"Have you seen a lot of deities and received many prophecies or not?"

I replied, "From the start, since my mother bore me, I have witnessed awareness holders, spiritual heroes, and dakinis. All of them gave me prophecies beyond measure. In particular, since I was accepted as a disciple by Supreme Orgyen [Guru Rinpoche], I've never experienced even a moment's separation from him. When I encountered Sangyé Ö Pakmé, Buddha Inifinite Light, in Great Bliss, the western pure land, I received the empowerment and scriptural transmission for the text outlining the means of accomplishment related to Great Bliss Pure Land. In that same fashion, when I met Sangyé Mengyila, Medicine Buddha, he gave me his means of accomplishment. When I encountered Dorjé Chang, Vajra Bearer, he gave me sacred pith instructions. When I encountered the eight awareness holders, they gave me the empowerments and scriptural transmissions for the eight classes of accomplishment. When I met Zurpoché Shakya Jungné and Zurchung Shérab Drakpé, they gave me Great Perfection teaching cycles. I met Longchen Rabjam three times and he bestowed upon me the complete view and meditation of Great Perfection.

"Pachik Dampa Gyagar [Padampa Sangyé], Sole Father of Holy India, advised me precisely regarding the meaning of the key points of the view of emptiness. When I met Machik Labdrön, Sole Mother Lamp of Lab, she gave me the profound sacred instructions of Severance of Evil Forces. When I encountered Jampal Yang, Gentle Splendor Melody, he gave me the empowerment and scriptural transmission for "Gentle Splendor Matrix of Mystery". When I met Chenrézi, All-Seeing Eyes, he gave me the empowerment and scriptural transmission of his means of accomplishment, as well as that of Lhachen Mahadeva. When I encountered Sangdak Chana Dorjé, Lord of Secrets Vajra-in-Hand, he gave me the complete empowerments and scriptural transmissions of the Lord of Secret's own means of accomplishment, as well as those of Nöjin Marnak, Dark Red Noxious Spirit; Za, Planetary Lord; Tsen, Sorcerer; and Damchen Dorjé Lekpa, Doctrine Guardian Vajra of Excellence. When I met Jampal Mawé Sengé, Gentle Splendor Lion of Speech, he gave me the profound instructions of Supreme Transference. Furthermore, how many times I've seen and received prophecies from deities, lamas, yidams, mantra protectors, and mamos is countless: There is no limit to what I could relate.

"As for the present outer turmoil, I think it will be very difficult to turn back the rain of blood. What's going to happen in Sertal?"

"That son of mine keeps very honest law, so there won't be any grave danger in that region," he said.

"Is there going to be major unrest?" I asked.

"I don't have to explain. It's easy to understand [that it's going to be very bad]. Holy individual, I have this offering for you." He gave me a single stone box. "I'm giving you a gem from Shar-nyenpo Yu-tsé. This treasure comes from the Chinese [Pacific] Ocean. It was given to me as a gift by Lumo Rinchen, Jewel Naga Goddess, Princess of Dzamling Wangmo, Queen of the Land of Jambu. Venerate it! If your family line doesn't leave this area of Serlung, in the future and long term, virtuous and favorable conditions will always be theirs. Before long, without delay, return to your homeland. The army's combat will block the way."

Then the woman from before said, "It's time to go." It felt like she was blowing on my face, which caused me to wake up. It was dawn.

CLOSE TO THE END of the first spring month I prepared to return home. After setting off on the journey, I arrived in the latter part of the middle summer month. In the last summer month, when omens of an impending major battle emerged, all the other common folk said, "We must escape!" As I considered that we probably needed to take up our encampment [and move], I saw the noble exalted Drolma, Liberating Mother. She assured me, "My child, you don't need to escape this year. There won't be any danger from a human army. An army of wicked murderous spirits will materialize as a miraculous manifestation of the barbarian border people. Even if you try to escape from them, you won't manage to." Then she vanished without a trace.

IN A DREAM AT NIGHT on the eighteenth day of the first autumn month, I saw crowds of Chinese people covering the earth. Someone called Damtsik Lhamo Pramoha [one of the eight mamos of the sacred sites] came from a gap in space saying this:

> This evil contingent of the Chinese army
> Is led by demons of corrupt aspirations.
> For that, persevere in the means to get yourself through this:
> Perform the meditation and recitation practice of Sengdongma, Lion-
>   Faced Dakini,
> Constantly perform reversal rituals,
> And enter a month-long retreat on the meditation of Wangchuk
>   Chenpo, Magnificent Ruler Deity.

Then she vanished.

New Flower of Her Praise

IN A DREAM AT NIGHT on the fifteenth day of the last winter month, Dakini Yeshe Tsogyal appeared in an expanse of dense clouds and rainbows, only revealing the upper part of her body. She sang,

> Kyé! Listen, my child, and I will give you profound advice in a few
>   words.
> Composing your life story
> Is consistent with the tradition of victors past.
> For the sake of your excellent, fortunate disciples,
> Don't procrastinate! Quickly finish it!
> Let Gyalsé Zhenpen Tayé, Victors' Heir of Infinite Benefit to Others,
> And Réchung Dorjé Drakpa, Young Cotton-Clad One of
>   Vajra Renown,
> Correct any faults in your writing.
> Now, because of nonsensical chatter and mental befuddlement,
> Look at how your body and mind are all tangled up!

When she said this, I responded, "Gyalsé Zhenpen Tayé already advanced to the pure lands and Réchung Dorjé Drakpa has done the same. They're unavailable, so what are you talking about?"

> Hé Go Na! Gyalsé Zhenpen Tayé [has taken rebirth]
> As Dong-rik Lungtok Gyatso, Ocean of Scripture and Realization of the
>   Dong Clan:
> If he doesn't repeatedly apply himself to longevity practice,
> He'll not live for long and will instead set out for basic space.
> Réchung Dorjé Drakpa [has taken rebirth]
> As Dong-rik Kyenrab Gyatso, Ocean of Omniscience of the Dong Clan.
> If he doesn't keep to unfixed mountain locales,
> He won't have the fortune to live very long.
> Therefore, don't put this off any longer:
> Make haste to write your life story and bring it to completion!

Regarding the significance of events that will soon transpire,
A poisonous tree will ripen on iron,
The stirring of the wind of circumstances
Will lead to the takeover of many passes and valleys.
The force of a vicious demonic official's corrupt aspirations,
Accompanied by a trio of black owls,
Will draw together the armies of western owls
That rend the poisonous tree with an ax.
A tempest's gale
Will press it under a black cloth.
It will be twice stirred by the upper wind.
Since hordes of southwestern demons
Were resurrected by evil vow-violation spirits,
Their minds became inflamed with cruel jealousy.
Due to this, a widespread arsenal will disseminate,
And flowers of human heads will be twice scattered.

Flocks of borderland birds will invade the central parts of the country.
The birds of those central areas will be thrown into suffering.
The movement of the iron wind
Will shear the braids of Naga King Jokpo,
And the turbulence from the depths of the ocean
Will throw waves in every direction.
Wind will rock the trees; the trees will shake each other,
And in all regions of Tibet
The acute pain of misery will rear up in myriad ways.
Although meteorite lightning arrows won't fall
Upon the hub of the central regions' land,
The roar of thunder will make your lungs and heart quiver.

In the eastern city of wicked birds,
A torrent of blood will fall three times.
It will become wretched to stay there,
So all the tiny multicolored birds in that area will flee in every direction.
As for those lesser birds in the place of garudas,
Have you not witnessed their garuda cries resound?
The eastern ogre city

Will invite messengers
Aligned with the red-spark vow-violation spirits.
Grabbing after resources and wealth,
They will defeat and annihilate themselves in the end.
Flocks of birds that are humans with animal faces
Flying on the garuda's wings
Will assail the central land
Together with the hordes of ghouls of Supreme Mountain's summit.
Even life-sustaining medicines will become poison.
Various new forms of behavior will spread.
Power, influence, and wealth will be sold to others.
Birds of the forest will escape northward.
Northern flocks of birds will stay in the forests and mountains.
All the arrogant guardians of the doctrine
Turn their faces to [Chana Dorjé's] Willow Pure Land:
The status of beneficent and happy beings will be degraded.
All mamos and dakinis
Will turn their affection towards Supreme Mountain,
And look with hateful eyes at the doctrine and beings.
The profound lineages of the oceanic classes of sutra, mantra, and
    tantra
Will be severed by poisonous vapors.
That, as well, will be the magical emanation of demons of corrupt
    aspirations.
During this time of havoc, these arsenals of weapons
Are the magical projection of malevolent demons, black defeating
    demons,
And the noxious spirit Gömaka.
The red-spark vow-violation spirits,
Male demons, and black rokti demons
Will collect beings' flesh, blood, and life-breath.
Since this evil era smothers everything,
They will strike many times. Do you understand?
Do you understand these symbols or not?

Your mother sets off for unmanifest basic space.
As for those individuals who keep their tantric commitments,

If they desire lasting happiness,
They must cast away worldly activity
And practice Buddhism in isolated mountain retreats in unfixed places.
There's no defeat or fault in that.
In the sun of blazing, pervasive clarity,
The mamos and dakinis will inspire their minds,
And the wisdom deities will reveal their faces within.

From the Celestial Enjoyment Pure Land,
I have come to visit your homeland.
In supreme indivisibility with me,
Depart for the land of Spontaneously Present Array.

Having spoken, she stroked my head and vanished without a trace.

In that way, as she advised me, and in response to my faithful disciples, I undertook the hardship of composing my own story in words. Sometimes, due to teaching the doctrine and so forth, it was delayed by other tasks, but just as the dakini advised, I've completed it quickly. While ending with such a meager account isn't proper, I've forgotten most things and I didn't write down events for which I couldn't recall the year, month, and day. I've gathered here only the rough outlines of what I consider to be important. That's what I think.

Colophon and Concluding Verses

AT A TIME BYGONE, in the Male Earth Bird Year [1888], my disciple Lama Tsé-chu, a holy, sublime individual who was prophesied in the texts, requested [the composition of my life story] and offered me a silk scarf, an exceptional drum for Severance practice beautifully inlaid with jewels, and a pair of human thighbone trumpets endowed with all the proper characteristics.

Jampal, a disciple endowed with unwavering faith, also gave me a lion-patterned banner for the drum, a multicolored cloth with a glorious knot emblem, turquoise, and coral, all of which he accompanied by insistent requests for this text.

After that, many fortunate vajra-brother and -sister disciples from Lama Rong in Serjong together offered me many material gifts, including silver, brocade, and bricks of tea. They accompanied their requests for this text with a monumental offering of spiritual practice, each according to his or her ability: Some pledged for the rest of their lives to live without worldly work and to stay in isolated places, while others promised to give themselves over to meditation practice for thirteen years, eighteen years, and so forth. In response, I began to write.

Recently, numerous students have yet again repeatedly requested this of me. Thus, I, Dudjom Dorjé, composed this text. Kyenrab Gyatso, Gélek Palzang, and others completed the scribe work. The reincarnation of Kéwang, Powerful Learned One, called Pema Lungtok Gyatso, carried out the superlative editing.

May this work long remain, flourishing and spreading throughout all times, directions, and circumstances!

> Within the supreme, stainless, unchanging basic space of awareness,
> He holds the treasure of a spontaneously perfect ocean of qualities.
> This masterful adept, vanquisher of every demon's attack,
> Is the glorious vajra-accomplished master, our eternal refuge.
>
> The nature of his amazing life story,
> Until he reached sixty, with two years added,

Is a clear presentation of the acts of his wisdom body, speech, and mind
That will bring to spiritual maturity and liberation anyone who sees,
    hears, or recalls it.
The keeper of secrets, Chief Dakini Tsogyalma,
Made an excellent offering of this new flower of her praise to him
Along with her request. In later times it will surely prove to be of great
    benefit for beings and the doctrine.
This her vajra words foretold.

As for accounts of nonvirtuous acts to defeat enemies and protect dear
    ones,
And activities of uncertain value, such as moving, sitting, doing, and
    toiling:
To undertake the hardship of writing those things down
Is commonly exaggerated as a life story. This composition and those
    ordinary ones are not comparable.
Innumerable exalted deities accepted him as their own.
The sweeping expanse of his realization, born from meditation,
    naturally overflowed.
He impartially spread the nectar of his profound treasure teachings
And was adept in myriad teaching methods. He demonstrated this in
    these writings.

Should anyone not beholden to anguished demons
Examine this life story even briefly,
With a spirit of total impartial honesty,
They will think it praiseworthy and amazing. How can it be seen
    otherwise?

In the final analysis, he is the primordial emanation of the compassion
Of the Original Victor, the array of his enlightened qualities,
Of one taste with the wisdom body, speech, and mind of all buddhas.
His life can only truly be seen by omniscient beings.
Therefore, although this is a finished composition,
It's like a drop of water taken from a massive sea.
He bestowed this fraction of his insight
According to the mental capacity of his present ordinary students.

Those whose minds are greatly stirred by the winds of jealousy,
Whose eyes and intellects are veiled by cataracts of bias,
Will feel acute distress on reading this life story.
Although they vainly consider themselves learned, their own karma is
   to blame for their lowly state.

Looking back on what has been written here, it did not come from
Mundane body, speech, and mind. It has many exceptionally exalted
   qualities:
Even the words used are not mere conceptual creations, ornaments of
   literary language;
They welled forth from the strength of his individual innate awareness.

Those victors abiding in the pure lands in the infinite ten directions, and
   their spiritual heirs,
The hosts of the three regions' spiritual heroes and dakinis,
And the deities and ocean of accomplished awareness holders
Showed him their delighted smiling faces. Who can falsely contradict
   that?

Ocean of doctrine guardians—carry out your assigned duties
Regarding this extremely secret life story:
Conceal it from those ill-fated with corrupt views,
And spread it among assemblies of fortunate individuals.

What store of good there is in this undertaking
Will pacify times of decline, including periods of disease, famine, and
   warfare
Everywhere on this wide earth!
May we be forever nurtured by happiness and glory.

May the strength of those supreme awareness-holding lamas' altruistic
   resolve,
The unhindered wealth of others and myself,
And the general and supremely secret profound Buddhist doctrine
Spread and flourish at all times and in all directions!

> May the supreme spiritual approach, beyond small-minded attitudes of
> doing and striving,
> Lead all sentient beings without exception to swift attainment of the
> magnificent state
> Of the Original Lord Protector—
> May the city of cyclic existence's deluded phenomena be emptied!

Thus, the universal embodiment in which all victors converge, the supreme treasure revealer and Buddhist king—his name, though difficult to utter, yet spoken for this purpose, is Rikzin Dudjom Dorjé Drolö Tsal. This account of his life until he reached sixty-two years constitutes an oral composition transcribed in his presence.

As for these concluding verses, Dudjom Lingpa gave his permission for their composition and my vajra brother who honors the tantric commitments, Kyenrab Gyatso, asked me to write them. In the knowledge that such a request was due to Terchen Rinpoche's own supreme loving-kindness in accepting me as his disciple, I placed the dust of his feet on the crown of my head with steadfast, unwavering faith and composed these lines. Signed, the individual who vainly considers himself slightly trained in the treatises of both the New and Ancient Schools, known by the name of the man of only three concerns [eating, sleeping, and defecating] Pema Lungtok Gyatso, or by another name, Lozang Tenpé Gyaltsen, Brilliant Mind Victory Banner of the Doctrine.

May all be entirely virtuous!

Printing Dedication

Om Swasti Siddam!

Infinite lord Pema Déwaché, Lotus of Supreme Bliss,
In the form of the executioner of those difficult to tame, crazy
    Drowolö—
You have intentionally taken rebirth, posing as a treasure revealer,
Vanquishing every kind of ruthless demon. In you I have utmost faith.

Whatever stories there are of your wondrous style of magical illusion,
Their unfathomable vastness can't be measured by immature minds.
At the request of a few karmically endowed disciples, with great loving
    compassion
You extracted this [life story] from the excellent vase of vajra songs.

Your revelation of definitively true, secret subjects destroys clinging to
    existence and peace as real.
Your great lion roar of fearlessness has resounded completely,
Intimidating lesser minds and placing those of sharp acumen in the
    state of highest joy.
In this time of conflict, you considered taking form

As the representative of the doctrine of Buddha Ever-Excellent's wisdom
    mind—
Your immediate and supreme reincarnation, Yeshe Dorjé [His Holiness
    Dudjom Rinpoche],
Requested this polished, impeccable doctrinal gift,
A text finely printed, intended to be cherished by open-minded
    disciples.

By this virtue, may the lotus feet of the glorious lamas and their spiritual
    heirs
Always be stable and may their activities extend to the ends of space.

May the flawless tradition of Ati Great Perfection, the victorious summit
    of the nine levels of practice,
Pervade the scope of all directions.

May all on the path of the contemplative practice of space, in which
    dualistic fixation is self-liberated,
Who see, hear, or recall this life story
Decisively leave the contaminated aggregates [of the body] in this very
    lifetime and depart as the rainbow body.
May the depths of cyclic existence be emptied, and may auspiousness
    and glory blaze!

To fulfill the wishes of the patrons [of this edition], including Namgyal
Palmo, Victorious Glorious Goddess, who made a connection through her
outstanding activity, I have accepted the sovereign of the wheel [of great
bliss at the crown of my head], Jikdral Yeshe Dorjé's, precious command [to
compose this dedication prayer]. I, Kusali Sangyé Dorjé [Chatral Rinpoche,]
wrote this with positive intentions and aspirations. Siddhi Rastu.

The Secret Autobiographies

A Clear Mirror

An Account of Supremely Secret Meditative Experiences

*From the Cycle of Treasures called Wisdom's
Infinite Matrix of Pure Phenomena*

Details of My Lifetimes

É Ma Ho! Wondrous! The primordially pure body of ultimate
    enlightenment is free from limiting formulations,
The utter enjoyment body displays spontaneously present bodies and
    wisdoms,
Compassion's natural radiance that tames beings is manifest—
Lotus King, in whom these three bodies are spontaneously present,
    shelter me!

In my past life as the adept Nüden Dorjé, I prayed,
"During the doctrinal era of the thousand buddhas of this fortunate
    aeon
May I continuously nurture disciples
With one billion of my own emanations."

I thus voiced my resolve. By the force of that pure aspiration,
One of those emanations arose specifically as me in this life.
When I reached forty years of age in the Dog Year,
At night on the twenty-fifth day of the first summer month,
In the appearing aspect of mingled sleep and clear light,
Ekazati, the empress of basic space,
Appeared from the wide-open expanse of all-encompassing space
Within a dense canopy of rainbow light.
She flaunted her face, blazing brilliant as the sun,
And said this with intense love and affection:

"Kyé Ho! Sublime individual, Dudjom Lingpa,
Before this life of yours,
What exactly was your succession of births?
If you remember, present it in song,
As it is of great significance to me."

So speaking, she stayed before me in a respectful manner.

In response, I sang this as I recalled my previous births,

> Kyé Ho! Wisdom dakini, listen to me!
> In a former life as the adept Nüden,
> To the thousand buddhas of this fortunate aeon
> I bestowed empowerments, gave names, and foretold their
>   enlightenment.
> In that lifetime I was Dorjé Chang, [Buddha] Vajra Bearer incarnate.
> By the force of my resolve and aspiration,
> Hundreds of my emanations appeared
> One after the next, at the beginning, the end, and in between:
>
> In the presence of Shakyamuni Buddha, I was Shariputra,
> Who maintained the manner of a hearer and fostered disciples.
> Anyone connected to me was established on the path of freedom.
>
> After that, at Drakmar Cliff, which sheltered birds,
> I was Supreme Hungkara,
> Who hoisted the banner of the doctrine of Secret Mantra.
>
> Heedful of disciples in the land of Tibet,
> I emanated as Drokben Khyé-u Lotsawa.
> Those connected to me were placed at the stage of everlasting happiness.
>
> Once again, the time was propitious to help beings.
> As the accomplished adept of Drum, called Karnak,
> I unlocked the portal of profound treasures and nurtured disciples.
> Anyone connected to me was placed on the path of freedom.
>
> Yet again, in order to continue working for the sake of beings,
> I was renowned as Hépa Chökyi Jungné.
> Revealing the path of freedom to disciples,
> I ignited the torchlight of the Secret Mantra doctrine.
>
> Furthermore, as Traktung Dudul Lingpa,
> I nurtured disciples through unpredictable conduct
> And wandered to many kingdoms' sacred sites and places,

Disseminating the sun's thousand lights of the Secret Mantra doctrine.

Once again, I appeared as the subsequent Dudul emanation
Who transformed Lo and Mön into virtuous dominions.
I subdued savage, malicious gods and demons
And strove at prodigious acts for others' benefit.

I've had many other lifetimes.
I've taken the form of treasure revealers to subdue beings
And I've maintained the lifestyle of village adepts who held the doctrine.
If I relate all the details of my lifetimes, there will be no end to it.

Yet again, this incontrovertible, strict order came down, as spoken by Supreme Orgyen:

Kye Ho! Hear me, sublime being of excellent fortune.
At the present time, in this five-hundred-year degenerate era,
The sun of Great Perfection is setting.
The supreme secret teachings are plummeting into the depths of
    darkness.
Individuals born at this time are cruel and wild,
Deceived by the tainted incantations and substances of barbarians.
Disciples are extremely difficult to guide,
Yet an assembly with aspirations, karmic propensity, and good fortune
    does exist.
It's time for them to become your disciples.
To have them enter the definite secret path,
Engage in various kinds of unpredictable conduct
To nurture your students, guiding them in ways attuned to their needs
    and circumstances.
Arise now as a wisdom body in human form!

So he spoke, and I responded,

Kyé! Supreme eternal refuge, [Orgyen] Rinpoche,
Superb universal embodiment of all buddhas of the past, present, and
    future,

Heed me with your love and compassion,
And grant me permission [not to return].

In many bygone lifetimes,
I used skillful means and enlightened activity attuned to others' needs
To take responsibility for the welfare of others and to accept disciples.
These days, in the last part of the aeon,
Sentient beings of the degenerate age are difficult to guide;
The dogma of demons with corrupt aspirations flourishes;
Border people pour into the central parts of country, seizing those
    areas.
Barbarian substances and incantations
Have overpowered the gods and demons of apparent existence—
Their thoughts and deeds are driven into wickedness.
They send various human and livestock epidemics,
And frost, hail, insects, and year-long diseases.
Myriad sufferings develop and become widespread.
Wild and cruel beings act terribly.
In such an epoch of meager fortune,
Someone like me would find it too difficult to guide disciples,
So there's no point in me assuming the body of a sentient being.
Therefore, guru, grant me your permission!

When I made this request, once again he issued a command:

Listen to me, Dudul Drakpo Tsal!
Sentient beings of this degenerate age are difficult to guide,
Yet there are three thousand fortunate individuals
Connected to you through their previous lifetimes' aspirations and
    karma—
These are your disciples.
More than five hundred sublime beings among them
Can gain freedom in one lifetime.
Reincarnations of the king and his subjects
Will arise as twenty-five envoys of your activity.
Moreover, ten emanations of treasure revealers
Will truly serve beings.

Emanations of seven Secret Mantra teachers
Will reincarnate as your own children.
They will benefit beings—have no doubt!
Therefore, you, sovereign awareness holder,
Arise as the wisdom body of Dorjé Drolö,
And these fierce dharma protectors will accompany you as companions.
You will appear as a child
To parents with whom you have a previous karmic connection.
The time to enact my enlightened activity has arrived. Now go!

As he commanded, I assumed a human body.

I made my home during the Wood Sheep Year,
When the garuda was lord of the house,
As its ten soldiers arrived.
When the radiance of the seven horses'rays shone forth,
Rainbows and lights coalesced
And our yak-hair tent was visibly engulfed by rainbows.
The roaring sound of a symphony was perceived
At the time I emerged from my mother's womb.[16]

WHEN I REACHED FOUR YEARS OF AGE, from a thorny grove, I heard this pleasant song sung by a wee nightingale:

É! Listen to me, fortunate child of the lineage.
I am Wisdom Dakini Ekazati
Come from a leafy garden in southern Mön
As the messenger of Buddha Ö Tayé, Infinite Illuminator.
You have the strength of many lifetimes' training,
Glorious Nüden Dudul Dorjé!
In the pure land of Lotus Light you rose in a wisdom body with form
And now assume the guise of a child who likes to play,
Yet your wisdom mind doesn't know how to be deluded in relation to
    the basic space of the nature of reality.
In the space of the pristine sky of fundamental clear light,
Dawns your youthful sun of true understanding of the meaning.
Without mistake, this is the seal of the vajra of awareness.

My child, keep this insight as security for your life force.
Bear it as supremely formidable armor
Against evil demons' countless obstacles.
Five human years from now
I will return once again into your presence.

Then she vanished within the forest.

When I related this to my parents, they said, "Either he's lying or it's a bad omen."

ONE NIGHT in the latter part of that same year, I had a dream that unfolded like this: A young woman told me, "Together, mother and child, let's go east-ward to see the Eastern Conch Mountain." Once she said that, I felt like we were in motion.

At the border of a land that was neither China nor Tibet, we reached a white mountain that rose high into space. A trio of young monks were seated there; someone said they were the lord protectors of the three kinds of beings. I saw their elegant palace, three stories in height, and the monk seated in the upper level told me,

Kyé Ho! Listen to me, child of my spiritual family.
I am Jampal Zhonnu, Youthful Gentle Splendor.
This mountain is the white Conch Mountain.
This empowerment is the wisdom body's vase empowerment:
Dudul Drakpo, I bestow it upon you.
It's meaning is for the energy-wheel of great bliss [at the crown of
    your head].
You won't be traveling to other mountain realms.

He then poured vase water on the crown of my head.

The monk seated in the middle level held a skull-cup of nectar in his hand:

Listen to me, fortunate child of my spiritual family.
This is the Conch Mountain's terrace.
I am Tukjé Chenpo, Supreme Compassion.
This empowerment is the supreme speech empowerment:
Dudul Drakpo, I bestow it upon you.

It's ultimate meaning is for the energy-wheel of enjoyment [at your
     throat].
You won't be traveling to other earthly realms.

Then he placed the nectar on my tongue.

I arrived at the lowest level where a monk was holding a blue vajra in his
hand.

Kyé Ho! Fortunate child of my spiritual family.
This is the Conch Mountain's base.
I am Chana Dorjé, Vajra-in-Hand.
This empowerment is the sublime insight-wisdom empowerment:
Dudul Drakpo, I bestow it upon you.
It's meaning is for the energy-wheel of the teachings [at your heart].
You won't be traveling to far-off realms.

Then a sound woke me from sleep.

Once again I described this to my parents, who said it was surely due to a
ruler demon or demoness.

WHEN I REACHED FIVE YEARS OF AGE, on the tenth day of the fourth month I
saw some juniper in a grove on a mountain cliff. I went there, and at the bottom of a juniper bush I saw a golden wasp, flying and hovering about. I heard
it sing this song:

É É! Time is impermanent—there is past and future:
The year is impermanent, with summer, winter, autumn, and spring.
The months are impermanent, appearing as the moon's waxing and
     waning phases.
The days are impermanent, always shifting between daytime and night.
People are impermanent, moving from infancy to youth to early
     adulthood, then into decline and death.
Livestock and wealth are impermanent, akin to magical illusions.
My child, do you recall death? Consider it well.

In the past, in the realm of southern Mön
You were called Pal Nüden Dudul Pawo.

In the interim you stayed in Lotus Light Pure Land.
Finally you miraculously appeared as a person in this human land.
First I was called Gyaza Kongjo,
The [Chinese] queen who pleased and fulfilled the wishes of the
    Tibetan king [Songtsen Gampo].
In the interim I lived in Potala Pure Land.
Now I'm an animal, a little bee skilled in song.
Listen here to this pleasant song I warble:

A single goose has arrived from southern Mön
To the grove of the great lake in the north.
From the center of southern Mön, Pu, and Kongpo,
Flies a vulture, slicing through the heaven's heights,
Circling the northern grove of red Lhotrak.
In Celestial Enjoyment Pure Land and Lotus Light,
From the ranks of assembled deities, spiritual heroes, and dakinis,
Those endeavoring for the sake of beings through their loving
    compassion
Are groups of glorious awareness holders and bodhisattvas.
Just as I, a bee, circle around ambrosia,
They gather round the god-king of awareness holders.

Then she vanished into a gap in space.

Spiritual Heritage

UNTIL I WAS FIVE YEARS OLD, Wisdom Dakini Yeshe Tsogyal was always with me and protected me as would a mother. When I reached seven years of age, I went together with two children to a place a short distance away. In the center of a large turbulent river, I spotted the top of a boulder and immediately thought, "Wouldn't it be delightful to go up there?" Instantly I stood right on it without having moved, planted there as if waking from a dream. At that time, there were many dakinis all around, and I heard their song:

> Ah Ho! In the east looms a white snow mountain soaring into space;
> At the mountain's summit stands a crystal stupa.
> Within its vase is someone called Dorjé Tsémo, Vajra Summit,
> A god who truly enjoys laughter.
> One hundred glowing light rays will strike that place.
> Their sheen suffuses this world, the Land of Jambu, illuminating and
>   beautifying it.
> At the snow mountain's base, a poisonous snake wound round a cliff
> Has magically changed its black venom into a lake.
> If you see its waves, your lungs and heart will quiver.
> Apart from the clout of magita potion,
> Other substances' potency is ineffective against it.
>
> In the south, in a far-off place a long distance away,
> Stretches a great lake like a wide turquoise plain.
> At it center rises a mountain of jewels and gold.
> You'll see its summit soaring up into space,
> And there stands a golden stupa blazing with light.
> Within its vase is someone called Rinchen Gyalpo, Jewel King,
> A good and glorious god who controls the emanations [of those
>   below].
> Together, the dawning seven-horsed sun and the stupas' sheen
> Dispel the darkness of the land of southern Jambu.

At the mountain's base are fish and frogs all tangled up.
Mustering their great strength, they're on the cusp of destroying this
     world, the Land of Jambu.
For that, apart from the three kinds of salt,
How is it possible to kill them with other substances?

In the west, at the summit of the red clay cliff,
Stands a ruby stupa resplendent with light.
In its vase is Wangdü Pema Ö, Overwhelming with Lotus Light—
Look at how his body's radiance fills the three planes of existence.
At the mountain's base are a white lion mother and cub at play.
Seeing the lions' mighty force drives the pack of monkeys mad.
If the lions don't encounter lifesaving medicine,
How will they gain the power of recollection?

In the north, the king of the forested mountain's summit soars into
     space.
At the mountain's peak stands a manifest turquoise stupa.
Within its vase is someone called Trinlé Yongdrub, Complete
     Enlightened Activity.
Even though his embodied emanations fill the world,
Their benefit and harm is merely a blossomed lotus garden.
At the mountain's base is an Indian tiger, with aggressive mighty
     force.
Its roar incites the wild animals of all directions.
Craving the flesh of every single one, he prepares to devour them.
For that, apart from the white lioness,
Who else can overwhelm his brilliance?

In the center, at the zenith of the wish-fulfilling tree,
A garuda spreads its wings with impressive power.
Not only can it defeat the hostile border people,
It can also shadow the sun and moon above.
Cutting the path of the planets and stars, the great poison moves.

These are emblematic omens of both gods and demons.

These are symbolic metaphors of both the Buddhist path and mundane
  existence.
Do you understand these symbols?

Thus she asked as she vanished into space.

Then two people came along who, as if swimming in the water, led me
back. They chastised and beat me, then disappeared. In the meantime, my
previous propensities awakened and I explained the doctrine to other small
children. I would tell them many stories that I had remembered.

WHEN I TURNED EIGHT YEARS OLD, I went with my sister and a friend to look
for a lost calf. At nightfall, a drop of blood fell from the sky onto a rock. As
soon as I saw that, I slipped into a terrified panic. I asked myself, "What was
that?" even though it was the miraculous apparition of a demon. That incident forced me to flee for home.

When I got into bed that night, the world and everything inside it collapsed into emptiness, like the dense evening darkness of summer. Above in
a great black expanse, a waterfall descended. Its thundering roar was like the
roar at the end of time. Just as I reached a state of utter terror, this was intoned
from the din of the waves:

Destroy, destroy, now is the destruction of the aeon.
Empty, empty, it is emptied out into empty space.
Vanish, vanish, vanishing into nonexistence.
Pacify, pacify, the three realms become empty and peaceful.

If what is primordially nonexistent has no being,
How can you be afraid of an abiding presence?
If what is originally empty has no being,
It is always empty—what is there to fear?
If what was previously nonexistent has no being,
And suddenly ceases to exist, where does it disappear?
That which appears while nonexistent is wrong:
Nonexistent in the present, where does it go?

First, where does this blood come from?

> From the sky, an empty space without foundation.
> These dense waves of blood
> Have no source and lack any basis or root.
> See everything animate and inanimate in the three realms from that
>   perspective!
> Cyclic existence is unbearable suffering.
> If you don't foster fearful panic toward that,
> Why are you afraid of blood?
> This lake of blood lacks intrinsic existence, yet it appears.
> This will continue until you reach twenty-two years of age.
> If you don't see existence to be just like this,
> I, the queen of existence, will show it to you!

Henceforth, throughout that same year, when I got into bed and closed my eyes, those kinds of sights were constant until dawn arrived.

I told my father and mother repeatedly about them, and they became distraught. They asked others, who did divinations. Some said it was a ruler demon's magical projection. Some said that it was sorcerers' contaminating influence. They asked a lama to give me empowerment and to perform ablution rituals. The sublime lama said, "This child has virtuous roots. This is an early portent of him awakening to his spiritual heritage." Then my parent's minds were relieved, and they didn't tell anyone else, keeping it to themselves.

> I didn't do anything at all in reaction to those chaotic sights.
> When that terrified panic repeatedly returned,
> I contemplated things incisively, looking at the way things really are.
> Seeing that existence is an ocean of blood,
> Sometimes from above, within emptiness,
> Red light dawned in the middle sky.
> At times, from the dark basic space of emptiness,
> For just as long as a flash of lightning,
> My own body and the world, the environment and its inhabitants, were
>   luminously apparent;
> Then once again they dissolved within that emptiness.

> When apparent existence entered into the continuity of emptiness,
> Sometimes even my own body didn't appear.

In that expanse like empty space,
The entire world and its contents were just like the moon's reflection on
    water,
Naturally appearing, self-arisen on their own.

At times, within the expanse of empty space,
My own body was a great river of blood,
Inside of which lived all sentient beings of the six "cities,"
As if they were life-forms that live in water.
Sometimes the blood dissolved into the beings.
Sometimes the six types of beings dissolved into the blood.
Sometimes it would alternate, with erratic scenes unfolding.
Sometimes that river of blood would pour from the upper part of my
    body,
And the lower part of my body would appear as the ocean of blood.
Within that, all animate and inanimate beings of the three realms
Appeared like planets and stars reflected on a lake.
Sometimes both the appearances and the domain of the appearances
Were nondual, pristine, and vividly illuminated.
When I shifted into that experience, that manifest indwelling state
    opened out into infinity.
Through that crucial experience I concluded
That the entirety of apparent existence, cyclic existence and
    transcendence,
Is utterly self-manifest and has equal value.
Supreme nonduality was made apparent.
The expanse of the wisdom mind of Great Perfection overflowed
And I gained control of the space treasury of the nature of reality.
This inaugurated a state of everlasting happiness.

DURING THE LATTER PART of that same year, at night on the eighth day of the
tenth month, Dakini Sukhasiddhi, Attainment of Bliss, sang to me,

Kyé Ho! Sublime individual of excellent fortune,
All gods and demons, [who are] the happiness and suffering of
    apparent existence,
Are merely the false impressions of delusion.

The entirety of the outer and inner world and its contents
Do not exist, though they appear—they are emptiness.
All outer phenomena
Are nonexistent, haven't arisen, and haven't come into being.
Look into that state and realize its nature!

Then I experienced her dissolving into me.

A Little Boy with Excellent Fortune

In the Rabbit Year [when I turned nine,] during the afternoon of the fifth day of the Saga Constellation Month, I saw a naked, iridescent child riding on a saddle. He ogled me with a hateful glare, saying, "If you're skilled, you can shoot this arrow. I'm an extraordinarily strong child. What do I like? I like arrows. Fire an arrow and I'll wait."

I shot a barberry arrow. It missed the child and struck the bottom part of the stirrup, piercing straight through as if it were clay. The child laughed with tremendous delight, saying,

> I am Dorjé Lekpa, Vajra of Excellence.
> This is a sign that emptiness is true, not a lie.
> Iron pierced by wood
> And grasping at what is nonexistent as having existence is childish
>   perception.
> Therefore, look at that perception vanishing into basic space.

Once he said that, everything except the saddle disappeared.

In the year I turned ten, at night on the eighth day of the Yugu Constellation Month, Dakini Yeshe Tsogyal suggested, "Let's go to meet Supreme Orgyen." We went up into the sky, and immediately, in the arena of unstructured space, I saw an immense vajra canopy of rainbow light. In its expanse sat the three male and female appearances of Orgyen, [namely, Guru Rinpoche, Yeshe Tsogyal, and Mandarava]. They were youthful, resplendent with the buddhas' marks and signs of physical perfection, and surrounded by one hundred thousand spiritual heroes and dakinis. I was instantly captivated by the sight. Once I had offered respectful prostrations and performed circumambulations, I placed myself before them and implored,

> Kyé Ho! Essential fusion of all buddhas,
> Treasure trove of the holy tantras,
> Master of the assembly of the exalted spiritual community—

You who are the three jewels, heed me!
Essence of the highest lamas,
Lord of the ocean of chosen deities,
Great expanse of the mamos and dakinis—
Convergence of the three roots, heed me!
The essence, the unformulated body of ultimate enlightenment,
The nature, the spontaneously present utter enjoyment body,
Responsive compassion, the all-pervasive manifest body—
Union of enlightenment's three bodies, heed me!
Tormented by unbearable pain
In the ocean of suffering that is cyclic existence,
The entire mass of sentient beings has no refuge.
Shelter us with your impartial compassion!

I spin ceaselessly in the cycle of senseless delusion,
Blind without a guardian.
Protect me!
Lacking stable independence,
Experiencing unceasing suffering:
Protect me, a sentient being of cyclic existence!
Having fallen under the sway of demons on a corrupt path,
Immersed in bad karma without any self-control,
I was propelled to boundless miserable existences—
Protect me, a careless lunatic!
Throughout my series of lifetimes immemorial,
I've engaged in the causes and results of suffering,
Tormented by the fruition of what I've done—
Protect me, this evildoer with bad karma!

I made this piercing supplication, and immediately Guru Rinpoche smiled and spoke with great joy:

Kyé Ho! Listen to me and consider this, child of my spiritual family.
When you reach twenty-five years of age,
You will unlock my profound treasure.
Nurture disciples, guiding them in ways attuned to their needs and
    circumstances.

In the dregs of the aeon of this evil time,
Wild and cruel sentient beings are difficult to subdue.
Therefore, for companions, rely on those capable of overpowering—
[The protector] Maru Tségyal, Victorious Summit of Maru, and
    Wangchuk Chenpo, Magnificent Ruler.
Hordes of demons with corrupt aspirations will rise up as adversaries;
The karmic retribution of lawsuits and legal contention will come.
For them, dispatch the one-eyed mamo [Mantra Protectress Ekazati]
And the vicious malevolent Za, Planetary Lord.
Exert yourself in repeating their practices many times.
Without delay or a long wait, this will put an end to your troubles.
Linked through thirteen lifetimes,
Your highest deity is Dorjé Drolö—rely on him.
You are truly Phurba, Dagger, incarnate—
Therefore practice the secret methods of Dorjé Phurba, Vajra Dagger.
When you were Supreme Hungkara,
You served as chief of the secret treasures of the dakinis—
Persevere in the practice of the dakinis' three bodies of enlightenment.

He spoke and then placed his left hand on the crown of my head, saying, "You are my holy, supreme son. Henceforth from today, you and I will be companions without separation for even an instant, and you can speak with me as any two people would. Until the fundamental state of the nature of reality becomes apparent to you, it's certain that we will meet again and again." Then he dissolved into me, and in equanimity, I woke up.

THAT SAME YEAR, in a dream at night on the tenth day in the Mindruk Constellation Month, someone appeared saying he was Lord Gesar of Ling. He wore armor and a helmet and had a belt wrapped three times around his waist. I saw him moving through space. As he descended next to me, I heard him languidly singing this song:

Yé Yé! Ah La Ho! Surely you recognize me—do you?
If you don't recognize me,
I am the great lion king of this world, the Land of Jambu.
During this aeon, in times past,
I was the four-faced supreme god Brahma from above,

Who became the son of Lord Shakyamuni.

During the middle period, in this world's human realm,

My emanations guide disciples in ways attuned to their needs and
    circumstances.

In this aeon, during the middle period,

I was known as Gesar, resident of the Land of Jambu.

Its upper part is India, the exalted land;

The middle part Tibet, the land of snows;

And the lower part China and Mongolia—

My fame spread throughout all these lands.

I was the protective keeper of wealth and treasures in Tibet.

I significantly helped the southern Land of Jambu in general

And traveled everywhere taming gods and demons.

I concealed the highest treasures, which represent the earth's essence,
    throughout all lands.

I was then the great adept Maha Hungkara

And emanated as someone called Ling Mépo Tragen, Ancestor of the
    Continent, Striped Old Man.

I acted as chief of thirty treasure cycles.

I completely defeated ruthless enemies and vow-violation spirits.

These days I'm a little boy—that's you!

Now you are a little boy with excellent fortune.

The phenomena of this life are impermanent like a dream;

Know that and recite the six-syllable mantra.

Your dear companions and family are like people in an illusion;

Your wealth and possessions are akin to the projection of an optical
    illusion;

Know that and recite the six-syllable mantra.

Forms are impermanent like images in a mirage;

Sounds are impermanent like an echo:

Smells are impermanent like a mirage;

Tastes are impermanent like a water bubble;

Touch is impermanent like a reflection;

Think of that and recite the six-syllable mantra.

The year is impermanent, changing with both summer and winter;

The months are impermanent, with the moon's waxing and waning
    phases;
The days are impermanent, shifting between daytime and night;
Time is impermanent, changing with morning and afternoon;
Recall that and recite the six-syllable mantra.
Ponder impermanence and death all the time.
At the end of this human life of yours
You will undoubtedly accomplish something very meaningful.

Then he dissolved into my heart. From that point on I contemplated the doctrine.

THAT SAME YEAR on the twenty-fifth day in the month of the Victorious Constellation Month, during the last part of the night, in a dream of pure vision, I saw Orgyen Tsokyé Dorjé, Orgyen Lake-Born Vajra, surrounded by an assembly including King [Trisong Deutsen] and his Tibetan subjects. Nöjin Shenpa Marnak, Dark Red Noxious Spirit Butcher, was in front, encircled by his eight emissaries and the eight tribes of gods and demons, like the gods' battalion or a human army. I saw them filling the entire realm of space. At that moment, Supreme Orgyen showed his joyful face to me and said,

Kyé Ho! Fortunate child of my spiritual family,
Listen to me with a reverential attitude.
This deity to whom you are karmically connected throughout your
    series of lifetimes
Is especially exalted compared to all others.
If you practice Shenpa, Butcher, you will accomplish without difficulty
What you intend—the four activities' enlightened action.
He is exceptionally superb in performing magnetizing and wrathful
    activities.
Therefore, I'm bestowing this upon you.

Then he placed the golden vajra in his right hand on my head, and said, "I'm giving this guardian to you as your inseparable companion and as sentinel of your accomplishment of the [four] enlightened activities. Nondual with Pal Tachok Wangyi Gyalpo, Glorious Supreme Steed Powerful King

[Tamdrin,] his prodigious force is unrivaled by anyone in the three worlds, and the clout of his wrathful virtuosity is greater than one hundred meteorite lightning bolts. The speed of his might is far swifter than a lightning flash. His great liberating power controls appearing existence. Thus it is bestowed. I confer upon you the power of his life force."

As soon as he spoke, Shenpa appeared taking the oath—he promised with words of honor to accompany me. Once again Supreme Orgyen spoke:

> Kyé! Listen to me, individual of excellent fortune.
> When you practice this arrogant deity,
> Possessing his spirit stone is a vital point regarding his life force.
> The vital point for the crucial instruction of tethering is this:
> To create the sacred circle for your practice, place the torma in a hidden place
> And surround it with an enclosure of a wrathful collection [of ritual daggers].
> Write down the enemy's name and clan
> And place it inside the heart of a red dog
> Or a maroon painted effigy.
> Place it in the secret hiding place [hole]
> And repeat the drawing in and embedding four times.
> Persevere in this summons with great insistence:
> É Hé Maru Tséguna Hri Tri Samaya Dza Dza!
>
> With monumental resolve, persist in drawing in the spirit.
> At that time, the victors of the ten directions and their spiritual heirs,
> And all the wisdom and worldly protectors
> Take on the appearing aspect of your creation-phase deity, [Shenpa],
> And dissolve into the deity you've created and meditate upon,
> Just like pouring water into water.
> Visualize that again and again.

From time to time [perform this visualization as well]:

> The animate and inanimate arena of cyclic existence and enlightenment—

The entirety of what dwells and is stable—
Is every trace of the Noxious Spirit Shenpa's wrathful might.
All of this, along with Wild Za, Planetary Lord of the five elements,
Is invited to take the form of that arrogant one's appearance,
And everything conceivable dissolves into your visualization of Shenpa
    again and again.
Imagine that, like the waxing moon,
This causes his mighty capability, brilliance, tenacity, and strength to swell.
Once you've swept together entirely all of cyclic existence and
    enlightenment, with nothing left out,
Meditate that it is gathered within him.

Constantly keep your mind on unimpeded appearances as that deity.
Continuously recite the mantra, halting ordinary language.
Repeat the visualization of summoning many times.

Your practice deity is nonexistent from the start;
Since it's created by mind, be vigilant in your visualization.
When you're making offerings and fulfillment offerings,
They are like a dream's miraculous images:
Send forth offerings as instantaneous sensory pleasures and a wealth of
    enjoyments.

By reciting the following lines, you will accomplish your wishes:

Kya! Arise in the wisdom form of the master of the activity
Of all buddhas of past, present, and future.
My mind multiplies actual and imagined offerings
In the vault of space.
I produce in the five senses' domain
Anything whatsoever that is desireable
To satisfy the wisdom mind of Nöjin Shenpa Marnak, Dark Red Noxious
    Spirit Butcher,
And to satisfy the wisdom minds of his consort and emissaries.
To you all, I petition, make offerings, and confess breaches and
    violations.

Fully enact the infinite enlightened activities
Of pacifying, increasing, magnetizing, annihilating, and direct wrathful
    conduct, I pray.

"As described, be diligent in this every day. You will accomplish your aims
through these vital instructions." He moved to the crown of my head and told
me, "I grant you investiture as the regent of all victors. I confer empowerment upon you as Buddhist king of the three realms. I give you the power to
empty cyclic existence from its depths." As he dissolved into the crown of my
head, the experience of the equal purity of cyclic existence and enlightenment
dawned within me.

Appearances as the Deity

WHEN I TURNED THIRTEEN, I fell asleep one day at the head of the Nyiyi Shukchen Pass. In the deluded appearances of a dream, in wide-open space to the east, I saw a white cloud like a tent, the color of conch. I gazed at it for a moment and right away a white woman appeared saying she was Dakini Mamaki. She sang,

> Look directly in front of you
> At the base of that red rock—
> There's a small scorpion.
> Strike that place in the rock garden with a stone.
> You'll find an auspicious knot, [a representation] of wisdom mind.
> I'm giving it to you, fortunate child.

I immediately woke up and then went to the rock garden. At its base was a small scorpion. When I struck the rock with a stone, it opened up. From the crevice in its surface, I retrieved a beautiful auspicious knot made of copper.

THAT SAME YEAR, in the early part of the morning on the eighth day of the Ox Month, someone called Orgyen Térdak Gyalpo, Treasure Lord King, holding a golden hook and a mongoose flaunted himself amid one thousand noxious spirits. I saw him projecting an array of magical manifestations. I offered prostrations to him and then said, "We beings who are tormented by poverty implore you to shelter us with your compassion."

When I said this, his face glowed as he smiled and looked at me. He replied,

> Kyé Ho! Fortunate one endowed with providence,
> At the end of this five-hundred-year period
> I have emanated as Wangchuk Chenpo, Magnificent Ruler.
> For individuals who practice me
> I am actually present in front of them:
> I grant spiritual attainment.

In response I asked, "What is the text outlining your means of accomplishment? If we practice it, is it a technique that doesn't waste time and energy? I beseech you to reveal its profound teaching!"

When I made that request, Supreme Orgyen's face shifted to the southwestern direction: "For my practice, you have to imagine in this way." The very instant he said that, I saw a vast and wide sanctuary in a cliff made of precious gold. Its topmost point rose into the center of space. This sheltered a large and spacious celestial palace made of various jewels. At its center stood an immense ruby throne with high cushions and a half-moon on top. He sat there, naked, jolly, and magnificent, endowed with a smiling demeanor, both peaceful and wrathful. His braids were dark blue and reached the ground. A half-moon appeared at the crown of his head and a sun shone at his navel. He held a hook in his right hand and brandished a lasso of sun rays in his left. He leaned back against the golden cliff. To his left stood his naked consort, red in color, her radiant face exquisitely gorgeous, with greenish-blue braids that reached the ground. She flourished a hook in her right hand and a jewel in her left. Her body touched his as she glanced sideways amorously. Encircled by a retinue of four red activity dakinis, they all shimmered brilliantly and blazed such that it was impossible to look at them directly.

"My child listen to me without distraction. Place a heart-shaped torma on a sacred circle in the form of a red magnetizing half-moon. To the left of that, place a food-offering torma that is lovely and appealing. Around that, place four smaller tormas in the shapes of the four activities. Arrange lavish offerings—material necessities for the vajra feast. Then without letting your mind wander elsewhere or interrupting your practice with human words, and never allowing the heat of your cushion to fade, exert yourself in reciting this mantra:

OM MAHADEVA HRING HRING HARINISA SAMAYA DZA DZA

"Once signs arise, append the additional mantras for the activities and recite those. By practicing me, it's certain that you will accomplish without impediment the entire infinitude of enlightened activities. Therefore, don't harbor any doubts!

"Child of my spiritual family, to swiftly and easily accomplish any deity and any activity you practice, say a declaration of truth incantation and make aspirations for what you desire, then recite the 'Heart of Interdependent

Origination' formula four hundred thousand times. Hold fast to this key instruction. For whoever performs recitation in that way, failure to accomplish their activity is impossible."

> Kyé Ho! Listen to me once again fortunate child!
> Since all sentient beings of this evil era of degeneration
> Are controlled by their karma and afflictive emotions,
> It's difficult for them to increase possessions and wealth.
> First accumulate copious stores of merit;
> Next make vajra feast offerings;
> Persevere again and again in the methods of confession and
>   purification.
> Perform abundant fulfillment offerings, supplications, and other
>   offerings.
> Never separate from seeing appearances as the deity—know this crucial
>   point.
> If you recognize the sovereign view,
> That is the storehouse of precious treasures,
> The kingdom of Kuntuzangpo, Ever-Excellent.
> If you don't recognize the sovereign view,
> Even having done recitation practice will become the cause of cyclic
>   existence.

I responded with this request: "What is that view? Tell me, I pray!" He answered by saying this:

> The sovereign view is space:
> The environment and its inhabitants are the sweeping openness of
>   space.
> The view of space is equanimity.

Then he vanished like a magical illusion.

WHEN I TURNED FOURTEEN, at night on the fifteenth day of the first summer month, flowers and lotuses bloomed on the ground, a lattice of rainbows gathered in the sky, and gods and goddesses filled the surrounding space. Within a spacious jeweled mansion, enchantingly elegant and lovely, upon a very tall,

beautiful throne sat an individual said to be the great adept Hungkara. Dark
blue with a brilliant luster, possessing the attributes of a heruka, he appeared
like a beautiful rainbow in space. Showing me a pleased and loving attitude,
he said:

> Kyé Ho! Fortunate child of my spiritual family,
> In the past, when the trio of the abbot, the master, and the Buddhst
>   king
> Erected illustrious Samyé Monastery in Tibet,
> They raised the victory banner of the two doctrines [of sutra and tantra]
> And caused the cruel and malevolent Bön tradition to decline.
> At that time, holders of the Bön tradition who were demonic
>   emanations
> And many of the officials and subjects who sustained the Bön lineage
> Made corrupt aspirations. Through that karmic connection
> They became enemies, bandits, thieves, and soldiers.
> Their deeds and criticism—the karmic retribution of corrupt views—
> Will assail those who uphold the victors' doctrine,
> And the descendants of the victors, the treasure revealers.
>
> To captivate those [wrongdoers] and to overwhelm them with splendor,
> Utilize Lhachen Wangchuk Chenpo, Magnificent Ruler Deity.
> This is what that practice entails:
> The sacred circle, painted with vermillion and ocher,
> Is an elegant celestial palace.
> On this, gather various grains and medicines in mounds.
> In the middle, in a jeweled copper vessel
> Stands a jewel-shaped torma
> Painted red.
> When this is complete, to increase your merit,
> First present lavish vajra feast offerings.
> Arrange grains, medicines, meat, alcohol,
> The three white foods, and the three sweets in abundance.
> Arrange copious tormas
> Made of flour, anise, sugar,
> Molasses, honey, radish,
> Milk, and yogurt mixed together.

"Then clearly visualize yourself as your chosen deity, the deity of power [Tamdrin]. Imagine that before you stands a red letter *Hri* blazing intensely with light and light rays, which shine forth, destroying into emptiness the entirety of apparent existence—the environment and its inhabitants.

"Within emptiness, at the center of a wide and spacious terrain of red light, stands a celestial palace made of precious ruby. It's shaped like a half-moon with one door facing west. At the core of its vast and spacious interior sits a grandiose throne of great height made of various gems. The red letter *Hri* descends onto the throne's half-moon seat and radiates light that makes incalculable pleasing offerings to all the victors of the past, present, and future along with their spiritual heirs. All their splendor, empowerment, and spiritual attainment converges, dissolving into the *Hri*. Light rays radiating downward purify the negative acts, obscurations, karma, afflictive emotions, and habitual patterns of all sentient beings throughout the three realms. All their power, strength, and capability converges and dissolves into the *Hri*.

"The *Hri* changes entirely into Lhachen Wangchuk Chenpo, Magnificent Ruler Deity. Visualize that his body is bright red like a heap of rubies circled by a hundred thousand suns, shimmering and lustrously blazing. He flaunts his face in a smiling manner, both peaceful and wrathful. His braids are in a topknot, marked with a half-moon; the sun rises at his navel. His dark blue braids reach the ground. In his right hand he wields an iron hook that draws in the three realms, and his left hand brandishes a lasso that binds all apparent existence as his servant. He has renounced clothing and ornaments; his erect penis points upward.

"The goddess Umadevi, Chief Goddess, stands to his left. She is red and naked, having renounced clothing and ornaments. She holds the sovereign of magnetizing jewels in her right hand. With her left hand she proffers a food offering of a hundred flavors, serving this to her consort. She bows toward him and touches him; both feel yearning in the taste of pleasure and the dew of their passion gathers.

"The emanated goddesses surround them. One draws in, one binds, one stupefies, and one renders mad. They are naked, having renounced clothing and ornaments. They each hold their respective implements in their right hands, and in their left hands they brandish a white, yellow, red, or green lotus.

"Meditate that all these deities bring the three realms under their control and employ the three planes of existence as servants:"

Om Maha Déva Hri Hri Vajra Samaya Dza Dza

"As you recite this mantra, don't let your mind be distracted by anything
else, and remain inseparable with the clear appearance of the deity. Know
this to be a key instruction! When you finish that recitation, add the mantra
of overpowering and recite that. Always devote yourself to this practice and
retain its sacred vital instructions."

> Kyé! Fortunate holy individual,
> Once three years from now have passed,
> You will have to go to Lower Serlung.
> All three—gods, demons, and humans—will abuse you.
> No matter what you try to do,
> In that dark province of nefarious demons,
> You won't have the fortune to subdue disciples.
> You will be propelled eastward to the land of Golok
> By the momentum of the auspicious connections of your karma and
>   aspirations.
> It is a land of savage demons,
> Yet some people there, connected to you through karma,
> Will accompany you as you become the glory of the doctrine and
>   beings.
> Once three more years from then have passed,
> Bring forth the profound treasures of Supreme Orgyen
> In Lower Ser, from Ngala Taktsé
> And Sébo Drakdzong Dorjé.
> Steal the power of the demons who assault you.
>
> Six years from now,
> The enlightened wisdom mindstreams of Lord Orgyen, Vimalamitra,
> And the sovereign of adepts, Saraha,
> Along with the wisdom dakini, will move to you,
> Delivered as your trio of mind treasures.
> As leader of thousands of students,
> You will unlock the gateway to supreme freedom.

Then he spread the fingers of his hand. At his fingertips were drops of rainbow light, amid which the sacred circle of the eight herukas was displayed. He said,

> To you, fortunate child,
> I confer the empowerment of the eight herukas.
> May you gain the complete supreme empowerment
> Of all spiritual families and sacred circles:

Buddha Vajra Ratna Pema Karma Kaya Wak Tsitta Sarwa
Abikentsa Om Ah Hung Soha

As the lama, deities, and mantras dissolved into my heart, the experience of great bliss dawned within me.

That same year at night on the eighth day of the Chu Constellation Month, in the deluded visionary experience of a dream, a vulture, king of birds, descended in front of me from a gap in space like a meteor. It said, "Sit on top of me," and as soon as I did, we flew like an arrow into the sky. When we reached a very high plane, we soared southward. I saw Supreme Mountain standing at the utmost height. Its snowy summit soared into space; its middle section was made of crushed clay pebbles; its base was festooned with grass and flowers. On its plains stretched lakes and meadows, upon which many kinds of medicines grew. Various pleasant sounds made by different kinds of intelligent birds and wild animals resounded, and they boasted their beautiful forms in frolic and play.

One league above the mountain's summit, within a dense expanse of light and rainbows, a celestial palace made of myriad gems stood in a lovely and captivating garden. It was elegant and densely ornamented. The gate goddesses of action at the outer gates and the four classes of mighty ones at the inner gates carried out enlightened activity and guarded against obstacles.

At the center of that great palace, upon a very high jeweled throne, sat the trio of the sublime exalted Tukjé Chenpo, Supreme Compassion; Drolkar, White Liberating Mother; and Droljang, Green Liberating Mother. I saw them surrounded by the exalted bodhisattvas. I offered them prostrations and implored,

Obscured and overpowered by habitual patterns of unawareness,
I wander in cyclic existence.
Tukjé Chenpo, Supreme Compassion, grant me refuge, I pray!
Lead me away from this deluded cycle of karma and afflictive emotions,
And make my wisdom become manifest!

Once I made that request, the Exalted One, [Tukjé Chenpo,] spoke:

Individual of excellent fortune,
Recite one hundred million six-syllable mantras.
Now you and I are indivisible with each other—
Gain resolute confidence that any connection with you whatsoever will
    be meaningful.
May you fully receive the supreme vajra empowerment!

Once he spoke, they vanished without a trace.

The Nectar of Bliss-Emptiness

IN THE YEAR I TURNED FIFTEEN, on the eighth day of the Saga Constellation
Month, a girl dancing above a three-stone hearth told me:

> Kyé! Skillful young lad, you listen to me.
> I am the girl named Déwé Garken, Joyful Dancer.
> If you want to shoot an arrow, shoot at me.
> It won't pierce me—I have a vajra body.

When I launched an arrow, it didn't hit her; it struck a bronze vessel and
went right through the bronze to the other side. That girl sang,

> Kyé! In pervasive unimpeded space
> A girl appears like a magical illusion.
> This bronze or iron, like a magical display,
> Is pierced by the magical display of wood:
> This is a sign that all apparent existence is a magical illusion.
> By the power of the changeless truth of magical illusion,
> May you recognize magical illusory phenomena.

> The lama is all buddhas of the past, present, and future.
> This holy lama of yours is not a human being.
> He is Pema Jungné, Lotus-Born.
> In a previous life, in a time gone by,
> He was called Acharya Palyang, Scholar Glorious Melody—
> A manifestation of Garab Dorjé, Vajra of Utmost Joy,
> He emanated as the teacher of both gods and humans.
> With faith and respect for him,
> Request as many empowerments and scriptural transmissions as you
>   are able.
> That is an auspicious connection for the increase of your service to
>   beings.

Then she vanished into the magical illusion of the nature of reality.

IN THE YEAR I TURNED SIXTEEN, on the eighth day of the middle summer month, I went to shepherd some animals. At the noontime break I fell asleep. A red dakini appeared in a dream singing to me:

> My child, listen to me without distraction.
> Tomorrow your father will come
> And you will have to part with your lama.
> At that time, make aspirations like this:
> From now on, throughout all my series of lifetimes,
> May I never be separated from you, my lama.
> Nurture me with empowerment and sacred instructions,
> Ripen and liberate my mindstream!

Seven days later, my outstanding lama said, "The time has come for you to go to your homeland. Prior to now I've examined your substance and I see you as someone with exceptional qualities, superior compared to others. You should look at the advice to treasure revealers in *The Testament of Guru Rinpoche,* take it literally, and cultivate that experience. Considerable benefit for others will naturally ensue.

"In particular, on the subjects of transcribing your profound treasures and teaching the sacred pith instructions to others, first devote yourself to your own practice and you will see the face of your chosen deity. Invest yourself in the profound view and meditation, and you will see the truth of the nature of reality. These are the two key instructions—keep them as supremely sacred.

"I'm an old man whose life is over. From now on it will be difficult for us to meet one another." He touched his forehead to mine and expressed prayers of aspiration and auspicious wishes.

FROM THAT POINT FORTH, I practiced the great, exalted Tukjé Chenpo, Supreme Compassion, as my chosen deity. While I was reciting the six-syllable mantra in the year I turned seventeen, I went into retreat during the Go Constellation Month. During retreat, at dawn on the twenty-second day, a little boy saying he was Tukjé Chenpo told me,

My child, if you definitely want to practice me,
You must have the key points of the creation phase.
It's very important! If you don't have them,
You can recite many, many mantras, yet they won't produce any result.
Even if they produce something, on this earth you'll be at a dead end,
Like not having any food and calling guests.

As for the meaning and purpose of accomplishing deities,
It is to fuse this impure world to what is pure;
Your attachment to substance, existence, is the body of the deity;
The aggregates that you cling to as "I"
Appear clearly as the illusory body of wisdom;
Your speech and circulating energies are joined to purity as the sound
    of mantras;
And mind's union with purity comes from always being accompanied
    by appearances as the deity.
These are the supreme methods of practice.

Once he spoke, I responded,

Kyé! Lama, Lord Protector of Supreme Compassion,
The profound vital points of creation-phase practice,
Which join to purity all phenomena of impure cyclic existence—
Lord protector, I beseech you, teach them to me!

He replied, "Kyé, child of my spiritual family, listen well. Instill this in your mind, and I will teach you. First, if you haven't taken refuge, then you aren't a suitable recipient for profound Secret Mantra since you haven't entered the Buddhist flock. Therefore, first you must take refuge in the Three Jewels. If you haven't developed the highest sacred intention to be of benefit to others, then your practice will not become authentic. Therefore, you must develop that intention for the purpose of the welfare and happiness of all sentient beings.

"If you haven't destroyed into basic space this aeon of impure karmic [embodiment], then phenomena as the wisdom deity won't become apparent. Therefore, first imagine that all phenomena brought together by dualistic fixation collapse within the empty open space of the nature of reality, like waking into basic space from a dream—that is what we call 'emptiness.' Further, when you make apparent the wisdom of awareness—pristine, luminous, and unsullied—that is what we call 'clarity.'

"Awareness instantly arises as a white letter *Hri* with two adjacent circles; this is what we call 'the cause of clarity.' Light shines from the letter, entirely pervading the arena of empty, luminous space; the miraculous illusory manifestation of wisdom becomes a vast and wide foundation of light, equal in scope to the infinitude of space. Hills of medicinal grasses grow there, over which waft delicious aromatic mists. Everything is blanketed with beautiful flowers and blossoming lotuses of myriad colors. The entire sky is decorated with images of intersecting rainbow latticework. In the surrounding space, all things desirable, sumptuous, and magnificent gather like mist and clouds. Every spiritual hero and dakini dances, frolics, and sings.

"Absolutely everywhere in all directions, countless offering goddesses multiply [and send forth] oceanic clouds of offerings. In the four directions stretch four oceans of nectar endowed with the eight qualities [of the best water]. Their banks are adorned with shorelines of gems, sands of gold, and grasses of turquoise. Between those oceans, springs of purifying nectar gush and large wish-fulfilling trees flourish. In these trees are different kinds of emanated birds in various appearances. They are white in color like conch, yellow like gold, red like coral, green like emeralds, blue like beryl, and dark blue like lapis. Inconceivable and limitless in number, they flaunt their beautiful forms, intone pleasant sounds, and so forth. This is the design of the pure land, what we call 'a created pure appearance.'

"Once again, the *Hri* shines light without edge or limit. The entire display of the wisdoms and bodies of enlightenment converges into light, from which a celestial palace emerges. It is vividly white in the east, yellow in the south, red in the west, green in the north, and dark blue in the center. At its center, the letter *Hri* descends onto a seat made of a lotus, sun, and moon and shines light that makes immeasurable pleasing offerings to all the victors of the ten directions along with their spiritual heirs. All their empowerments, blessings, and spiritual attainments are garnered and dissolve back into the *Hri*.

"Light shines downward and purifies all the karma, afflictive emotions, and habitual patterns of every sentient being of the three realms and places them in the state of enlightenment. The light reconverges, and instantaneously, all beings' longevity and merit dissolve into the *Hri*.

"The *Hri* morphs completely into yourself as the sublime bodhisattva Tukjé Chenpo, Supreme Compassion. Your body is white and iridescent like the sun dawning on a snowy mountain, resplendent with light. Adorned with the buddhas' marks and signs of physical perfection, you have the bearing of a youth who has reached eight years of age. You are seated in vajra cross-legged posture. Among your four arms, the first two are joined in prayer at the level of your heart. The lower two hold a rosary and a white lotus. Endowed with the look of a peaceful, smiling face, you are ornamented with the complete regalia of the utter enjoyment body of enlightenment and sit within an expanse of five-colored rainbow light. This is clearly visualized, and is what we call 'clarity as the vajra body.'

"Meditate that at the center of a six-petaled white lotus [in the center of your body at the level of] your heart stands a white letter *Hri*. On the eastern petal is a white *Om*. On the second petal is a green *Ma;* on the third is a yellow *Ni;* on the fourth is a blue *Pé;* on the fifth is a red *Mé,* and on the sixth stands a dark blue *Hung*. Imagining that their own sounds resound from those letters like the roar of a thousand dragons, recite *Om Mani Pémé Hung*. That is what we call 'vajra wisdom speech.'

"With your mind not straying elsewhere, maintain unobstructed pride of yourself as the deity—this is what we call inseparable 'vajra wisdom mind.'

"If you've practiced without parting from these vital points, in this very lifetime your three doors of ordinary body, speech, and mind will become enlightened as the three vajras—enlightened body, speech, and mind. These constitute the unsurpassable profound pith instructions.

"You should meditate in this way, sending and absorbing light in order to receive empowerments, blessings, and spiritual attainments. Do so with intent diligence. From now on, for twelve human years, the two of us will not part from one another. In this form of a small child, I will reveal to you in dreams all the positive and negative things that you do." Then he vanished without a trace.

THAT SAME YEAR in the Go Constellation Month, in the presence of Jetsun Lama Jikmé, I stayed in a retreat based on the preliminary practices. At night on the tenth day of that month, an old woman saying she was Yeshe Tsogyal told me, "My child, let's go to receive spiritual attainment." I went with her and immediately we arrived in front of the lama. At that point, I couldn't see him—instead, in the midst of a rainbow canopy sat [a form of Guru Rinpoche] called Orgyen Nangsi Zilnön, He Who Overwhelms Apparent Existence with Splendor. To his right was the great King Namangbu [Namtösé, Heir of Hearers,] and to his left was Bodhisattva Namké Nyingpo, Essence of Space. They were encircled by the Tibetan king and his subjects who were Guru Rinpoche's disciples, elevated seven cubits in space. A generous stream of nectar flowed from their bodies, entirely filling a large copper vessel. The lama and his retinue considered me with love. Glowing with great kindness, they said,

> Kyé Ho! Fortunate child of our spiritual family,
> This is the spiritual attainment of the vase–wisdom body empowerment
> In the form of the nectar of bliss-emptiness.
> Today we bestow this upon you.
> Having accepted this, your physical obscurations will be cleansed,
> And the seed to attain the manifest body of enlightenment will be
>   planted within you.
> May you be ripened and liberated as the vajra body!

Then they dissolved into the crown of my head. The dakini told me, "Drink this nectar without leaving anything left over!" I gulped it down without leaving any remainder, and my entire body became drunk with the flavor of bliss and happiness. The dakini sang,

> This holy lama of yours is not a human being.
> He's really the Buddha incarnate.
> You, Drokben Khyé-u Chung Lotsawa,
> Are the heart son of Supreme Orgyen.
> By the strength of his pure aspirations,
> He appeared in an emanated body as a protector of beings.
> He planted the seed of freedom in the mindstreams
> Of individuals endowed with devotion and respect.

> He makes those who recite supplications and mantras
> Draw nigh to the level of omniscience.
> Therefore, offer the first portion of all your food and drink
> To this holy lama who is not a human being,
> But truly the Buddha.

Recite mantras and pray to him;

When you are walking, meditate that he is at your right shoulder;

When you receive empowerments, meditate on him in space before
    you;

When you meditate and when you go to sleep,

Meditate on him in your heart and merge your minds.

When you are eating or drinking, meditate on him in your throat.

When you are doing deity practice, meditate on him as the essence of
    the deity.

To sum up my point, at all times and in all circumstances,

All the lamas from whom you've received

Empowerment, scriptural transmission, and pith instructions are fused
    in this lama.

Meditate that in essence

He is supreme Dorjé Chang, Vajra Bearer, or Orgyen Pema Jungné,
    Lotus-Born.

Accept empowerment and spiritual attainment from him repeatedly,

Develop irreversible faith and respect,

And gain supreme spiritual attainment in this very lifetime!

Then she vanished into the space of the nature of reality.

What Is Called "Meditation"

IN A DREAM AT NIGHT on the twenty-fifth day, a holy individual appeared saying he was the Buddhist king Trisong Deutsen. He told me,

> Kyé Ho! Fortunate child of my spiritual family,
> There are countless sentient beings in cyclic existence,
> Yet look at how few gain a human body.
> Many gain a human body,
> Yet look at how few are endowed with the freedoms and resources [of
>   a precious human birth].
> Although many have gained the freedoms and resources,
> Look at how few make them meaningful.
> Since it's as if none make them meaningful,
> Look at how few attain liberation.
>
> These days, like appearances in a dream,
> Look at how even those who gain this precious human body
> Waste their human life
> Over the course of years, months, days, and moments.
> Of those early years of life,
> Look at how many are spent practicing the holy Dharma.
> Among the activities in that human life,
> Look at what point they have.
> The human beings who lived in the past
> Busied themselves with activities concerned with this life;
> Now that they're on the road toward death,
> Look at what sort of help these tasks are to them.
> For the welfare of children, grandchildren, dear ones, and family,
> They defeated enemies, protected friends,
> Farmed crops, stockpiled, and swindled,
> Yet now when they're on the road toward death,
> Look at the value and result of what they've done.
> Although ancestors and those before them,

Wore out their human lives in suffering
Thinking of future generations of children and grandchildren,
Is there anyone who remembers their kindness? Look at that.

Entirely everything you do
Is just the same as that, and since it's the same,
Concentrate on becoming self-sufficient.
From a universal monarch on high
To a little child born yesterday,
One hundred years from now,
The human beings now alive on this earth
Won't be anything but ashen corpses:
Everything is nothing more than appearances in a dream.

After a year has passed,
It's as if it was no longer than a mere instant;
Even if you manage to live one hundred years, it still feels like merely a
    moment.
At the time of death, the life you led seems like a dreamscape.
When the time arrives for the aeon of destruction,
Everything animate and inanimate in this world throughout the three-
    thousandfold cosmos
Will vanish into emptiness without a trace.

All the people who died in the past
And the dead you've actually seen all had the same attitude:
They strived and strategized to remain for many years;
Unsuccessful in those wishes,
They fell under the power of impermanence and death.
They left behind their wealth like dirt and rocks,
Lost their illusory body like tattered clothes,
And were divided from friends and family like people in a crowded
    marketplace.
They woke up from their lives' events as if from a dream
And wandered like a stray dog into the next world.
Without any control over where they're going,
They're driven from behind by the strong gale of karma.

Led helplessly by the Lord of Death's minions,
They plunge into what they don't want—the abodes of the miserable
　　existences—
To experience their sufferings all alone.
They wail in agony, crying out,
Yet apart from themselves, no one sees or hears them.
Think of that, and apply yourself to your own quest for enlightenment.

If hardship, hunger, cold, sickness, and suffering occur
For the sake of your spiritual practice,
And you find yourself exasperated,
Why aren't you fed up with experiencing the endless suffering
Of the agony of cold and heat known by hell beings,
The exhaustion, hunger, and thirst of starving spirits,
Or the mute foolishness,
Butchery, forced labor, and the like that animals must undergo?
If dismay with those states has arisen,
How can you possibly be annoyed with hardship in your spiritual
　　practice?

Don't forget these key points. Instill them in your mind.
Don't forget these key points. Hold them in your heart.
Take these as foremost among all profound pith instructions.
Don't forget! Don't forget! Don't forget death!
Don't be distracted! Don't be distracted! Don't be distracted in this
　　human life!
Don't give up! Don't give up! Don't give up what's helpful for your next
　　life!
Think about it! Think about it! Think about the suffering of cyclic
　　existence!
Concentrate! Concentrate! Concentrate on the holy Buddhist path!
Escape! Escape! Escape from the abodes of cyclic existence!
Pursue! Pursue! Pursue the trailhead of freedom.

This sovereign king's wisdom midstream shifts to you.
In the past, when I was Rikzin Jikmé Lingpa,

You were my maternal uncle renowned as a great meditator,
And you were unsurpassably kind to me.
Therefore, the fruition of that is my encounter here with you.
In this lifetime, we will be father and son.
In the future, in the northern land of Shambala,
You and I will accompany one another as king and official.

Then he vanished into the arena of intangible space.

THAT SAME MONTH on the night of the new moon, the supreme awareness holder Dudul Dorjé appeared within a canopy of dense rainbow light. I saw him as he considered me with affection. Joyfully he sang,

Kyé! Listen to me, you handsome-faced child.
You are my emanation, indivisible with me.
I will teach you profound pith instructions,
So listen with utmost care and hold them in your mind.

Adopt the ten virtuous acts;
Abandon as if they were poison the ten nonvirtuous acts.
All training and vows are subsumed in this.

Wherever you have been born in cyclic existence, high or low,
Is but a dark box of unbearable suffering,
Where there exists not even an iota of assured happiness.
Strive for supreme freedom!

If you seek refuge elsewhere, you will be deceived.
Take as your holy refuge the Three Jewels—
Whether happy or sad, at all times and in all circumstances,
Hold them with respect, indivisibly, in your mind.

Sentient beings are, by nature, your parents;
Develop deep confidence in the four boundless aspirations, and
Then focus on their welfare and happiness.
Constantly undertake what is helpful for beings.

Offer your body and possessions, along with the roots of your virtue,
With an attitude free from attachment and grasping,
To the supremely precious Jewels.

Fortified with the crucial instructions of the four antidotal powers,
Admit and purify your negative and nonvirtuous acts.

For refuge, rely on your superb lama, the eternal lord protector,
And proffer offerings to him or her.
Make supplications, take the four empowerments,
And at all times, without separation, depend on your lama as you
    would your own eyes.

Always practice the methods for accumulating merit.
Be diligent in the supreme practice of offering your body.
To train in the [practice of attaining] the pure lands,
Bring the pure lands to mind.
Cultivate the experience of the profound path of transference of
    consciousness.

To dispel outer and inner obstacles and impediments,
And to shift your three doors of body, speech, and mind to the
    adamantine city,
When you meditate on your chosen deity and recite mantras,
Never ever let go of the appearance of the deity.

Then he dissolved into my heart.

IN THE YEAR I TURNED EIGHTEEN, on the tenth day of the Miracle Month,
when I went to shepherd animals, I rested at the base of the Nélé Shar Cliff
and fell asleep for a moment. In the appearing aspect of a dream unfolding,
inside a mansion made of five kinds of gems, I saw a handsome young scholar
who told me he was Padampa Sangyé. He said,

Child, listen to me without distraction.
Your mind is inclined to Buddhist practice,

Yet you haven't differentiated between what is Buddhist practice and
   what is not,
Therefore I will make that distinction for you.

Virtuous acts of body and speech
Are not the perfect buddhas' practice.
If you've made present the nature of mind,
That is the perfect buddhas' holy practice.

Even if the force of your previous good karma has led you
To realize the view of infinite space,
Concentrate now on realizing the path
Of clarity-emptiness, without clinging, in your meditation.
This is the ultimate holy practice.
This is the innermost core of all Buddhist practices.
This is the most profound of all sacred instructions.
This is the swiftest among all paths.
This is renowned as the pith instruction in what is called "meditation"
By all lama adepts who appeared in the past.
Know it, child of my spiritual family.

Then he vanished into the expanse of space.

THAT SAME YEAR in the Ox Month, while I was sitting at the base of a cliff
called Marshar focusing my mind on a stone, I fell asleep. In my dream a
small child in white cotton attire was dancing on the treetops. He asked me,
"Child, why have you come here?"

I answered, "Lamas, monks, and tantric adepts of the past have said that
there's something to see and hear in what's called 'meditation.' So I'm sitting
here waiting."

To that the little boy sang,

When at first you receive pointing-out pith instructions,
Your body is like a roll of paper,
Your speech is akin to the sound of wind in a tube,
And your mind is the foundation of all cyclic existence and enlightenment.

This body is a like an empty house,
Your speech is like the sound of wind in a space,
And your mind is like a den of thieves.

In some spiritual paths, it's said multiple things—body, speech, and
    mind—are of one taste.
In some spiritual paths, it's believed they are separate.
In some spiritual paths, it's believed they are interconnected.
From among the trio of body, speech, and mind, we identify which is
    chief.
Now and later, and in the interim, at the start, at the finish, and always,
Who created cyclic existence and enlightenment?
Think very precisely about the way that is and functions.
Since what is called 'meditation' is originally nonexistent,
In waiting for something you can see or hear, you're really far off from
    what is called 'meditation.'

Then he burst out laughing, which woke me from sleep.

I recognized that as a sign
That I must examine this trio of body, speech, and mind.
As soon as I looked at them,
I saw that the vagrant in the miserable states of cyclic existence is the
    mind;
The one liberated on the ground of enlightenment is also the mind,
And the one perpetuating happiness and suffering is the mind as well.
If it's liberated, it's naturally liberated by itself
And apart from this, virtuous acts of body and speech alone aren't
    helpful.
I examined in detail minds' mode of being and its reasons, and so forth.
After that, I didn't know what I should do.
I rested within equanimity.

AT NIGHT ON THE NINTH DAY of the Tiger Month, as a dreamscape unfolded,
that little child from before appeared. This is what I told him:

As you said, I examined things—
The one that creates everything is the mind;
Therefore, I understand that among the three doors, the mind is chief.
Now what do I do? I know nothing at all.

In response the little child said,

If it is the mind that creates everything,
Regarding this mind, where does it initially come from?
In the interim, at what place does it abide?
In the end, where does it go and what is going? Investigate that!
Don't settle for mere understanding or just what you've heard,
You must believe with deep conviction.
Don't forget! Take this as the holy vital instruction.

Then he vanished into the continuity of space.

The month after that,
Once I examined further using that process,
I saw that there was no place to come from, nor something that comes,
No place to abide, nor something abiding,
And no place to go, nor something that goes. With all of that,
I concluded with certainty that there is no objective domain, basis, or
    root.
Having examined that again and again,
I saw it as the play of all-pervasive space.
I rested in vivid clarity
Within the indivisibility of mind and space.
When that was finished, I still didn't know what to do.

IN A DREAM at night on the first day of the following month, a young woman
saying she was Dakini Nangzéma, Illuminator of Appearances, told me,

Listen to me, fortunate child of the lineage.
Once you enter the paths of other spiritual approaches,
You produce or block discursive thoughts—

Either your mind blocks them or performs tasks,
Such as looking at one part of the mind with another.
The unpredictable phenomena of happiness and suffering
Suddenly erupt.
So in the doctrine, don't trust in and depend upon
Calculations of the paths and stages [of the general, lower approach].
The adept who has realized the indwelling nature
Of the indivisibility of mind and space
Makes space apparent in the arena of awareness.
This is the exceptionally profound swift path.
This is what you should trust in. Take it as the sacred meaning.
This is the heart essence of mamos and dakinis,
The supreme foundation of all profound pith instructions.
Cultivate this experience and you will surely gain liberation!

Then she vanished without a trace.

THAT SAME YEAR on the tenth day of the first winter month, I went to shepherd the animals. When I fell asleep at the base of a cliff called Götsang, a red dakini appeared saying, "This red cliff is the abode of a sorcerer. Inside here lies a treasure box and a stone statue of Méwa Tsekpa [a wrathful guardian deity]. Go where you see a black design, strike the earth with a rock, and take the treasure."

I woke up, and as soon as I struck that place with a rock, what remained of the rock face was a black iron stone the size of a vulture's egg, blazing with light. I took the wrathful deity statue made of stone, five finger widths in height, and carried it home. I showed it to our venerated lama, named Chödzin, Doctrine Holder. The next day he declared, "This is definitely the spirit stone of a god-demon. I dreamt that you must return it to where it was."

When he said that, both my parents told me, "Quickly take it back to its own place." As instructed, I put it back.

A dakini told me in a dream, "You took a jewel in your hand, then a demon gave you an incorrect prediction: You lost hold of the auspicious connection to gain one hundred statues. From this point on, abandon poor conduct of that sort!" Then she disappeared.

A Lucid Dreamer

IT WAS THE YEAR I TURNED NINETEEN. When I went to northeast Lower Ser, to Ngala Taktsé, I journeyed deep into an area of cliffs and forests. I kept going further and further until mountainous cliffs surrounded me. In the center stretched a meadow of blossoming flowers, circled by a perimeter of trees. I saw a red cliff that seemed to rise into the center of space, and at its base stood a very large cave. It looked like fingertips joined in a symbolic gesture. Inside I found a hearth, along with a place to sleep. As soon as I saw that, my mind become melancholy. As I sat in that place for a moment, a man riding a goat appeared. He sang,

> Do you know what place this is or not?
> If you don't know,
> This site is the Cliff and Forest Fortress.
> Machik Lapdrönma's superlative son,
> Tö-nyön Samdrub, Skull Madman Accomplisher of Wishes,
> Stayed here in retreat for ten months.
> This location is equal in blessings
> To the Indian charnel ground Spontaneous Pinnacle.
> This site's owner is Dorjé Drakpo Tsal, Fierce Vajra Adept,
> Who is sometimes accompanied by mamos and dakinis
> Attending the vajra feast in Celestial Enjoyment Pure Land.
> Sometimes he acts as the general of the eight tribes of spirits,
> As they suppress evil demons.
> Sometimes he accompanies hordes of ruler demons and sorcerers
> As they protect human beings.
> Sometimes he accompanies goblins and ghouls
> As they put to death unruly, wicked humans.
> Sometimes he acts as the leader of noble female practitioners
> As they destroy people who have transgressed promises and tantric
>   commitments.
> Sometimes he accompanies throngs of regional gods
> As they protect the doctrines of individuals who truly practice.

Although this is a place endowed with pristine qualities like these,
The assembled retinue of the great minister
King Yutreng, Turquoise Rosary, delight in evil—
They have converted to wickedness all the people of this area.
As a result of their deception, transgressed promises, and broken tantric
    commitments,
Their merit and glory have declined
And destitution, poverty, ghosts, and ghouls abound.

In the future, in the Sheep Year [1859],
Once you've unlocked the door of your profound treasures,
If the karma, fortune, and auspicious connections come into alignment
For the spread of those profound teachings throughout this area,
This region's influence will increase.

My child, return to your homeland.
On the west flank of this mountain stands the illusory wisdom body of
    Drolma, Liberating Mother,
Emanated in a form made of turquoise.
When you encounter her, offer prostrations,
Make mandala offerings, and your merit will increase.

Then he vanished without a trace into open space. As I returned, along the way, in a grove of a white medicinal herbs I saw a statue of Drolma, Liberating Mother, made of turquoise, two thumbs high. I did prostrations and made mandala offerings to her, and developed devotion such that I couldn't stand to be apart from her.

Later I went to my aunt's home. When I recounted my story she said, "Either you're lying or it was a goblin."

On the eighth day of the first summer month, I was at the crossroads of a place called Marshar. I brought forth awareness, and while I settled in evenness, I fell asleep. In my dream a young monk saying he was Bodhisattva Shariputra told me, "Child of my spiritual family, regarding the perfection of sublime insight, that is what is called 'meditation.' Apart from meditation, there is no other such thing as perfection of sublime insight, nor apart from the perfection of sublime insight is there any other such thing as meditation.

"What is sublime insight? It is to make apparent your original abiding insight—simply that. By their nature, the five aggregates are empty; you must see them correctly as such. Form is emptiness. Emptiness is form. Apart from form, there is no other emptiness. Likewise, sensation, perception, and all compositional factors are emptiness.

"Child of my spiritual family, accordingly, phenomena are emptiness, with no characteristics, no origin, no cessation, no defilement, no lack of defilement, no dearth, and no fullness. Therefore, there is no form in emptiness, nor is there sensation, perception, formation, consciousness, eyes, ears, nose, tongue, body, intellect, form, sound, smell, taste, touch, and phenomena. There is no sense-base of the eyes, [ears, nose, tongue, body,] or intellect. Furthermore, there is no sense-base of consciousness of the [eyes, ears, nose, tongue, body,] or intellect. Likewise, there is no suffering, no cause of suffering, no cessation, and no path. There is no wisdom, no attainment, and even no lack of attainment.

"Child of my spiritual family, therefore, bodhisattvas have nothing to attain, so they rely upon and dwell in the perfection of sublime insight. Because their minds are not obscured, they are without fear. Having utterly gone beyond ever turning back [to cyclic existence], they have fully perfected the transcendence of sorrow. Even all buddhas who abide in the past, present, and future have relied on the perfection of sublime insight to fully manifest buddhahood—unsurpassed and absolutely complete awakening."

He quoted this directly as it was written, then told me, "Child of my spiritual family, as described, know the meaning and indwelling nature of all cyclic existence and enlightenment as one taste in supreme emptiness. Make emptiness obvious. That is the inconceivable wisdom of the basic space of phenomena, so recognize it! Trust in it!" Then he dissolved into me, causing all appearances to spin into bliss and the experience of vivid, luminous awareness to dawn.

THAT SAME YEAR on the thirteenth day of the last winter month, along the way to work as a shepherd, I saw a whirlwind spinning clockwise. "That is a demon," I thought, and picked up a stone. I recited the four-Hung mantra and threw the stone. A naked little boy said to me,

> I'm not a demon or even a god;
> I'm not old, nor young, nor born,

Therefore I'm the little boy Namké Norbu, Gem of Space.
Demons have many forms.
All that the eyes see is an immense great city,
Where a maniacal demon darts about in the sensory realm of form.
If one is to subdue that demon, it will be subdued by an illusionist.
You don't recognize that. Alas!

All that the ears hear is an immense city
Where a maniacal demon pursues sounds.
If one is to subdue that demon, it will be subdued by someone skilled
    in echos.
You don't recognize that. Alas!

All that the nose smells is an immense city
Where a maniacal demon chases smells.
If one is to subdue that demon, it will be subdued by the child of an
    illusory smell-eating spirit.
You don't recognize that. Alas!

All that the tongue experiences is an immense city
Where a maniacal demon makes tastes apparent.
If one is to subdue that demon, it will be subdued by a dreamer.
You don't recognize that. Alas!

All that the body feels is an immense city
Where a maniacal demon makes touch perceptible.
If one is to subdue that demon, it will be subdued by someone skilled
    in water bubbles.
You don't recognize that. Alas!

Then he vanished into the magical illusion of the nature of reality.

THE YEAR I TURNED TWENTY, at night on the twenty-fifth day of the middle
summer month, to the west in a drought-stricken area I found the remains
of a spring. I saw a naga woman there, suffering from severe exhaustion, her
four limbs disease-struck, crippled, and dessicated. I asked her, "What causes
and circumstances produced such suffering?"

The naga woman uttered,

> Alas! How I suffer!
> A woman washed her body—
> The runoff entered my mouth as pollution and poison.
> That was the cause and condition
> For such suffering and disease as this.
> With the spring dried up, my homestead has vanished.
> My strength to walk and move is spent.
> If you're able to make water offerings to me,
> It will likely help.

She said that and I responded,

> Alas, you sentient being with wretched karma!
> I see unbearable suffering of this sort
> As the fruition of your previous negative karma.
> The means to reverse this won't come about from someone
>   like me.

When I said that, Bodhisattva Chenrézi, All-Seeing Eyes, appeared in space before me:

Kyé Ho! Fortunate child of my spiritual family, to protect this afflicted sentient being, you must perform this recitation and meditation:

> In an instant of recollection,
> I appear complete as Jikten Wangchuk Chenrézi, World Sovereign
>   All-Seeing Eyes,
> With one face and two arms, in standing posture.
> My right hand holds a precious jewel,
> And my left hand displays the gesture of supreme generosity.
> In my palm are a white Om, a red Ah, and a blue Hung,
> From which flow the nectar of uncontaminated great bliss.
> The suffering, karma, and afflictive emotions
> Of all beings of the three realms, in general, and of my focal subject,
> Are cleansed like a perfectly clear mirror—

And they gain an inexhaustible treasury of riches.
They actually attain the exalted state of the Bodhisattva!

Om Mani Pémé Hung

Nama Sarwa Tata Gata Ahwaloki Té Om Sambara Sambara
Hung

He said, "By performing that one hundred thousand times, signs of release from suffering will manifestly appear." Then he vanished.

As described, for seven days I made water offerings and performed that visualization and recitation many times. Rain fell at night on the eighth day. In the morning, water overflowed from what was left of the dried out spring, far in excess of what had flowed there before.

That night the naga woman appeared again. "Later I will give you naga wealth. Tonight I'm going to kill the woman who inflicted that suffering upon me."

I answered, "Don't kill that woman. Just send her something to make her heart unhappy."

In response, the naga woman told me, "If I don't take the living heart of a sentient being, I can't just sit here doing nothing." Then she flew into the sky. The next day at sunset hail fell and lightning struck a cow-yak hybrid, killing it.

In the year I turned twenty-one, on the twenty-ninth day of the first summer month, I spotted an egg in a snake's nest. Several days later, I returned there and saw a spectacle. It was a single egg the size of the top of my thumb, like an unmarred crystal outside and within. Inside sat an eight-petaled lotus that always faced upward, no matter how you placed the egg. I built a structure of rocks around it.

In a dream ten days later, that naga woman from earlier appeared. "That snake egg is naga wealth. This is my marvelous repayment for your kindness. For someone like you who endures suffering such as poverty and dwindled wealth, this alone will alleviate it. By merely possessing this egg, your wealth will grow greater than it was before." After that, I wrapped the egg in white wool and placed it in a small container. By keeping it as a sacred support, my wealth increased only slightly more than it was previously.

IN THE LATTER PART OF THAT SAME YEAR, my vajra companion named Lama Ten, Stable, said to me, "It's likely you're a lucid dreamer. Can you see in your dreams a mantra to increase my wealth?"

To do so, one night [before sleep] I recited a declaration of truth incantation, and in the appearing aspect of a dream, Dakini Lhacham Gyalmo, Queen Divine Wife, said,

> If that man desires wealth,
> He should imagine before him a golden castle, yellow in color.
> Inside stands a throne of precious gems.
> Upon this is the letter *Bé,* from which appears Gyalchen Namtösé,
>   Great King Heir of Hearers,
> Golden colored, holding a victory banner and mongoose.
> Adorned with silks and jewels,
> He majestically sits upon a white lioness
> Amid immeasurable light and brilliance.
> The yellow letter *Bé* at his heart
> Is encircled by the mantra garland, from which light shines,
> Inviting the deity from his own abode and causing him to dissolve into
>   the imagined deity.

> OM BÉ SHRAMANA YÉ SVAHA BÉ SAMAYA SARWA BASU SIDDHI
> SIDDHI HUNG

"Once he has recited that, if he makes offerings, fulfillment offerings, and supplications, then his wealth will increase, as will auspicious events." Then she vanished within the nature of reality.

Thirteen Holy Disciples

IN THE YEAR I TURNED TWENTY-TWO, in the appearances of a dream at night on the ninth day of the Miracle Month, a dakini appeared saying she was Yeshe Tsogyal. She sang,

> Kyé Ho! Fortunate child of my spiritual family,
> If you don't recognize me,
> I am, Tsogyal, noble lady of Karchen.
> I was commanded by Guru Supreme Orgyen
> To visit your place.
> Why have I come here?
> It's time for you to guide disciples.
> My child, listen to your mother's words.
> As soon as you see the glowing face of the snake,[17]
> A pair of superb steeds will arrive from the east.
> By the hot rays coming like light from above,
> Develop the agile strength of the five-faced one [a lion], and mount the
>   horse.
> Once you've reached the land of unruly wicked humans,
> The fruit of your seeing eyes will open
> And two branches with intelligence will grow.
> You will encounter a mountainous cliff of jewels and gold
> And obtain three wish-fulfilling jewels.
> You will encounter a mountain of rubies
> And both the sun and moon will rise in the sky.
> The manifestation of an enormous number of evil demons and vow-
>   violation spirits
> Will separate milk and water.
>
> You will encounter a precious earth treasure—
> Few disciples will practice that.
> As for the cycle called The Profound Doctrine Overflowing into the
>   Expanse of Wisdom Mind—

Even fewer disciples will practice that.
Wisdom's Infinite Matrix of Pure Phenomena will appear—
A great many disciples will practice that.
You will open the door of The Space Treasury of the Nature of Reality—
Many disciples will be trained through that.
Especially in relation to The Space Treasury of the Nature of Reality,
Anyone connected to that cycle will be propelled into the prescence of
    freedom.

Furthermore, due to the spread of their hostile evil,
In the ogre city of nefarious humans,
Many detractors of you and your doctrine
Will appear in the form of numerous emanations of demons and vow-
    violation spirits.

There will be many individuals with faithful intention
Connected to you through positive aspirations and karma.
Guide them in ways attuned to their needs and circumstances;
If you teach, the doctrine will gradually spread.

These days, in this degenerate aeon,
An emanation of a conquest demon, Langdarma,
Is renowned as a ruler among the people of Nyarong.
He has taken control of numerous mountain passes and valleys.
He holds in punishment many who are without fault.
And has destroyed many Buddhist centers.

In the east lives an ogre demon couple, male and female.
Together they've dominated many areas,
Controlling extensive mountain passes and valleys.
They are assisted in their evil venture
By a few people with corrupt aspirations
Who persevere in acts of fighting, incest, and murder—
This agitates hostile worldly gods and demons.
Sickness, famine, and epidemics will erupt.
The force of barbarian substances, incantations, and curses
Will lead people to engage in riotous wrongdoing,

Perpetually on the attack, with each deceiving the other.
The signs of the degeneration of this evil era are on full display.
To turn them back, rely on Dorjé Phurba, Vajra Dagger, and
Then exert yourself in the practice of Lhachen Wangchuk, Magnificent
    Ruler Deity.
If fortunate persons don't fall under demonic control,
A period of increasing merit will occur.

Then she vanished into the space of the nature of reality.

AT NIGHT on the tenth day of the Miracle Month, Dakini Yeshe Tsogyal appeared. She poured thirteen mustard seeds onto a pristine blue mirror, saying,

You are my heart's dearest child.
These mustard seeds, thirteen grains, are spiritual heroes
Who will, in the future, during the latter part of your life,
Manifest enlightenment in this very lifetime.
They will become your thirteen holy disciples
Equal to Buddha Dorjé Chang, Vajra Bearer.
Keep this mirror at your heart
And the realization of Great Perfection will overflow from the expanse.
I, the dakini, will also dissolve into you.
Realize the meaning of our nondual wisdom mind.

She dissolved into my heart and the experience of the wisdom of bliss-emptiness dawned.

IN THE APPEARANCES of a dreamscape at night on the tenth day of the Saga Constellation Month, the vajra body of Orgyen appeared. He placed a silver vase on the crown of my head, saying, "This is the vase wisdom-body empowerment." As he poured the vase water onto my head, it suffused my body and I was intoxicated by the flavor of bliss. Furthermore, he dissolved into the crown of my head.

Later, in the appearing aspect of the night of the eighth day in the Ling Constellation Month, someone said to be the vajra speech of Orgyen appeared. The vajra master's body was red in color and he had a skull-cup filled with impure shit. "This is the secret empowerment. Consume this without leaving anything behind," he told me. As soon as he placed it in my hand, I ate it with powerful devotion and respect, and it became nectar endowed with the nutritive qualities of one hundred tastes. It was suffused with qualities, such as being sweet, delicious-smelling, and appealing. I experienced the wisdom of bliss-emptiness, and the supreme master said, "Earlier you received the vase empowerment. Now you've received the secret empowerment. This constitutes the complete simultaneous empowerment of the buddhas of the past, present, and future, and of the protectors who guard their doctrine." Then he vanished into the space of the nature of reality.

THAT SAME YEAR in the Victory Constellation Month, Pachik Dampa Sangyé gave me numerous empowerments and profound instructions for the holy doctrine of the Pacification of Suffering. In particular, he spoke these lines again and again:

> This holy doctrine, the Pacification of Suffering,
> Is the core amalgamation of every pith instruction
> Of the sutras and tantras: It is their condensed essence.
> It makes apparent the nature of mind.
> It is awareness of the emptiness of the universe and its inhabitants.
> It is the view of appearing existence as self-manifest.
> It is the three realms as the display of mind.
> It binds together cyclic existence and enlightenment as emptiness
>   alone.
> It is gods and demons as positive and negative thoughts.
> It is happiness and suffering as the false images of mind.
> It is hope and fear as the messengers of demons.
> It is the essence of the grasping mind.
> It is the creator of the desiring mind.
> It is the metaphor for the magical illusion of mind as the reflection of
>   the moon on water.
>
> If you recognize this fundamental nature that is the view,
> To make that fundamental nature apparent is meditation.
> To gain self-reliant mastery in the fundamental nature is conduct.

The four evil forces are what should be severed into basic space.
The body's aggregates are what should be thrown out as food.
Happiness is what you should give to others.
Suffering is what you should accept.
Charnel grounds are the wild places where you should wander.
Unfixed and ever-moving is how you should be.
Fearlessness and great confidence is what you should gain.
Benefit for the gods and demons is what you should accomplish.

Today I am entrusting this to you.
This is the root of all profound pith instructions.
This is the truest of all paths.
This is how you will accomplish enlightenment in one lifetime.

Then he seemed to dissolve into me.

WHEN I WAS TWENTY-THREE, on the eighth day of the first summer month I went east to the region of Golok. In a dream at night on the tenth day, I was told,

Tomorrow, in that place,
Whatever auspicious connections occur, if you act according to them,
It's certain that the welfare of beings will ensue:
My child, look at what transpires and consider it.

So spoke Dakini Lékyi Wangmo, Queen of Activity, and also this:

In the pure celestial realms of great bliss
There are inconceivable qualities of bliss and happiness.
These are all my, the dakini's, array.

Then she vanished into the space of the nature of reality.

Furthermore, the next day when morning arrived, along the Mar Tak-yak Pass I met with a bridal procession. The bridal escorts told me, "Dismount and drink some alcohol." When I drank the alcohol as they said, I examined that auspicious connection. I saw that I would need to be a householder who relies on a female companion and engages in worldly activity. That's how I understood the event as a sign and portent.

THAT SAME YEAR in the first autumn month, when I saw the exalted Jikten Wangchuk, World Sovereign [i.e., Chenrézi], he spoke of texts outlining the means of accomplishment related to various deities:

> My child, previously, when you were seventeen years old,
> You practiced Jampal Mawé Sengé, Gentle Splendor Lion of Speech.
> You saw his face and received prophecies from him,
> Yet the consecrated pills [on your shrine] were gathered into the basic
>   space of the dakinis.
> Since your connection with that deity so far isn't very good,
> Exert yourself in that practice once again.
> If you recite twenty-one malas of mantra
> For one hundred days without interruption,
> The channel in your throat will open
> And a vast treasure trove of words and terms will overflow.
> If you don't visualize your own body as the deity's [form],
> Whatever mantra you've recited won't produce any result.
> If you don't possess this key instruction,
> Your writing will be faulty—everyone will disparage you.
> If you err in relation to the meaning, others will harbor doubts.
> The sophists of this evil era of degeneration
> Don't know how to evaluate the sharp efficacy of your blessings.
> Inspecting just your words, they lob criticism.
> In particular, those heavily bedecked with wealth, fame,
> Or the eight worldly concerns,
> And who seem visibly adorned with beauty,
> Lack any qualities, yet everyone grovels before them.

> Those with true aspiration and karmic destiny as treasure revealers
> Have been born in low situations, poor and humble.
> They mostly stay in mountain hermitages, cliffs, and caves.
> Some assume the guise of beggars.
> Some live as busy householders.

In order to foster humble disciples,
They renounce greatness, keeping to a low station.
To fulfill the necessity of meeting individuals connected to them
By positive aspirations and karma,
They journey throughout every land, wandering without a fixed locale.
Guiding fortunate individuals with skillful means,
Connections to them lead to the path of the great spiritual approach.
Each and every [true treasure revealer] commits themselves to practice,
And harbors minimal craving for wealth and livestock.
They delight in making respectful offerings to Pema Jungné, Lotus-Born.
They work for the benefit of disciples,
Persevering without chagrin or weariness through the hardships of
    helping others.
All treasure revealers manifest due to past aspirations and karmic
    affinity
Made with Pema Jungné, Lotus-Born.
Diligent in practice and happy to teach,
They accomplish impartial benefit for others:
If you want to guide disciples, do so with that example.

These days, in this five-hundred-year period of decline,
Many charlatans with false treasures
Practice in the wish for profit, fame, and renown in this lifetime.
They crave wealth and are greedy for food.
They aren't diligent in practice and conduct rituals to avert misfortune.
Traveling compulsively through all the townships,
They waste their human life searching for gain.
They save face with the high and detest the low.
Their desire and avarice are stronger than those of dogs in alleyways.
Making a connection with someone like that is utterly meaningless—
They're like leaders of the blind and nothing more.

You, individual of superlative fortune,
Possess the strength of training throughout your series of lifetimes.
Since you've already achieved magnificent benefit for yourself in the
    past,
The time has arrived for you to help others impartially.

Custodians of My Doctrine

IN THE YEAR I TURNED THIRTY, in the pure vision of a dream at night on the ninth day of the eighth month, Wisdom Dakini Tsogyal sang to me,

Regarding this woman below, Sönam Tso, Lake of Merit,
Although her family line is not appealing,
She is an emanation of a flesh-eating dakini.
Rely on her as your partner,
And next year Lord Garab Dorjé, Vajra of Utmost Joy, will be born
As your son endowed with the force of merit.
Through the might of pure aspiration,
If he's not overpowered by a bad companion,
For your doctrine it will be like the sun dawning—
It's even possible that it will pervade absolutely all directions.
Give him the name Sönam Tenzin, Meritorious Holder of the Doctrine.

Then in the Rabbit Year
Another son will be born—
Kyira Gönpo Dorjé, Vajra Lord Hunter.
If he lacks faith in your doctrine,
He won't be of any help. If you give him to someone else, it will be
    good.
As an omen that the protectors aren't pleased with him,
His merit and fame will be weak.
Due to the birth, that woman won't have the opportunity to stay.
She will [pass away,] vanishing into basic space.

North of here,
A woman with a garland of moles
Known by the name Sangyé, Buddha,
Is an emanation of Nyenmo Siddhi.
If you enjoy her as your partner,
A son will be born who is King Dza.

You'll see him in the Female Earth Snake Year.
He will cultivate your doctrine.

Further, in the next Rabbit Year,
One son will appear as the dance of the display of Mélong Dorjé, Vajra
    Mirror.
He will act for the welfare of beings
Who are intangible gods and demons.
He will conduct himself in a peculiar style.

Within the coiled recesses of the black Metal Snake [Year],
One son will appear, an emanation of Matok Rinchen.
He will help beings.

These two women are the first you need to live with.
To please the dakinis, you must rely upon them,
And although your influence and fame won't come from them,
They will be significant for you to complete your profound teachings.

Then she vanished into the sky without a trace.

IN THE YEAR I TURNED THIRTY-ONE, at night on the tenth day of the first
month, Master Prabahasti bestowed upon me the empowerment and scriptural transmission of Dorjé Phurba, Vajra Dagger. That same year at night
on the twenty-fifth day of the Saga Constellation Month, the wisdom dakini
Dorjé Naljorma, Vajra Adept, granted me the complete empowerment and
scriptural transmission for the heart practice called "Wisdom Sun," for the
complete sacred instructions of Severance, and for the text outlining the
means of accomplishment related to Tröma Nakmo, Wrathful Black Goddess. When that concluded, she gave me some prophecies and profound
advice, and finally vanished within nonreferential space.

IN THE YEAR I TURNED THIRTY-TWO, at night on the tenth day of the Tiger
Month, I saw Orgyen Pema Dudul, Lotus Demon Tamer, and he bestowed
upon me the sacred instructions of Great Perfection.

IN THE YEAR I TURNED THIRTY-THREE, on the fifteenth day of the Mindruk Constellation Month, Dakini Sukasiddhi gave me numerous pith instructions for the means of accomplishment related to Profound Severance of Evil Forces.

IN THE YEAR I TURNED THIRTY-FOUR, at night on the twenty-seventh day of the Victory Month, Master Supreme Hungkara told me, "You are the designated inheritor of my doctrine." He also gave prophecies regarding the future assembly of my karmically destined students and made aspirations. His appearance dissolved into me.

IN THE YEAR I TURNED THIRTY-FIVE, at nightfall on the fifth day of the first summer month, Jampal Mawé Sengé, Gentle Splendor Lion of Speech, appeared in the visionary experience of a dream. When I encountered him he bestowed upon me the complete empowerments and scriptural transmissions for the outer, inner, and secret texts outlining the means of accomplishment related to the five sacred families of Jampal. Once again, he granted me prophecies and profound advice.

IN THE YEAR I TURNED THIRTY-SIX, when I saw Lord Tsépak-mé, Boundless Life, he granted me the full empowerment and scriptural transmission for his means of accomplishment. Moreover, he taught me various details of creation and completion phases of the Great Bliss Pure Land practice.

IN THE YEAR I TURNED THIRTY-SEVEN, the supreme Bodhisattva Tukjé Chenpo, Supreme Compassion, appeared in the visionary experience of a dream. When I saw him, I received the nectar of his wisdom speech. He bestowed upon me the complete empowerments and scriptural transmissions for five texts outlining the means of accomplishment related to him from the highest level [of tantra]. He made aspirations and gave me his seal of entrustment again and again.

IN THE YEAR I TURNED THIRTY-EIGHT, Orgyen Nangsi Zilnön, He Who Overwhelms Apparent Existence with Splendor, appeared in the pure appearances of a dream. When I met him, he gave me the empowerments and scriptural transmissions for many texts outlining the means of accomplishment related to Awareness Holder Lama, both peaceful and wrathful forms, as well as many other sacred instructions.

IN THE YEAR I TURNED THIRTY-EIGHT, I encountered Orgyen Térdak Gyalpo, Treasure Lord King. He bestowed upon me the scriptural transmission and life-force entrustment for the text of the means of accomplishment related to the legion of the arrogant doctrine guardians.

IN THE YEAR I TURNED FORTY, in a visionary experience of clear light, I met the great adept Saraha. He granted me the complete empowerments and scriptural transmissions for The Space Treasury of the Nature of Reality cycle.

IN THE YEAR I TURNED FORTY-ONE, Dakini Yeshe Palbarma, Wisdom Torch, gave me many prophecies regarding my travel and residences.

IN THE YEAR I TURNED FORTY-ONE,[18] Dakini Sukasiddhi gave me the seventeen profound tantras of Severance of Evil Forces and its seven teachings. She granted me all these and remarked, "Although very few people are suitable recipients for these, I've bestowed them on you simply as an auspicious connection."

IN THE YEAR I TURNED FORTY-TWO, Dakini Sangdzö Dakmo, Keeper of the Secret Treasury, told me,

> You are Saraha:
> You needn't depend upon the path of explanation through words.
> Although you thoroughly comprehend all teachings,
> In order for disciples to develop confidence in you,
> You must meet Buddha Dorjé Chang, Varja Bearer.

Immediately Dorjé Chang arrived in space before me. He revealed the inner heart teachings of the tantras:

> Once cyclic existence and enlightenment become apparent to you
> As a perfectly contained display within supreme emptiness,

And its display manifests as spontaneously present perfection,
You've extracted the inner heart of the tantras.

Then he vanished.

IN THE YEAR I TURNED FORTY-THREE, Dakini Dorjé Naljorma, Vajra Adept, led me to Unsurpassable Spontaneously Present Pure Land. The teacher Nyima Wangpo, Mighty Sun, bestowed upon me 180 different types of buddha-family mantras and evil mantras.

AT THE END OF MY FORTY-FOURTH YEAR, I met Zhonnu Namgyal, Youthful All-Victorious, in the form of a young boy, and he granted me the pith instructions for drawing others under my control.

WHEN I WAS FORTY-FIVE, Dakini Nangdzé Wangmo, Queen of Creating Appearances, gave me prophecies telling me where to go and what to do.

WHEN I WAS FORTY-SIX, Dakini Yeshe Lhamo Yangchenma, Melodic Wisdom Goddess, from Unsurpassable Beautiful Pure Land, spoke of many texts outlining the means of accomplishment to gain wealth.

> My child, an obstacle to your longevity is close at hand.
> There is an emanation of Nor Gyünma, Stream of Wealth Goddess,
> Who has *Ka* in her name
> And comes from the Mukpo Dong clan.
> To extend your life span, increase your wealth, have your fame resound,
>   and to conserve your money,
> Rely on her as your consort—
> It will be immeasurely helpful to your doctrine.

She said things such as that, and gave many prophecies.

WHEN I WAS FORTY-SEVEN, I met Orgyen Tsokyé Dorjé, Lake-Born Vajra. He gave me extensive empowerments, scriptural transmissions, and profound instructions. I received the blessings of his vajra body, speech, and mind.

When I was forty-eight, in the pure vision of a dream, I encountered the sacred circle of Demchok Korlo, Supreme Wheel of Bliss, from Mount Kailash in India. I received his means of accomplishment and the complete empowerments and scriptural transmissions for the practice cycle of Dutsi Kyilwa, Swirling Nectar.

In the year I turned forty-nine, I met the teacher Supreme Dorjé Chang, Vajra Bearer, in Unsurpassable Blissful Array Pure Land. I received the complete empowerments accompanied by the scriptural transmissions for the practice of Kagyé, Eight Herukas, and six Garuda practices.

In the year I turned fifty, in the sublime land of Willow, I met the Lord of Secrets Chana Dorjé, Vajra-in-Hand. I received profound instructions on Great Perfection as well as many texts outlining the means of accomplishment related to dakini practice.

When I was fifty-one, I met the great adept Hungkara. I received permission for seven unique cycles of profound instructions on Direct Crossing.

> If the bridge of the lineage of the profound teachings is not broken
> Within your own family line,
> Your descendants will exclusively be male and female awareness-
>   holding adepts.

Having said this, he made many aspirations. He gave me nine dark blue *Ah* syllables all at once, saying, "By eating these, you will gain mental retention without forgetting anything." I swallowed them as instructed.

When I was fifty-two, I saw Master Namké Nyingpo, Essence of Space. He said this to me:

> My child, you are of my family line—
> Listen to what I give you, this cherished jewel of pith instructions:
> Within unborn, pristinely clear space
> The interdependent arising of all worldly phenomena
> Lack intrinsic existence, yet they appear—destroy them in basic space.

This is the abiding nature of the basic state of all things.
Once you've truly realized it, make that present
And you will have brought forth the heart of the six million [and four
    hundred thousand] tantras
Spread out in the palm of your hand.
My nephew, I entrust this to you—keep it.

He said this and gave many other profound instructions.

WHEN I WAS FIFTY-THREE, I encountered the sublime Bodhisattva Tukjé
Chenpo, Supreme Compassion, as if actually present. He told me this:

Your little boy Drimé Ö
Is the heir to the victors, Drimé Özer [Longchenpa].
This little boy Mipam Dorjé,
Is the hidden adept Kong-nyön.
The little boy Dzamling Wangyi Gyal, Mighty King of the Land of Jambu,
Is the Buddhist king, Trisong Deutsen,
As well as Dzamling Gesar Gyalpo, Gesar, King of the Land of Jambu.
That little boy called Kiso
Is an emanation of King Dza
And the Buddhist king, Murub Tsenpo.
That little boy Pema Dorjé
Is fierce Marpa Lotsawa, Marpa the Translator.
The little boy Namké Jikmé, Fearless Sky,
Is my own, the bodhisattva's, emanation.
The little boy Gönpo Dradul, Lord Protector Defeater-of-Foes,
Is an emanation of Chana Dorjé, Vajra-in-Hand.
The little boy Lhachen Tobden
Is Lhabu Tsangpa Dongzhi, Four-Faced Brahma,
As well as Great Glorious Dorjé Zhonnu, Vajra Youth.
Further still, there will be two more
Who are emanations of Chana Dorjé, Vajra-in-Hand, and Jamyang,
    Gentle Melody.

A child who should have come, an emanation of Wangchuk Chenpo,
    Magnificent Ruler,

Was unable to appear due to vow-violation demons' emergence.
Had he been born, there would have been various kinds of auspicious
    connections
For him to take control of appearing existence.
Although he previously entered the womb,
He's never for an instant been separate from you.

Now instill this in your mind:
I will tell you favorable and dire things about what's to transpire or not.
As for the individuals who are custodians of your doctrine,
If they preserve your doctrine, that will be good.
If they do anything other than that, they will have extensive obstacles.
If they solely perform meritious work for your profound doctrine,
It will be virtuous in the past, present, and future.

Then he vanished into the basic space of phenomena.

WHEN I WAS FIFTY-FOUR, Yeshe Tsogyal showed her face to me. She gave predictions regarding the assembly of individuals who would be custodians of my doctrine. I'm reluctant to write too much, so I won't relate it here. She revealed 119 treasure teachings.

WHEN I WAS FIFTY-FOUR, a great many pure visions of importance arose.

WHEN I WAS FIFTY-FIVE, Dakini Dorjé Kunzikma, All-Seeing Vajra, gave me prophecies regarding the doctrine in general.

WHEN I WAS FIFTY-SIX, Dakini Kunkyen Yeshe-ma, Omniscient Wisdom, bestowed prophecies concerning supreme individuals.

WHEN I WAS FIFTY-SEVEN, Dakini Dorjé Dudulma, Vajra Demon Tamer, gave me prophecies regarding future emanations of wicked demons.

WHEN I WAS FIFTY-EIGHT, Rikzin Dorjé Drakpa, Awareness Holder Vajra Renown, foretold the personal and family names of eighteen awareness holders who would attain rainbow body. I've recorded them elsewhere.

W<small>HEN</small> I <small>WAS</small> <small>FIFTY-NINE</small>, Tröma Nakmo, Wrathful Black Goddess, said, "There will be five hundred individuals who practice me and become indivisible with me." Once she spoke, the pure sky of basic space entered basic space and I let go into infinity.

W<small>HEN</small> I <small>WAS</small> <small>SIXTY</small>, I met the body of the teacher of ultimate enlightenment Dorjé Chang, Vajra Bearer, who appeared in my self-manifest experience as a nonhuman teacher. He trained me in many spiritual and worldly activities:

> Four of your supreme students are pillars.
> As for the great eastern pillar, Chö Dorjé, Vajra Doctrine,
> Due to the actions of his evil family clan,
> He will turn against your teaching.
> Nevertheless, in the year you turn sixty-five he will return,
> And there will be no damaged connection between you. Rejoice,
>   forgive, and bless him.
> This is meaningful for the happiness of yourself and others.

Then he vanished into the sphere of space.

W<small>HEN</small> I <small>WAS</small> <small>SIXTY-ONE</small>, I encountered the body of ultimate enlightenment Dorjé Chang, Vajra Bearer. He gave me the profound instructions of conjoined skillful means and sublime insight.

> Many among your disciples, who have become your subjects,
> Will be supreme awareness holders of the rainbow body
> And reach the ground of freedom.
> I too proclaim powerful positive aspirations for you.

He said this and placed his palm on the crown of my head and made aspirations and then vanished into basic space.

W<small>HEN</small> I <small>WAS</small> <small>SIXTY-TWO</small>, once again I met Supreme Orgyen. He conferred upon me many kinds of empowerments and predictions, and then vanished into basic space.

WHEN I WAS SIXTY-THREE, Wisdom Dakini Dudulma, Demon Tamer, gave me many empowerments and profound instructions. In the end, she also granted many kinds of prophecy and sacred advice.

WHEN I WAS SIXTY-FOUR, I met Rikzin Dorjé Töpa, Awareness Holder Vajra Skull. He bestowed upon me the complete empowerments and scriptural transmissions for my three cycles of pure visions and the earth treasures in their entirety.

> Prior to now, these dawned as the dynamic expression of your own
>   awareness—
> Although the power [of your treasures] was already naturally complete,
> To instill confidence in them, I've given these teachings to you.

Then he appeared to dissolve into me.

> Thus, in chronological order,
> I've written down a few of my pure visions.
> I was unable to turn away the insistent requests
> Of my faithful disciples, so I've recorded just that much.
> There is scant necessity
> To describe all my visions,
> And out of fear of wasting paper,
> I haven't said more than just this much.

Colophon

AT THE OUTSET, based on insistent requests made by one hundred of my disciples, I finished writing just the first part of this text. Later I completely finished it in the presence of Lama Orgyen Rangshar. This was composed by Traktung Dudjom Dorjé. May it be wholly virtuous! Virtue! Virtue! Virtue!

[Note on the present edition:]

This is the middle-length autobiographical account of the great treasure revealer Dudjom Dorjé. At Kalzang Monastery in Upper Li, I, Trogyal Dorjé [Chatral Rinpoche], a monk of the lowest caste, copied out and double-checked this edition based on the actual manuscript that had belonged to the treasure revealer himself.

The Secret Autobiography That Briefly Relates Replies to the Queries of a Wisdom Dakini

Ah Ho! Don't you recognize me?
If you don't recognize me,
I am she who traverses all abodes, regions, and charnel grounds.
I am the illusionist who appears as anything at all, doing absolutely
     anything.
With unpredictable styles, I have a thousand names.
I am cyclic existence. I am enlightenment.
I am the supreme lady of nondual basic space.
I am the chieftess—Ekazati.
In utmost peace, I reveal myself as the primordial Buddha.
If I am wrathful, I show off both the boons and faults of existence.
If I consume, both cyclic existence and enlightenment are hidden in my
     belly.
When I'm hungry, I destroy everything into emptiness.
When I'm thirsty, I'll drink anything in equanimity.
No one can come to a definite conclusion about me.
Those who have come to a conclusion wander in delusion.
Apart from me, there is no entryway;
These entrances appear to each individual, so numerous are they.
Wherever paths are traveled, they remain within my expanse.
In that way, I am the supreme pervading empress.
From the sweeping expanse that lacks characteristics,
Why do I take this guise of form through skillful means?
I'm encouraging you with this lovely melodic song
To express, in like manner, your own superb qualities!

So she spoke, and this is what I sang in reply:

Kyé Ho! Universal empress of cyclic existence and enlightenment,
I am the original primoridal Buddha.
Within the basic space of the supreme equal purity of cyclic existence
     and enlightenment,
Unaltered by any faults and qualities,
I am the pervading lord Kuntuzangpo, Ever-Excellent.

I don't know how to stray from the basic space of phenomena.
The naturally occurring bodies and wisdoms of enlightenment

Don't have characteristics or truncated limits.
I am Nampar Nangdzé, Illuminator of Appearances.

Within the dynamic expression of the play of spontaneously present
    great bliss,
I am not fabricated by anything at all.
My wisdom vajra of natural liberation destroys the two obscurations.
I am Chana Dorjé, Vajra-in-Hand.

Within the radiance of the nature of reality, free from elaboration and
    extremes,
I appear as the illusory wisdom body in the presence of disciples'
    devotion,
Like the dance of the moon on water.
I am Pema Jungné, Lotus-Born.

With the great radiance of my indestructible vajra,
I destroy the demon hordes of conceptuality.
Wrathful from the sphere of ferocious wisdom,
I am Vajra Anger.

My ultimate nature is as I've described,
Yet hear me further, daki-ma.
Sometimes, in the appearing aspect of magical illusion,

From eight years of age,
As a sign of seeing the truth of the nature of reality,
I saw existence as waves of blood.
Unable to fathom its depths and edges,
Unbearable terror and panic ensued for a long time.
When my fears subsided, that catalyst
Caused me to understand appearing existence as simply self-manifest.

At the age of ten,
I met Orgyen Tsokyé Dorjé, Lake-Born Vajra
And received from him the empowerments, blessings, and permission
Of complete liberation from cyclic existence.

He declared me to be the supreme emanation
Of the great and magnificent Dorjé Drolö.

Later, in self-manifest pure visions
Time and again I met Lord Pema Jungné, Lotus-Born;
He granted me reassurance through the vast and deep [empowerments
    that foster] maturation and the [instructions that lead to] liberation,
And promised me we would never, for even an instant, be apart.

After that, a wisdom dakini
Poured thirteen mustard seeds
Onto a clear blue mirror saying,
"Superb individual, you are Dorjé Drolö.
Keep this mirror, [a representation of] wisdom mind,
At your heart. This is the sublime insight-wisdom empowerment.
These mustard seeds represent thirteen spiritual heroes.
In the latter part of your human lifetime,
They will become disciples who actualize the exalted state
Of Dorjé Chang, Vajra Bearer, in this very life.

Following that, on occasion in dreams and meditative experiences,
I encountered many buddhas and bodhisattvas.
In particular, I met Jampal Yang, Gentle Splendor Melody,
And was entrusted with the profound doctrine of the sutras and tantras.

In self-manifest ultimate Unsurpassable Pure Land,
The great and magnificent Dorjé Drolö
Blessed me as indivisible with him.

In self-manifest Celestial Enjoyment Pure Land,
I met the eight supreme awareness holders
And received the doctrinal empowerment of the eight herukas.
In the self-manifest Copper-Colored Mountain,
I received from the eight great adepts,
And especially from Awareness Holder Supreme Hungkara,
Empowerment in the sacred circles of Vajrayana tantras
And the seal of entrustment for their doctrines.

In the expanse of self-manifest Lotus Light,
I met the illusory wisdom bodies of
Drimé Özer, Jikmé Lingpa,
And Drubwang Kunzang Shenpen,
And received the seal of entrustment of the profound Heart Essence
    cycle.

In the expanse of the Magical Matrix of Clear Light,
Sangdak Chana Dorjé, Lord of Secrets Vajra-in-Hand,
Gave me the innermost core instructions of the supreme secret tantras.
"You, a superlative individual, and I, Lord of Secrets,
Are now inseparable. This is my vajra word.
Henceforth, from you through three generations of transmission of the
    lineage,
One hundred awareness holders will attain rainbow body
If the profound seal of sacred teachings remains unbroken."
Thus he spoke, and then conferred upon me the doctrinal
    empowerment
Of the profound pith instructions for the self-liberation of dualistic
    fixation.

Once again, in self-manifest Great Bliss Pure Land,
In the palace of the manifestation of clear light,
I met the supreme adept, Lord Garab Dorjé, Vajra of Utmost Joy.
From that Buddha's own mouth this was spoken:
"Listen to me Dudjom Trolö Tsal!
King Dza, sovereign of great secrets,
Has emanated as your son to revive the doctrine and beings.
His fame and renown will fill the three planes of existence
And he will vanquish the nine dark countries which are demons'
    domains.

I too have emanated as your child.
When I steal the life force of the eight tribes of arrogant spirits,
I will work for the benefit of intangible gods and demons,
And bring the sunrise of the Secret Mantra doctrine.

Shri Sengha has emanated as your child.
He will raise the banner of the clear-light doctrine
And lead a circle of five thousand followers.
He will plant the tree trunk of the Heart Essence doctrine.

Yudra [Nyingpo] will emanate as your nephew,
And act as the key to the profound treasure trove.

Until your family line reaches its end,
It will always be composed of holy awareness holders."

Then he granted me further prophecies and empowerments.

Moreover, in self-manifest pure visions,
I saw the faces of immeasurable hosts
Of buddhas, bodhisattvas, and dakinis
As the magical illusory appearances of wisdom.
They gave me inconceivable empowerments and prophecies.
In particular, Supreme Orgyen accepted me
Without separation for even an instant.

As described, these special substantial qualities—
Empowerments, prophecies, blessings, and transfer of the wisdom-
    mind lineage to my mind—
Make me outstanding.

Listen to me further, my darling.
Throughout this human life, from beginning to end,
Although I haven't relied upon a human lama,
My karmic destiny through previous training awakened,
And I arrived effortlessly at the state of an awareness holder.
I didn't depend upon words or metaphors,
Yet the treasury of the vast expanse of the nature of reality overflowed.
All appearances arose as signs and metaphors.
I became aware of the supreme equal purity of cyclic existence and
    transcendence.

All phenomena were purified as naked awareness.
I gained virtuosity in Great Perfection.

Through the wide eyes of sublime insight and wisdom,
I saw the truth of the nature of reality.
My inner strength ensured that I had no need to sightsee in the realm
    of the five senses.

With monumental power as an autonomous king,
I gained the unassailable state directly within myself.
My inner strength ensured that I had no need to pay attention to
    others' appraisals.

All of the supreme qualities of Kuntuzangpo, Ever-Excellent,
Are not concealed: I've reached their indwelling state.
I didn't need to depend upon oral teachings and study.

I saw the quintessential equality
Of cyclic existence and enlightenment as nothing apart from myself.
My inner strength ensured that I didn't need to adhere to [spiritual
    approaches that make] calculations and lists.

Within myself, I gained Great Perfection
In which all paths and stages are but one.
My inner strength ensured that I didn't need to meditate with clinging,
    fetters, and tightness.

I attained the fusion of the profound innermost essence
Of the oceanic classes of sutras and Secret Mantra tantras:
I didn't need to go out in the world, seeking like a beggar.

In that way, I gained mastery of the supreme treasury
Of the expanse of the bodies and wisdoms of enlightenment.
My strength ensures that there exist disciples, fortunate men and woman,
Connected with me through aspirations and karma.
Through the momentum of securing their inheritance—the lineage of
    wisdom mind—

They become awareness holders and that alone.
This is without a doubt the doctrine of Pema.

These are qualities far more exalted than others'.

Thus I spoke.
The wisdom dakini sang,

Well then, at a time in the future,
This song of your outstanding qualities
Will be of great purpose. Therefore put this into writing.

She spoke, then vanished into the magical illusion of the nature of
    reality.

A Supernova of Blessings

*A Brief Supplication to the Life Story
of the Treasure Revealer Dudjom Dorjé*

Namo Guru Byé! Homage to the Lama!

The body of ultimate enlightenment, primordially pure, unborn, and unformulated;

The spontaneously perfect enjoyment body, the five spiritual families of Buddha Great Glacial Lake;

The inconceivable emanations that skillfully guide disciples in ways attuned to their needs and circumstances:

To the glory of these spontaneously present three bodies, I pray!

Pema Jungné, Lotus-Born, illustrious protector of beings,

You appear as a teacher of disciples

For fortunate individuals whose karma, aspirations, and auspicious connections have converged

To produce a self-manifest teacher who subdues their own minds: To you I pray!

A nonhuman in a human emanation, like the moon's [reflection] on water,

You arose as a wisdom body with a form attuned to others' karma, aspirations, and auspicious connections.

To nurture your disciples like the dakinis' own children,

You demonstrated a wondrous emanation body like a radiant rainbow: To you I pray!

From your birth until nine years of age,

The wisdom dakini cared for you like her own adored child.

With myriad visible and invisible emanations,

You actualized your own benefit [by attaining realization]: To you I pray!

Collapsing the division of cyclic existence, you used a variety of skillful means

[That lead to] liberation in the basic space of wisdom

To actively distinguish between suitable and unsuitable minds and outlooks among your disciples.

Creator of unpredictable magical projections, to you I pray!

From age ten through twenty-five,
You received prophecies and empowerments from spiritual heroes and
    dakinis.
You gained the capacity and forceful power to direct beings' minds to
    awakening
And to have your activities succeed and flourish: To you I pray!

From age twenty-six to thirty-seven,
You received three cycles of pure vision treasures and the rocky cliff
    earth treasure
And unlocked the vast treasury of those four profound doctrinal cycles,
Bringing all beings to spiritual maturity and liberation: To you I pray!

Opening the gateway of Great Perfection, the utmost pinnacle of the
    vajra approach,
You led beings skillfully, guiding them in ways attuned to their needs
    and circumstances;
Among them, destined individuals attained the rainbow body of
    supreme transference.
Teacher of the supreme approach: To you I pray!

From age thirty-eight to fifty-seven,
You used the meditative concentration of steering the minds of
    beings—
Human or nonhuman, visible or not—
To impartially carry out what was beneficial for others: To you I pray!

You launched a festival of the profound teachings of the utmost
    pinnacle of the nine vehicles
That make basic space and awareness apparent in clear-light Direct
    Crossing.
In concert with the minds of others, you assumed a humble position,
And skillfully guided them: To you I pray!

Although enlightened as Ever-Excellent from the start,
As wisdom's dynamic display, you appeared like the moon's [reflection]

In the water vessel that is your disciples' experienced phenomena.
Supreme sovereign of compassion: To you I pray!

From age fifty-eight to sixty-eight,
Within the context of impermanent, composite reality,
You used symbolic means to demonstrate that phenomena are illusory.
Superb adept of magical illusion: To you I pray!

The cruel beings of this degenerate age are hard to subdue,
Yet you employed myriad responsive skillful means and conduct
To guide the fortunate assembly connected to you through [excellent]
    karma and positive aspirations.
Subduer of the remaining disciples [not previously awakened]: To you I
    pray!

For all beings, lofty and humble, directly and through the lineages of
    others,
You donned the armor of awakened intent and spurned weariness,
Causing a timeless deluge of the teachings night and day.
Impartial protector of beings and the Buddhist doctrine: To you I pray!

The moment I hear or recall the deeds of you, the master,
With sincere devotion and confidence,
May the awareness-holding lamas of the entire three lineages of
    enlightened mind, symbolic, and aural transmission,
Transfer the blessings of the enlightened mind transmission to my
    mind!

Bound to cyclic existence since time immemorial,
My karma continues endlessly.
In this very lifetime may I travel swiftly
To the magnificent state of full and complete enlightenment.

May I and all sentient beings with whom I have a connection,
Effortlessly awaken to our inner nature
And now, simultaneously, attain manifest enlightenment
Within the all-illuminating ultimate body.

This supplication to my life story, entitled "A Supernova of Blessings," was insistently and repeatedly requested by my own student, the adept Ngawang Trinlé. In response, I, Awareness Holder Dudjom Dorjé blurted out whatever nonsense came to mind. May it be virtuous in the beginning, end, and middle. May auspiciousness prevail!

Appendix 1: An Exalted Family Line

Eight Incarnate Sons

IT'S INTERESTING TO NOTE THAT, through one circuitous route or another, four of Dudjom Lingpa's eight children are reincarnations of Longchen Rabjam (1308–1363), one of the most renowned Ancient Tradition masters. It's not unusual for realized masters to see their teachers, colleagues, and students reappear as their own children. Likewise, some of Dudjom Lingpa's contemporaries took rebirth as his children.

Dudjom Lingpa received extensive prophecies regarding his ensemble of reincarnate children; the earliest prophecy occurs in his secret autobiography, *A Clear Mirror: An Account of Supremely Secret Meditative Experiences* and gives details about his first five children. Dudjom Lingpa's first son was the Third Dodrupchen Jikmé Tenpé Nyima (1865–1926), who did indeed arrive in the year foretold. He went to receive teachings from the eminent Patrul Rinpoche (1808–1887) where he progressed with miraculous ease, and Patrul Rinpoche had Dodrupchen, who was only eight years old at the time, give the annual teachings on *The Way of the Bodhisattva* to a large assembly at Dzagyal Monastery. Stories relate how Dodrupchen, who became a foremost scholar, challenged his father in traditional Tibetan debate. Despite Dudjom Lingpa's lack of formal education, father bested son, finishing with a pithy remark about his son's paltry knowledge compared to the overwhelming vastness of wisdom mind. Later, Dodrupchen's colleagues, renowned scholars of the Gelukpa order, told him they also wished to debate his father. Dodrupchen assured them they wouldn't win.[19]

Dudjom Lingpa's second son was predicted to arrive in the Rabbit Year, which corresponds to 1867. This likely refers to Drupchen Tulku Péma Dorjé, who was born sometime between 1865 and 1868. Tulku Péma Dorjé went on to live at Dodrupchen Monastery and later became the institution's administrator and the caretaker of his eldest brother's projects.

Another son was slated to arrive in the Female Earth Snake Year, 1869. However, it appears that this son, the reincarnation of the legendary wild adept, Do Khyentsé Yeshe Dorjé, Khyentsé Tulku Dzamling Wangyen

(1868–1907) appeared one year early. Of course he announced himself to Dudjom Lingpa beforehand in a dream. He was enthroned at both Dodrupchen and Nizok monasteries, though he remained with his father. Some stories relate that Do Khyentsé, whose unpredictable and sometimes intimidating demeanor were similar to Dudjom Lingpa's, announced his arrival to his future father before he even passed away. The two met on horseback on a mountaintop and drew swords as if to fight. Dudjom Lingpa told Do Khyentsé they needed nothing from each other, insinuating that each were complete in their realization. Do Khyentsé countered, saying that he would need to rent a room from Dudjom Lingpa soon. This is thought to allude to his subsequent reincarnation.

The birth of another son was predicted for the following Rabbit Year, 1879. This child was foretold to be a reincarnation of Drupchen Mélong Dorjé (1243–1303), another great treasure revealer. This could refer to Chewö Rikzin Chenmö Tulku Mipam Dorjé although he passed away in early childhood with no confirmed birth date.

The last child mentioned in the prophecy was to appear in the Metal Snake Year, 1881. Longchenpa Tulku Drimé Özer did arrive on schedule.[20] Tulku Drimé, who chose not stay in a monastic institutional setting with his eldest brother, taught extensively throughout Eastern and even Central Tibet. He did much to preserve and further his father's doctrine. Unfortunately, his Collected Works, said to have totaled eighteen volumes, were lost in the Chinese invasion of Tibet in the 1950s. This extraordinary father-son connection prevailed as they were reunited a generation later; Drimé Özer took rebirth as Dungsé Thinley Norbu Rinpoche, the eldest son of His Holiness Dudjom Rinpoche, Dudjom Lingpa's own reincarnation.

In addition to the five children above, three more incarnate sons were born, preceded by their own unique portents. Apang Kuchen Tulku Lhachen Tobgyal arrived in 1885. His conception was even more miraculous than usual. Through the concentration of Dudjom Lingpa's wisdom mind, the child was conceived from afar in his mother's womb who happened to be a nun with pure vows. At age eight this remarkable child was taken to Katok Monastery and enthroned as the reincarnation of Zhichen Tulku Rinpoche. He became a revered master with extraordinary disciples, including his own children. Apang Terchen's death was as extraordinary as his conception. Announcing his intention to help the Sakya lineage, one of the four major orders of Tibetan Buddhism, he passed away deliberately and reincarnated as His Holiness the Sakya Trizin, the current head of the Sakya tradition.

The seventh son did not receive any less fanfare than his brothers. One night in a dream, Dudjom Lingpa's primary doctrine guardian appeared with news that Patrul Rinpoche, who had recently passed away, would soon arrive. In fact, he did return in 1888 as Dudjom Lingpa's son, Dza Patrul Tulku Namké Jikmé. He eventually went to live in Dzachukha, where his previous incarnation had formerly resided.

In 1890, Yeshe Tsogyal informed Dudjom Lingpa that an emanation of the bodhisattva Sangdak Chakna Dorjé, Lord of Secrets Vajra-in-Hand, would appear as his son. The following year Sangdak Tulku Dorjé Dradul (1891–1959) was born. He eventually became Dudjom Lingpa's successor at Kalzang Monastery.

Generations of Awareness Holders

DUDJOM LINGPA'S LONG GENETIC LINE would also become exceptional spiritual heirs. He received numerous visionary missives emphasizing the majesty of generations to come. The great master himself reincarnated at least three times, two of which were as the children of his own sons. The first such incarnation was Sungtrul Kunzang Nyima (1904–58), whose father was Dudjom Lingpa's third son Khyentsé Tulku. Born in Pemakö in Southern Tibet, he was invited to return to Sertal, Dudjom Lingpa's homeland, where he studied under Terchen Lerab Lingpa. Kunzang Nyima was a master of Great Perfection and taught throughout Eastern Tibet. His son, Tulku Tekchok Rinpoche, currently teaches and transmits his father's and Dudjom Lingpa's lineages worldwide.

Dudjom Lingpa's second incarnation to appear as his own grandson was Sönam Deutsen (1910–58), whose father was Tulku Drimé. A treasure revealer with disciples in Golok, he lived and taught at Dudjom Lingpa's seat, Kalzang Monastery.

Dudjom Lingpa's granddaughters have also continued to act as steadfast stewards of his lineage. Sémo Kunzang Wangmo, the daughter Dudjom Lingpa's seventh son Dza Patrul Tulku, is renowned for teaching and spreading the doctrine of both Dudjom Lingpa and the New Treasure (Tersar) tradition of Dudjom Rinpoche throughout Eastern Tibet and China. Her prolific activities, including trips to twenty-one provinces in China, continued until she departed from this world in July 2009.[21]

Apang Terchen's daughter Taré Lhamo (1938–2003) was recognized as a reincarnation of Lushül Khenpo, one of the four great scholars of Dodrupchen Monastery. Taré Lhamo was a treasure revealer who taught extensively throughout Eastern Tibet.

Appendix 2: A Living Legacy

THE GREAT LAMA who acted as the vital link between Dudjom incarnations was Dza Pukhung Gyurmé Ngedön Wangpo. He was a student of Dudjom Lingpa and teacher to his immediate reincarnation, His Holiness Dudjom Rinpoche. Born in the Dergé region of Eastern Tibet, Gyurmé Ngedön Wangpo met the exceptional teacher Jamyang Khyentsé Wangpo at age fifteen. After seven years, this renowned guide sent his young student back to his homeland to fulfill a meaningful connection with Dudjom Lingpa. Due to their karmic connection over many lifetimes, their meeting was joyful, and Dudjom Lingpa bestowed his entire treasure transmission upon Gyurmé Ngedön Wangpo and fully empowered him as a custodian of the Dudjom doctrine.

In accord with Dudjom Lingpa's final testament and secret prophecies, Gyurmé Ngedön Wangpo went to Pemakö in Southern Tibet when his teacher passed away. He taught extensively throughout that region. There in Pemakö, as Dudjom Lingpa himself predicted, this superb disciple once again met his teacher, discovering Dudjom Lingpa's immediate rebirth in a young boy who became known as Dudjom Rinpoche Jikdral Yeshe Dorjé (1904–1987). Every lineage that converged in Gyurmé Ngedön Wangpo was passed on flawlessly to the reincarnation of his teacher. By serving this supreme master through two incarnations, he guaranteed the seamless continuation of the Dudjom lineage into the modern world.

Dewé Dorjé (1892–1940), known as Sera Khandro, is located in history just one generation after Dudjom Lingpa. She stands out as a realized adept and a practitioner who sustained his doctrine in myriad ways. Born to nobility in Lhasa, Sera Khandro received early predictions that she would be a great treasure revealer and teacher. Surprisingly, this would take place not in Central Tibet but in the frontier of Eastern Tibet, near Dudjom Lingpa's homeland. Despite dramatic obstacles, Sera Khandro and Dudjom Lingpa's fifth son, Tulku Drimé Özer, eventually become consorts and worked together as equal partners, revealing treasures, exchanging esoteric practices, and preserving his father's lineage.

After the tragic death of Tulku Drimé, Sera Khandro relocated to Sera

Monastery in Eastern Tibet, and at age thirty-four launched a prolific teaching career. This included bestowing the empowerments, scriptural transmissions, and explanations of the treasure revelations of Dudjom Lingpa and Drimé Özer upon monastics, lamas, and the residents of religious encampments. In Sera Khandro's autobiography she also notes giving the "entire father and son" treasure teachings at a place called Vairocana Cave.

In addition to transmitting the Dudjom lineage, Sera Khandro dedicated herself to the comprehensive collection and production of Dudjom Lingpa's Collected Works. This vast project commenced in 1930 and included gathering Dudjom Lingpa's writings from disparate locations, editing the writings, and compiling the volumes into a form that others could copy by hand. There is evidence of at least one sponsored printing of these works, along with Drimé Özer's canon. However, the carved woodblocks that would have been created for such printing were never found. The modern incarnation of Sera Khandro's compilation endeavor is an exquisite computer-input version published in 2004. These volumes were produced in Bhutan under the direction of Lopön Nikula, a close disciple of Dudjom Rinpoche. Through practice, teaching, and archiving, Sera Khandro sustained the Dudjom lineage in essential ways, creating a crucial link to the present.

One of Sera Khandro's close students, and one of the greatest lamas living today, is Chatral Sangyé Dorjé Rinpoche. He was born in 1913 in Nyarong, an area of Eastern Tibet not more than a few hundred miles from Dudjom Lingpa's birthplace. Chatral Rinpoche's boundless energy and the integrity of the lineages he holds are legendary. In every aspect—studies, retreat, teaching, and outer service to the doctrine and beings—his activity surpasses what we would normally consider possible. Chatral Rinpoche studied under his root master, Katok Khenpo Ngawang Palzang (1879–1941) in Eastern Tibet. Following formal studies, Rinpoche spent decades living as hermit in secluded retreat, often moving around to avoid persistent followers, including many high lamas, who came to request teachings and benedictions. Relentless in his personal practice, it has been reported that Rinpoche has completed the practices of fourteen full cycles of teachings. In addition, he went on to build temples, stupas, and three-year-retreat centers throughout India, Nepal, and Bhutan.

This supreme master represents another vital bridge between Dudjom incarnations over three lifetimes. Chatral Rinpoche received Dudjom Lingpa's lineage from both Sera Khandro and Dudjom Lingpa's youngest son,

Sangdak Tulku Dorjé Dradul, in Tibet. Later Chatral Rinpoche became His Holiness Dudjom Rinpoche's regent and a principal custodian of his lineage. When Dudjom Rinpoche took rebirth in 1990, Chatral Rinpoche assumed responsibility for his young reincarnation's enthronement and much of his Buddhist education.

Chatral Rinpoche currently lives in Nepal with his daughter Saraswati, who is a reincarnation of Sera Khandro. Like Dudjom Lingpa, Chatral Rinpoche was never recognized or enthroned as any specific tulku, though his activities in this lifetime are nothing short of miraculous in scope and profundity. After meeting Chatral Rinpoché in 1968, Father Thomas Merton, is reported to have said, "That is the greatest man I ever met. He is my teacher." It is this realized lama, who so perfectly embodies the noble qualities of the doctrines he holds, that brings us to the present moment of the Dudjom lineage.

Bibliography

Doctor, Andreas. 2005. *Tibetan Treasure Literature: Revelation, Tradition, and Accomplishment in Visionary Buddhism*. Ithaca: Snow Lion Publications.

Dorje, Jikdrel Yeshe. 1991. *The Nyingma School of Tibetan Buddhism: Its Fundamentals and History*. Translated and edited by Gyurme Dorje and Matthew Kapstein. Boston: Wisdom Publications.

Gayley, Holly. "The Scions of Dudjom Lingpa." Published at the Tibetan Buddhist Resource Center (www.tbrc.org), January 21 2010.

Gyatso, Janet. 1998. *Apparitions of the Self: The Secret Autobiographies of a Tibetan Visionary*. Princeton: Princeton University Press.

Jacoby, Sarah Hieatt. 2007. "Consorts and Revelation in Eastern Tibet: The Auto-biographical Writings of the Treasure Revealer Sera Khandro (1892–1940)." PhD diss., University of Virginia.

Khenpo, Nyoshul. 2005. *A Marvelous Garland of Rare Gems: Biographies of Masters of Awareness in the Dzogchen Lineage*. Translated by Richard Barron [Chökyi Nyima]. Junction City: Padma Publishing.

Lingpa, Dudjom. 1994. *Buddhahood Without Meditation: A Visionary Account Known as Refining One's Perception (Nang-jang)*. Translated by Richard Barron [Chökyi Nyima]. Junction City: Padma Publishing.

Rabjam, Longchenpa. 1989. *The Practice of Dzogchen*. Translated, annotated, and introduced by Tulku Thondup. Ithaca: Snow Lion Publications.

Ricard, Matthieu. 2001. *The Life of Shabkar: The Autobiography of a Tibetan Yogin*. Ithaca: Snow Lion Publications.

Sky Dancer (movie). 2009. Directed and Produced by Jody Kemmerer.

Terrone, Antonio. 2009. "Householders and Monks: A Study of Treasure Revealers and Their Role in Religious Revival in Contemporary Eastern Tibet," in Sarah Jacoby and Antonio Terrone, eds. *Buddhism Beyond the Monastery*. Leiden: Brill.

Thondup, Tulku. 1986. *Hidden Teachings of Tibet: An Explanation of the Terma Tradition of Tibetan Buddhism*. Boston: Wisdom Publications.

———. 1996. *Masters of Meditation and Miracles: Lives of the Great Buddhist Masters of India and Tibet*. Boston: Shambhala Publications.

Tsogyal, Yeshe. 1993. *The Lotus-Born*. Hong Kong: Rangjung Yeshe Publications.

Tsogyal, Yeshe. *Orgyen gu ru padma 'byung gnas kyi skyes rabs rnam par thar pa rgyas par bkod pa padma bka yi thang yig ces bya bzhugs so*. English: 1978. *The Life and Liberation of Padmasambhava*. Emeryville: Dharma Publishing.

Notes

1. Personal communication with Lama Tséring Gyaltsen, September 2009.
2. Personal communication with Lama Tharchin Rinpoché, September 2010
3. Nagas are a class of water-dwelling beings who are able to shape-shift into human-like forms. They are considered wealth and treasure guardians.
4. *An Encyclopedic Tibetan-English Dictionary,* s.v. "dkor."
5. This is the perspective presented in Thondup 1986: 61-62, although vision treasures are a category with numerous interpretations.
6. For this translation I used the computer-input version of Dudjom Lingpa's *Collected Works* produced in Bhutan. The autobiographies, including the colophons, final verses, and Chadral Rinpoché's appended printing dedications, constitute Volume Dza, pp. 1-368. [Translator's note].
7. The majority of Dudjom Lingpa's stories take place either on particularly auspicious and powerful days in the Tibetan calendar, or on the eve of or the day after these special days. For instance, he is born on the tenth day; the tenth day of any month is known as Guru Rinpoché Day, perhaps the most important day in terms of practice and general auspiciousness. Other days to keep in mind on a monthly basis are the twenty-fifth day, known as Dakini Day, the eighth day, known as Medicine Buddha Day, the fifteenth day, full moon, and the thirtieth and last day of the month, which is new moon. The first day of the first month is Tibetan New Year (Losar). Dudjom Lingpa states that is was born in the Bird Month, which could be the eighth month according to the Mongolian calendar he refers to throughout, or the sixth month based on other commonly used systems. With that ambiguity in mind, when months are given names rather than numbers, they are left as such. [Translator's note].
8. In Tibetan tradition, an individual is considered to be one year old at birth. With this in mind, at this point Dudjom Lingpa is actually two years old in Western terms. This custom is maintained throughout the narrative. [Translator's note].
9. A torma is an object offered to request the activities or blessings of deities, doctrine guardians and so forth. They are usually made from flour and other edible material infused with consecrated substances; tormas vary greatly in size, shape, and purpose, and are generally sculpted in a specific design related to their purpose. [Translator's note].
10. This meaning of this line in the text is unclear: *grol bai ltas su ming de 'dzin.* [Translator's note].
11. *Sa-tsas* are small reliquaries traditionally made from clay.
12. The timing of this episode is unclear. The text indicates that Dudjom Lingpa remained

in retreat for one year with his students, but his subsequent account suggests he left after five days.

13. This refers to a Tibetan saying, referring to the belief that when you reach a place where you can't hear someone shouting from where you left, you're far away. {Translator's note.]

14. In Tibetan, the tiger in this episode says in a playful or mocking tone, "pi pi ling ling," which refers to the slang word "pi-ling" used throughout Eastern Tibet to refer to foreigners from outside of Asia, i.e., Westerners. [Translator's note.]

15. These verses song and the previous concluding verses are both composed in a unique Tibetan style that incorporates one of Dudjom Lingpa's names, Dudjom Dorje, Demon Vanquisher, into the words of the first verse. [Translator's note].

16. The first four lines indicate the time of Dudjom Lingpa's birth: 1835 was the Female Wood Sheep Year; "garuda" refers to the Bird Month; "ten soldiers" indicates his birth on the tenth day at dawn, "the seven horses' rays" being a poetic reference to the sun. [Translator's note].

17. This refers to the Snake Year and several lines later, "mount the horse" refers to the following year, the Horse Year. [Translator's note].

18. The year Dudjom Lingpa is forty-one appears twice in the text. [Translator's note].

19. Personal communication with Lama Tharchin Rinpoche, April 2008.

20. An English translation of Tulku Drimé's biography (a treasure revelation of his consort Sera Khandro) is currently underway, although there is an abundance of information on his life, including excerpts from his biography, in Jacoby 2007.

21. An excellent documentary called *Sky Dancer* chronicles the incredible life of Kunzang Wangmo.

Index

CPSIA information can be obtained
at www.ICGtesting.com
Printed in the USA
JSHW011526190723
45053JS00010B/714

9 789627 341673